PINEAPPLE ANTHOLOGY OF FLORIDA WRITERS

Volume 1

James C. Clark, Editor

Pineapple Press, Inc.
Sarasota, Florida

To friends old and new: Cathy and Craig Cook, Rona Gindin,
Nancy Young, Gerald Higgins, Erica Lee, and Mark Reid. And to
my wonderful colleagues in the University of Central Florida
History Department. I am grateful for your support and friendship.

Inquiries should be addressed to:
Pineapple Press, Inc.
P.O. Box 3889
Sarasota, Florida 34230

www.pineapplepress.com

Library of Congress Cataloging-in-Publication Data

Clark, James C., 1947–
    Pineapple anthology of Florida writers volume 1 / James C. Clark. — First edition.
        pages cm
    Includes bibliographical references and index.
    ISBN 978-1-56164-609-8 (pbk. : alk. paper)
        1. Florida—Literary collections. 2. Literary landmarks—Florida. 3. Florida—In litera-
    ture. 4. Florida—Biography. I. Title.
    PS558.F6C57 2013
    810.8'09759—dc23
    [B]

                                                                                        2013000760
First Edition
10 9 8 7 6 5 4 3 2 1

Design by Shé Hicks
Printed and bound in the United States

CONTENTS

INTRODUCTION

THE LITERARY TRADITION in North America began in Florida. Nearly a century before the Pilgrims reached New England, or the members of the Virginia Company arrived in Jamestown, the French and the Spanish were writing about Florida, producing histories, adventure stories, and poetry.

For five hundred years, Florida has attracted great writers, men and women who are almost universally known by their last names: Dos Passos, Williams, Hemingway, and scores of others. Some got their start in Florida, others came to combine writing with an escape from weather or jobs or family, and many used Florida as the backdrop for their stories.

This is the first of three volumes to be published by Pineapple Press to mark the five-hundredth anniversary of the European discovery of Florida. As this volume does, the future volumes will include a wide range of authors who have written about Florida. The authors in this volume wrote over a period of two hundred years, beginning when the population of Florida numbered in the thousands and ending with the population in the millions.

This volume contains profiles and writing of twenty-four authors whose work has left a mark. There are poets, novelists, a playwright, and even a president of the United States. Selecting the authors was difficult as there were literally hundreds of choices. Some were selected because of their role in bringing attention to Florida with their writings. For example, Harriet Beecher Stowe was most famous for *Uncle Tom's Cabin,* but while she lived in Florida, she provided a boost to the state's tourist industry, which was in its infancy.

The poets, including Elizabeth Bishop and Tennessee Williams, captured Florida in verse. Frederick Remington and Ned Buntline wrote of the rough-and-tumble era of Florida. Writers Carl Hiaasen and Dave Barry have captured modern Florida with its zaniness and threats to its future.

Every attempt has been made to use a complete selection from the author, whether it is a poem, short story, or article. In only a few cases was it necessary to use excerpts.

ACKNOWLEDGMENTS

THIS BOOK REQUIRED great amounts of help and inspiration from others. Kevin M. McCarthy, the godfather of Florida literature, and the author of *The Book Lovers Guide to Florida* (Pineapple Press), showed the way with his groundbreaking research in more than two dozen books. He is also the editor of *Florida Stories* and *More Florida Stories* (University Press of Florida), which helped in the selection process. Maurice O'Sullivan and Jack Lane of Rollins College edited *The Florida Reader: Visions of Paradise* (Pineapple Press), which was a major aid.

At the University of Central Florida, Jon Findell and Ryan Retherford provided vital technical assistance in assembling the manuscripts. Without their help, this project would have been almost impossible. As always, Adam Watson of the State Archives of Florida provided invaluable assistance. My colleagues at the University of Central Florida could always be counted on for encouragement and advice.

This is my third book published by Pineapple Press, and editor June Cussen has always worked hard to make my writing better and cleaner. She and David Cussen embraced the idea of a three-volume anthology without hesitation. And Shé Hicks and Kris Rowland at Pineapple provided huge amounts of patience and good humor in putting all the pieces together.

JOHN JAMES AUDUBON

1785–1851

JOHN JAMES AUDUBON was an unsuccessful storekeeper in Kentucky when he made a dramatic career change, becoming a portrait painter, traveling from town to town to seek clients willing to pay him in a frontier where paintings were considered unnecessary by most. As he traveled, he drew the birds he saw and soon received encouragement from ornithologist Alexander Wilson. He began seeking financing for an unprecedented undertaking—drawing the birds of North America.

He first came to Florida in 1831 during a lull in the fighting with the Seminole Indians. He went to St. Augustine, the largest town in the territory, but a backwater that Audubon disliked. He stayed at a tavern but complained about the other residents, mostly fishermen. He wrote to his wife asking her to send more socks. "I wish thee to forward me some good socks . . . the salt marshes through which I am forced to wade every day are the ruin of everything."

Painting birds was hard work: "We get into a boat, and after an hour of hard rowing, we find ourselves in the middle of most extensive marshes, as far as the eye can reach. The boat is anchored, and we go wading through mud and water, amid myriads of sand-flies and mosquitoes, shooting here and there a bird." He tried to hire assistants but found the St. Augustine residents too lazy to work.

He gave up on Florida after a few months, complaining about the alligators and worried about his dog, Plato, going into the gator-infested waters. He returned to Charleston but decided to try Florida once again, sailing to Key West. He was told there were scores of bird species and the trip would be worth it. He arrived in April 1832 and settled at 205 Whitehead Street. His information was correct; he found the nearly extinct white-crowned pigeon as well as the great white heron.

While St. Augustine was a disappointment, Key West was paradise for Audubon. "Seldom have I experienced greater pleasures than when on the Florida Keys, under a burning sun, after pushing my bark for miles over a soapy flat, I have striven all day long, tormented by myriads of insects, to procure a heron new to me, and have at length succeeded in my efforts."

He wanted to return to Florida for a trip along the state's west coast in 1837, but the outbreak of the Second Seminole War forced him to cancel his plans. He was able to go to Pensacola, but could go no farther in Florida.

Although Audubon is known for his paintings of birds, he also wrote stories as he traveled. In "Death of a Pirate," Audubon tells a story he heard while in the Keys. It is impossible to tell whether it is fiction or nonfiction, or contains some facts, stretched to make a better story. In it, an officer comes across a dying pirate on an island near the Florida Keys. There was a small boat stained with blood and two bodies inside. The man urges the pirate to confess his sins.

Death of a Pirate
by John James Audubon

In the calm of a fine moonlight night, as I was admiring the beauty of the clear heavens, and the broad glare of light that glanced from the trembling surface of the waters around, the officer on watch came up and entered into conversation with me. He had been a turtler in other years, and a great hunter to boot, and although of humble birth and pretensions, energy and talent, aided by education, had raised him to a higher station. Such a man could not fail to be an agreeable companion, and we talked on various subjects, principally, you may be sure, birds and other natural productions. He told me he once had a disagreeable adventure, when looking out for game, in a certain cove on the shores of the Gulf of Mexico; and, on my expressing a desire to hear it, he willingly related to me the following particulars, which I give you, not perhaps precisely in his own words, but as nearly so as I can remember.

"Towards evening, one quiet summer day, I chanced to be paddling along a sandy shore, which I thought well fitted for my repose, being covered with tall grass, and as the sun was not many degrees above the horizon, I felt anxious to pitch my mosquito bar or net, and spend the night in this wilderness. The bellowing notes of thousands of bull-frogs in a neighbouring swamp might lull me to rest, and I looked upon the flocks of blackbirds that were assembling as sure companions in this secluded retreat.

I proceeded up a little stream, to insure the safety of my canoe from any sudden storm, when, as I gladly advanced, a beautiful yawl came unexpectedly in view. Surprised at such a sight in a part of the country then scarcely known, I felt a sudden check in the circulation of my blood. My paddle dropped from my hands, and fearfully indeed, as I picked it up, did I look towards the unknown boat. On reaching it, I saw its sides marked with stains of blood, and looking with anxiety over the gunwale, I perceived to my horror, two human bodies covered with gore. Pirates or hostile Indians I was persuaded had perpetrated the foul deed, and my alarm naturally increased; my heart fluttered, stopped, and heaved with unusual tremors, and I looked towards the setting sun in consternation and despair. How long my reveries lasted I cannot tell; I can only recollect that I was roused from them by the distant groans of one apparently in mortal agony. I felt as if refreshed by the cold perspiration that oozed from every pore, and I reflected that though alone, I was well armed, and might hope for the protection of the Almighty.

Humanity whispered to me that, if not surprised and disabled,

I might render assistance to some sufferer, or even be the means of saving a useful life. Buoyed up by this thought, I urged my canoe on shore, and seizing it by the bow, pulled it at one spring high among the grass.

The groans of the unfortunate person fell heavy on my ear, as I cocked and reprimed my gun, and I felt determined to shoot the first that should rise from the grass. As I cautiously proceeded, a hand was raised over the weeds, and waved in the air in the most supplicating manner. I levelled my gun about a foot below it, when the next moment, the head and breast of a man covered with blood were convulsively raised, and a faint hoarse voice asked me for mercy and help! A death-like silence followed his fall to the ground. I surveyed every object around with eyes intent, and ears impressible by the slightest sound, for my situation that moment I thought as critical as any I had ever been in. The croaking of the frogs, and the last blackbirds alighting on their roosts, were the only sounds or sights; and I now proceeded towards the object of my mingled alarm and commiseration.

Alas! the poor being who lay prostrate at my feet, was so weakened by loss of blood, that I had nothing to fear from him. My first impulse was to run back to the water, and having done so, I returned with my cap filled to the brim. I felt at his heart, washed his face and breast, and rubbed his temples with the contents of a phial, which I kept about me as an antidote for the bites of snakes. His features, seamed by the ravages of time, looked frightful and disgusting; but he had been a powerful man, as the breadth of his chest plainly showed. He groaned in the most appalling manner, as his breath struggled through the mass of blood that seemed to fill his throat. His dress plainly disclosed his occupation:—a large pistol he had thrust into his bosom, a naked cutlass lay near him on the ground, a red silk handkerchief was bound over his projecting brows, and over a pair of loose trousers he wore fisherman's boots. He was, in short, a pirate.

My exertions were not in vain, for as I continued to bathe his temples, he revived, his pulse resumed some strength, and I began to hope that he might perhaps survive the deep wounds he had received. Darkness, deep darkness, now enveloped us. I spoke of making a fire. "Oh! for mercy's sake," he exclaimed, "don't." Knowing, however, that under existing circumstances, it was expedient for me to do so, I left him, went to his boat, and brought the rudder, the benches, and the oars, which with my hatchet I soon splintered. I then struck a light, and presently stood in the glare of a blazing fire. The pirate seemed struggling between terror and gratitude for my assistance; he desired me several times in half English and Spanish to put out the flames, but after I had given him a draught of strong spirits, he at length became more composed. I tried to staunch the blood that flowed from the deep gashes in his shoulders and side. I expressed my regret that I had no food about me, but when I spoke of eating he sullenly waved his head.

My situation was one of the most extraordinary that I have ever been placed in. I naturally turned my talk towards religious subjects, but, alas, the dying man hardly believed in the existence of God. "Friend," said he, "for friend you seem to be, I have never studied the ways of Him of whom you talk. I am an outlaw, perhaps you will say a wretch—I have been for many years a pirate. The instructions of my parents were of no avail to me, for I have always believed that I was born to be a most cruel man. I now lie here, about to die in the weeds, because I long ago refused to listen to their many admonitions. Do not shudder when I tell you—these now useless hands murdered the mother whom they had embraced. I feel that I have deserved the pangs of the wretched death that hovers over me; and I am thankful that one of my kind will alone witness my last gaspings."

A fond but feeble hope that I might save his life, and perhaps assist in procuring his pardon, induced me to speak to him on the subject. "It is all in vain, friend-! have no objection to die—am glad that the villains who wounded me were not my conquerors—I want no pardon from any one—Give me some water, and let me die alone."

With the hope that I might learn from his conversation something that might lead to the capture of his guilty associates, I returned from the creek with another capful of water, nearly the whole of which I managed to introduce into his parched mouth, and begged him, for the sake of his future peace, to disclose his history to me. "It is impossible," said he, "there will not be time; the beatings of my heart tell me so. Long before day, these sinewy limbs will be motionless. Nay, there will hardly be a drop of blood in my body; and that blood will only serve to make the grass grow. My wounds are mortal, and I must and will die without what you call confession."

The moon rose in the east. The majesty of her placid beauty impressed me with reverence. I pointed towards her, and asked the Pirate if he could not recognise God's features there. "Friend, I see what you are driving at," was his answer,— "you, like the rest of our enemies, feel the desire of murdering us all. Well — be it so — to die is after all nothing more than a jest; and were it not for the pain, no one, in my opinion, need care a jot about it. But, as you really have befriended me, I will tell you all that is proper."

Hoping his mind might take a useful turn, I again bathed his temples and washed his lips with spirits. His sunk eyes seemed to dart fire at mine — a heavy and deep sigh swelled his chest and struggled through his blood-choked throat, and he asked me to raise him for a little. I did so, when he addressed me somewhat as follows, for, as I have told you, his speech was a mixture of Spanish, French and English, forming a jargon, the like of which I had never heard before, and which I am utterly unable to imitate. However I shall give you the substance of his declaration.

"First tell me, how many bodies you found in the boat, and what sort of dresses they had on." I mentioned their number, and described their apparel. "That's right," said he, "they are the bodies of the scoundrels who followed me in that infernal Yankee barge. Both rascals they were, for when they found the water too shallow for their craft, they took to it and waded after me. All my companions had been shot, and to lighten my own boat, I flung them overboard, but as I lost time in this, the two ruffians caught hold of my gunwale, and struck on my head and body in such a manner, that after I had disabled and killed them both in the boat, I was scarce able to move. The other villains carried off our schooner and one of our boats, and perhaps ere now have hung all my companions whom they did not kill at the time. I have commanded my beautiful vessel many years, captured many ships, and sent many rascals to the devil. I always hated the Yankees, and only regret that I have not killed more of them. I sailed from Matanzas. I have often been in concert with others. I have money without counting, but it is buried where it will never be found, and it would be useless to tell you of it." His throat filled with blood, his voice failed, the cold hand of death was laid on his brow, feebly and hurriedly he muttered, "I am a dying man, farewell."

Alas! It is painful to see death in any shape; in this it was horrible, for there was no hope. The rattling of his throat announced the moment of dissolution, and already did the body fall on my arms with a weight that was insupportable. I laid him on the ground. A mass of dark blood poured from his mouth; then came a frightful groan, the last breathing of that foul spirit; and what now lay at my feet in the wild desert? — a mangled mass of clay!

The remainder of that night was passed in no enviable mood; but my feelings cannot be described. At dawn I dug a hole with the paddle of my canoe, rolled the body into it, and covered it. On reaching the boat I found several buzzards feeding on the bodies, which I in vain attempted to drag to the shore. I therefore covered them with mud and weeds, and launching my canoe, paddled from the cove with a secret joy for my escape, overshadowed with the gloom of mingled dread and abhorrence.

NED BUNTLINE

1823–1886

THERE IS NO doubt that Ned Buntline was a thoroughly disreputable person. The list of people wronged by Buntline would fill one of his dime novels, and yet his name lingers on, linked to two events, only one of which happened. Buntline is forever linked to the Buntline Special, a special revolver he supposedly gave to Western lawmen like Wyatt Earp and Bat Masterson—an exciting but ultimately false story. And he is also linked to the dime novel, making the western lawmen heroes to millions of readers.

Edward Judson first came to notice when he committed a heroic act, saving drowning people in New York's East River while working on a ship. He was honored by President Martin Van Buren, who gave him a Navy commission at the age of sixteen. That commission brought him to Florida, where he served in the Florida Keys during the Second Seminole War.

He adopted a nautical name (as Samuel Clemens would do decades later). Buntline is a rope attached to haul up the sail. He was executive officer on the *Otsego*, a ship on the Florida Squadron, which patrolled along the east and west coasts of south Florida and into the Everglades, where the Seminoles fled after battles. There was no Miami yet—that was half a century away—just the Army base at Fort Dallas.

Fleeing before his creditors became something of a habit for Buntline, along with getting married (we can only estimate the number of wives he had because he sometimes married while still married to someone else). He was also known for starting riots, which resulted in deaths in New York and St. Louis, and for being a leader in the anti-Catholic Know-Nothing Party.

He started a number of magazines, always encountering failure sooner or later. Although he was a heavy drinker, he traveled around the country giving temperance lectures, preaching against the evil of drink. While on one of his temperance tours, he met William Cody, a buffalo hunter and winner of the Congressional Medal of Honor. Buntline wrote a serial novel about Cody for the *New York Weekly* in 1869. Titled, *Buffalo Bill, the*

King of the Border Men, it was largely fictional but became a best seller and made Cody an instant legend.

Buntline realized he had struck gold and began cranking out what became known as dime novels—in all, more than 400. In 1872 Buntline came up with the idea of combining his showmanship with Cody's fame. He wrote a play called *The Scouts of the Prairie* starring Cody and a huge cast. The show toured for a decade, playing before large audiences before Cody launched his own Wild West Show.

While he is best known for his stories of the Old West—and the false tale of the Buntline gun—Florida provided a wealth of story ideas early in his career. Buntline was the first popular writer to come to the state, and while his stories were largely fictional, they were read by those who were ready to believe his tales of battles and Indians. For the readers of his stories, Florida became a wondrous place full of adventure. Stories such as "A Cruise in Lake Okeechobee," "A Chase in the Everglades," "The Capture and Trial," and "Indian Key: Its Rise, Progress and Destruction" made Florida seem exciting. Buntline made a fortune, becoming one of the wealthiest writers in the nation, but spent more than he earned and died broke. He wrote stories for the *Western Literary Journal,* which he and a partner owned. He did not own it long: facing bankruptcy, he fled and stuck his partner with the bills.

He set some of the dime novels in Florida. They were often expanded versions of newspaper or magazine articles, ranging from forty to eighty pages and were a leading form of literature in the late 1800s. His Florida books included *Matanzas; or, A brother's revenge. A Tale of Florida.* Though this story was just 46 pages long it proved to be extremely popular. One of his longest books was *The White Wizard, or, The Great Prophet of the Seminoles,* which he wrote in 1858. It originally appeared as a serial in the *New York Mercury,* then as a book in 1862. It mixed fiction with fact, blending the names of real people from Buntline's time in Florida with characters he created. He also wrote *The Red Revenger, or, The Pirate King of the Floridas: A Romance of the Gulf and its Islands.*

Buntline clearly loved Florida. In one of his stories, he wrote, "I love a

Florida winter. I do not mean one of your northern winter evenings, only rendered clear through the intense frigidity of the stiffened atmosphere. I allude to one where the bright-faced moon and dancing stars look down on forests clothed in the rich beauty of perennial greenness, on an earth covered with luscious, air-perfuming fruit."

Ned Buntline's short story "The Fast Duel, a Sketch from Life" appeared in *The Family Friend,* a newspaper in Monticello, Florida, on April 20, 1861.

The Fast Duel, a Sketch from Life
by Ned Buntline

Maybe you have read the "Fastest Funeral on Record" and other fast stories written by fast men, but I'll bet a sixpence to a kid of mush, that you never heard of the fast duel.

It occurred ten or twelve years ago—yea, thirteen of them—when I was a young man aboard the sloop of war *Boston,* in the West Indian Squadron.

We had just got in from a cruise up amongst the Windward Islands, and had not had much fun for some time, for 'twas in the hurricane season, and we had seen heavy weather enough to satisfy any old Blowhard that ever smelt salt water.

The very day we came to anchor at Pensacola, however, we had a godsend in the shape of a fresh caught midshipman, who, coming from the back woods of Alabama, had never seen anything higher than a flat boat, and was as green as a prairie colt in harness, and pretty near as wild. His name was Ezra Blizzard, and the Commodore ordered him aboard of us, as we had a couple of vacancies, one of our men being shot in a duel and the other having done worse by falling in love with an heiress ashore, marrying her and resigning.

Mr. Blizzard therefore was as I said before a perfect godsend. He was soon initiated into the duties of keeping his own watch and watch for some of the rest of us occasionally; taught how to pay over his mess money; persuaded out of a dash of wine for his "footing," and made the victim of a few harmless tricks; such as having his hammock cut down by the head, when he was asleep in it, being baptised by a sailor, by getting a bucket of salt water poured over him when he was with his mouth open; finding a dead rat or two occasionally in his pocket, or salt instead of sugar in his coffee, etc., all of which he bore so mildly that we began to consider him a regular spoony, and not calculated to become a credit to his mess in particular or the service in general.

To settle the point and determine his quantum of spunk, it was voted that he must be made to fight a duel, and a plot was made up between three of us, that it should be a harmless one, just to try his spunk. Accordingly Hogan B., one of the best shots in the squadron, by the way, insulted him in due form, and much to our astonishment, was knocked down for his pains. He arose as wrathy as a mad bull, and would have pitched into his opponent on the spot, had we not interfered and insisted upon the quarrel being settled according to the "code of honor." Hogan therefore challenged Blizzard, at the same time insisting with us that the fight should be real, and not fun with cork balls as at first proposed. But we overruled him, inasmuch as the insult he had given was uncalled for; and the youngster accepted the writer's volunteered service to act as his second.

"Must I fight him with pistols?" he asked; "I could wollup the life out of him in my own way."

"Gentlemen only use pistols—you struck him, and of course must give him gentlemanly satisfaction. I hope you are a good shot—he is," I replied.

"I never shot off a pistol in my life, but I'm some with a rifle."

"Rifles are not allowed in the code; pistols are the only weapons, and Hogan has a first-rate pair, has killed two reefers already!"

I could see that Blizzard didn't like this news, but he tried to look calm, and asked when he would have to fight.

I told him we would have it out that afternoon, as it was bad to let the blood cool over such affairs. And accordingly, in an hour afterwards we managed to get ashore with the case of pistols wrapped up out of sight in an old pea jacket.

We immediately went out to the old Spanish graveyard, back of the town. To heighten the effect and as luck would have it, we found a freshly dug grave, which was probably to be tenanted on the morrow. Blizzard looked at it and wanted to know what that was for. We told him that the death of one or the other party only could atone for a blow, and that the grave had been prepared for the one that fell. The youngster turned a shade paler as he heard this, but still he gave no stronger signs of backing out.

Reaching a little orange grove near the newly dug grave, we halted, picked out and measured the ground. Myself and the other second now opened the pistol case and commenced preparing the pistols. Hogan coolly lighted a cigar, looking as ferocious as a meataxe at his opponent, who nervously watched our movements.

"Blast the luck," I exclaimed, pretending to try the lock of one of the pistols. "The main spring of the pistol is broken—what shall we do?"

"Fight with the other—toss up which shall have the first shot," growled Hogan in a fierce tone.

"Yes," said his second, "that's fair."

"No it ain't. Supposed he gets the first shot, he'll kill me without me getting a shot at him," said Blizzard.

"Yes, sure as winking," I added, "but then if you get the first shot you are safe. Trust to luck, my boy, you'll stand as good a chance as he."

Very reluctantly, B consented, declaring that he never had any luck; but to his delight and our surprise, won the first fire.

He was now more nervous than ever, and, as I handed him the pistol, loaded very heavily with powder only, his hand shook so that he could hardly handle it.

"If I should miss him, he'll kill me sure," he muttered to me.

"Yes," said I, "but you mustn't miss him. Take good aim. I'll give the word very slow, bore him right through the heart, for you're dead if he gets a shot at you."

They were placed—the distance only ten paces, and Hogan stood with his arms folded, full breast to the toe, scowling at him as if he wanted to blast him.

"Are you ready, Mr. Blizzard?" I asked.

"Yes—but I-I don't like to shoot at him so, as he is standing there without a chance."

"Come—be quick—no trifling—it's *my* turn next," said Hogan in a bitter tone.

Blizzard's hand trembled worse than ever, but his eye flashed and he answered, "I'm ready now—I'll see if it's your turn next."

As I gave the word very slow, he raised the pistol, not as I had shown him, but with both hands, taking sight as he would with a rifle, and fired. Having held it too close to his nose, the recoil of the heavy loaded weapon nearly knocked him down, drawing the claret from his nose. But to his utter horror and astonishment, the first sight that met his bewildered eyes was Hogan standing there with his arms folded, a most diabolical smile on his face, and evidently untouched.

"Oh Lord!" he exclaimed, "how could I have missed him. I was sure I had killed him."

"You grazed his ear—that was pretty close!" I said by way of a comforter.

"Bear a hand and load the pistol—I'm hungry—want to punish him and go to supper!" cried Hogan, sharply.

Poor Blizzard. He looked as though he would sink into the earth—he was pale as a ghost, but he had stopped trembling. He was evidently trying to nerve himself to meet his fate like a man.

"Is there anything I can do for you after you have gone, my friend?" I asked coolly.

"Yes," he replied, hoarsely, "write to my father and tell him that Ezra Blizzard died like a man—just as he told me—and cut off a lock of my hair (here his voice trembled) and send it to Mary Neal in the same letter; poor gal, she'll break her heart for this. That's all—good-bye, Buntline!"

"Good-bye, Blizzard, I am sorry for you, but it can't be helped," I replied, putting my handkerchief up to my face as if to hide my tears, but really to conceal the laugh that was trying to break adrift in spite of my efforts to look serious.

"Give the word slow!" said Hogan fiercely.

"The devil is in his eye—he'll kill him for sure!" I muttered just loud enough for Blizzard to hear me. I could see the poor fellow begin to tremble.

"Are you ready?"

"No," said Hogan, "wait a moment till I finish this cigar."

Blizzard's tremor increased every moment—suspense was too severe. I added to his agony by again remarking in an undertone that I never saw Hogan so deliberate and murderous.

At last Hogan said he was ready—and again said, "Give the word slow, now!"

"By heavens, I can't stand this, it's murder!" I cried, as if dreadfully agitated. "Run, Blizzard, run!"

My earnest cry, added to what he had already endured, decided poor Blizzard, and off he started like a wounded buck.

"Stop, stop till you are killed!" yelled his second.

"Go it, Blizzard!" I shouted, at the same moment seizing a half-rotten orange from the ground and hurling it with all the force I could after him.

The orange struck him plum upon that portion of his body named by philosophers as the seat of honor, bursting and deluging him with its juice at the very instant that Hogan fired his pistol.

Poor Blizzard heard the shot, felt the orange, and tumbled forward flat on his face, close beside the new-made grave.

"Are you killed!" I cried rushing up and kneeling by his side.

"Oh Lord—oh Lord!" he groaned—"dead-shot in the back, too. Oh

Lord—tumble me into the grave—I don't care, only I'm shot in the back."

"Maybe I can stop the blood!"

"No, don't try, I don't want to live. I'm shot in the back!" he groaned.

"Don't let Mary or father hear of it—bury me as soon as I am cold!"

"Don't the wound hurt you?"

"No, no, nothing hurts me but being shot in the back. What did you tell me to run for? It was all your fault. I was ready to die like a man."

I could hold in no longer! I burst into a yell of laughter, and lifted up my principal to his feet. Hogan and his second came up and the cat was let out of the bag—everything explained.

About the maddest person that I think I ever saw in my life was that same Ezra Blizzard just at that time. He was utterly wolfish. He wanted to fight all of us on the spot one after the other, and nothing but our assurance that we were satisfied that he was true to the very backbone would satisfy him.

He afterwards became a smart and popular officer, and in real service by my side in the swamps of Florida, proved himself a trump card, and, though wounded on two occasions, he was never "shot in the back," except in that "Fast Duel."

JOHN MUIR

1838–1914

JOHN MUIR WAS eleven when his family came to the United States from Scotland to settle on a farm in Portgage, Wisconsin. He fled to Canada during the Civil War to avoid military service, returning after the war and taking a job making wagon wheels. He became a valued employee, helping improve the rudimentary machinery and making invaluable suggestions for increasing production.

He might have stayed at the factory for the rest of his life, but a tool he was working with slipped and severely damaged his eye. The doctors could recommend no more than rest in a dark room for six weeks, and prayers that his vision would return. At the end of the six weeks, his vision was normal, but his entire view of life had changed. He wrote, "God has to nearly kill us sometimes, to teach us lessons."

He quit his job and dedicated the rest of his life to the study of nature. While sitting in the darkened room, he planned his future; he would set on an unbelievable journey, walking from Indiana to Florida. He took care of personal business, and on September 1, 1867, took a train from Indianapolis to southern Indiana, walked across a bridge to Kentucky, and began his journey.

It took him ten days to pass through Kentucky, then another five days before he reached the Great Smoky Mountains and a week later he entered Georgia, presumably following the tracks of the Augusta and Waynesboro Railroad and then the Georgia Central Railroad into Savannah in early October.

He was passing through what two years earlier had been the heart of the Confederate States of America, and he could still see the damage caused by General William Sherman's March to the Sea as he moved through Georgia. He entered Florida on October 15, recording in his diary, "Today, at last, I reached Florida."

He stopped at Fernandina Beach, today a charming resort town, but then one of the state's larger cities. It was a bustling seaport, bringing in thousands of tourists who came by steamship, and serving as a shipping hub. Three days later, he reached the small community of Gainesville and wrote, "Obtained food and lodging at a sort of tavern." He was following the tracks of the state's first railroad, which ran from Fernandina to Cedar Key, although much of it was damaged during the war.

He reached his goal, Cedar Key, on October 23. Like Fernandina, Cedar Key was a thriving community and the wooden-pencil capital of the world. Two years earlier, Eberhard Faber built a mill, and the Eagle Pencil Company followed with its own mill, utilizing the cedar wood that seemed to be available in inexhaustible supply. The railroad, wrecked by Union soldiers during the war, was being repaired, and the community was thriving.

At Cedar Key, Muir put his mechanical skills to use, helping to fix machinery at a local sawmill. He came down with malaria, a not uncommon occurrence in Florida, where mosquitoes were everywhere and a solution was decades away. He recovered at the home of the sawmill manager while working on his writings. His original plan had been to go to South America to continue his walk, but his health would not allow it. He was finally able to leave Cedar Key in January on a schooner for Cuba.

Cedar Keys

An excerpt from *A Thousand-Mile Walk to the Gulf*

by John Muir

Today I reached the sea. While I was yet many miles back in the palmy woods, I caught the scent of the salt sea breeze which, although I had so many years lived far from sea breezes, suddenly conjured up Dunbar, its rocky coast, winds and waves; and my whole childhood, that seemed to have utterly vanished in the New World, was now restored amid the Florida woods by that one breath from the sea. Forgotten were the palms and magnolias and the thousand flowers that enclosed me. I could see only dulse and tangle, long-winged gulls, the Bass Rock in the Firth of Forth, and the old castle, schools, churches, and long country rambles in search of birds' nests. I do not wonder that the weary camels coming from the scorching African deserts should be able to scent the Nile.

How imperishable are all the impressions that ever vibrate one's life! We cannot forget anything. Memories may escape the action of will, may sleep a long time, but when stirred by the right influence, though that influence be light as a shadow, they flash into full stature and life with everything in place. For nineteen years my vision was bounded by forests, but today, emerging from a multitude of tropical plants, I beheld the Gulf of Mexico stretching away unbounded, except by the sky. What dreams and speculative matter for thought arose as I stood on the strand, gazing out on the burnished, treeless plain!

But now at the seaside I was in difficulty. I had reached a point that I could not ford, and Cedar Keys had an empty harbor. Would I proceed down the peninsula to Tampa and Key West, where I would be sure to find a vessel for Cuba, or would I wait here, like Crusoe, and pray for a ship. Full of these thoughts, I stepped into a little store which had a considerable trade in quinine and alligator and Cedar Keys rattlesnake skins, and inquired about shipping, means of travel, etc.

The proprietor informed me that one of several sawmills near the village was running, and that a schooner chartered to carry a load of lumber to Galveston, Texas, was expected at the mills for a load. This mill was situated on a tongue of land a few miles along the coast from Cedar Keys, and I determined to see Mr. Hodgson, the owner, to find out particulars about the expected schooner, the time she would take to load, whether I would be likely to obtain passage on her, etc.

Found Mr. Hodgson at his mill. Stated my case, and was kindly furnished the desired information. I determined to wait the two weeks likely to elapse before she sailed, and go on her to the flowery plains of Texas, from any of whose ports, I fancied, I could easily find passage to the West Indies. I agreed to work for Mr. Hodgson in the mill until I sailed, as I had but little money. He invited me to his spacious house, which occupied a shell hillock and commanded a fine view of the Gulf and many gems of palmy islets, called "keys" that fringe the shore like huge bouquets—not too big, however, for the spacious waters. Mr. Hodgson's family welcomed me with that open, unconstrained cordiality which is characteristic of the better class of Southern people.

At the sawmill a new cover had been put on the main driving pulley, which, made of rough plank, had to be turned off and smoothed. He asked me if I was able to do this job and I told him that I could. Fixing a rest and making a tool out of an old file, I directed the engineer to start the engine and run slow. After turning down the pulley and getting it true, I put a keen edge on a common carpenter's plane, quickly finished the job, and was assigned a bunk in one of the employees' lodging-houses.

The next day I felt a strange dullness and headache while I was botanizing along the coast. Thinking that a bath in the salt water might refresh me, I plunged in and swam a little distance, but this seemed only to make me feel worse. I felt anxious for something sour, and walked back to the village to buy lemons.

Thus and here my long walk was interrupted. I thought that a few days' sail would land me among the famous flower-beds of Texas.

But the expected ship came and went while I was helpless with fever. The very day after reaching the sea I began to be weighed down by inexorable leaden numbness, which I resisted and tried to shake off for three days, by bathing in the Gulf, by dragging myself about among the palms, plants, and strange shells of the shore, and by doing a little mill work. I did not fear any serious illness, for I never was sick before, and was unwilling to pay attention to my feelings.

But yet heavier and more remorselessly pressed the growing fever, rapidly gaining on my strength. On the third day after my arrival I could not take any nourishment, but craved acid. Cedar Keys was only a mile or two distant, and I managed to walk there to buy lemons. On returning, about the middle of the afternoon, the fever broke on me like a storm, and before I had staggered halfway to the mill I fell down unconscious on the narrow trail among dwarf palmettos.

When I awoke from the hot fever sleep, the stars were shining, and I was at a loss to know which end of the trail to take, but fortunately, as it afterwards proved, I guessed right. Subsequently, as I fell again and again after walking only a hundred yards or so, I was careful to lie with my head in the direction in which I thought the mill was. I rose, staggered, and fell, I know not how many times, in delirious bewilderment, gasping and throbbing with only moments of consciousness. Thus passed the hours till after midnight, when I reached the mill lodging-house.

The watchman on his rounds found me lying on a heap of sawdust at the foot of the stairs. I asked him to assist me up the steps to bed, but he thought my difficulty was only intoxication and refused to help me. The mill hands, especially on Saturday nights, often returned from the village drunk. This was the cause of the watchman's refusal. Feeling that I must get to bed, I made out to reach it on hands and knees, tumbled in after a desperate struggle, and immediately became oblivious to everything.

I awoke at a strange hour on a strange day to hear Mr. Hodgson ask a watcher beside me whether I had yet spoken, and when he replied that I had not, he said: "Well, you must keep on pouring in quinine. That's all we can do." How long I lay unconscious I never found out, but it must have been many days. Some time or other I was moved on a horse from the mill quarters to Mr. Hodgson's house, where I was nursed about three months with unfailing kindness, and to the skill and care of Mr. and Mrs. Hodgson I doubtless owe my life.

Through quinine and calomel "in sorry abundance" with other milder medicines, my malarial fever became typhoid. I had night sweats, and my legs became like posts of the temper and consistency of clay on account of dropsy. So on until January, a weary time. As soon as I was able to get out of bed, I crept away to the edge of the wood, and sat day after day beneath a moss-draped live-oak, watching birds feeding on the shore when the tide was out. Later, as I gathered some strength, I sailed in a little skiff from one key to another. Nearly all the shrubs and trees here are evergreen, and a few of the smaller plants are in flower all winter. The principal trees on this Cedar Key are the juniper, long-leafed pine, and live-oak. All of the latter, living and dead, are heavily draped with tillandsia, like those of Bonaventure. The leaf is oval, about two inches long, three fourths of an inch wide, glossy and dark green above, pale beneath. The trunk is usually much divided, and is extremely unwedgeable. . . . It is a grand old king, whose crown gleamed in the bright sky long ere the Spanish shipbuilders felled a single tree of this noble species.

The live-oaks of these keys divide empire with the long-leafed pine and palmetto, but in many places on the mainland there are large tracts exclusively occupied by them. Like the Bonaventure oaks they have the upper side of their main spreading branches thickly planted with ferns, grasses, small saw palmettos, etc. There is also a dwarf oak here, which forms dense thickets. The oaks of this key are not, like those of the Wisconsin openings, growing on grassy slopes, but stand, sunk to the shoulders, in flowering magnolias, heathworts, etc.

During my long sojourn here as a convalescent I used to lie on my back for whole days beneath the ample arms of these great trees, listening to the winds and the birds. There is an extensive shallow on the coast, close by, which the receding tide exposes daily. This is the feeding-ground of thousands of waders of all sizes, plumage, and language, and they make a lively picture and noise when they gather at the great family board to eat their daily bread, so bountifully provided for them.

Their leisure in time of high tide they spend in various ways and places. Some go in large flocks to reedy margins about the islands and wade and stand about quarrelling or making sport, occasionally finding a stray mouthful to eat. Some stand on the mangroves of the solitary shore, now and then plunging into the water after a fish. Some go long journeys in-land, up creeks and inlets. A few lonely old herons of solemn look and wing retire to favorite oaks. It was my delight to watch those old white sages of immaculate feather as they stood erect drowsing away the dull hours between tides, curtained by long skeins of tillandsia. White-bearded hermits gazing dreamily from dark caves could not appear more solemn or more becomingly shrouded from the rest of their fellow beings.

One of the characteristic plants of these keys is the Spanish bayo-net, a species of yucca, about eight or ten feet in height, and with a trunk three or four inches in diameter when full grown. It belongs to the lily family and develops palmlike from terminal buds. The stout leaves are very rigid, sharp-pointed and bayonet-like. By one of these leaves a man might be as seriously stabbed as by an army bayonet, and woe to the luckless wanderer who dares to urge his way through these armed gardens after dark. Vegetable cats of many species will rob him of his clothes and claw his flesh, while dwarf palmettos will saw his bones, and the bayonets will glide to his joints and marrow without the smallest consideration for Lord Man.

The climate of these precious islets is simply warm summer and warmer summer, corresponding in time with winter and summer in the North. The weather goes smoothly over the points of union be-twixt the twin summers. Few of the storms are very loud or variable. The average temperature during the day, in December, was about sixty-five degrees in the shade, but on one day a little damp snow fell.

Cedar Key is two and one half or three miles in diameter and its highest point is forty-four feet above mean tide-water. It is sur-rounded by scores of other keys, many of them looking like a clump of palms, arranged like a tasteful bouquet, and placed in the sea to be kept fresh.

Others have quite a sprinkling of oaks and junipers, beautifully united with vines. Still others consist of shells, with a few grasses and mangroves, circled with a rim of rushes. Those which have sedgy mar-gins furnish a favorite retreat for countless waders and divers, especially for the pelicans that frequently whiten the shore like a ring of foam.

It is delightful to observe the assembling of these feathered people from the woods and reedy isles; herons white as wave-tops, or blue as the sky, winnowing the warm air on wide quiet wing; pelicans coming with baskets to fill, and the multitude of smaller sailors of the air, swift as swallows, gracefully taking their places at Nature's family table for their daily bread. Happy birds!

The mockingbird is graceful in form and a fine singer, plainly dressed, rather familiar in habits, frequently coming like robins to doorsills for crumbs —a noble fellow, beloved by everybody. Wild geese are abundant in winter, associated with brant, some species of which I have never seen in the North. Also great flocks of robins, mourning doves, bluebirds, and the delightful brown thrashers. A large number of the smaller birds are fine singers.

Crows, too, are here, some of them cawing with a foreign accent. The common bob-white quail I observed as far south as middle Georgia. Lime Key, sketched on the opposite page, is a fair specimen of the Florida keys on this part of the coast. A fragment of cactus, Opuntia, sketched on another page, is from the above-named key, and is abundant there. The fruit, an inch in length, is gathered, and made into a sauce, of which some people are fond. This species forms thorny, impenetrable thickets. One joint that I measured was fifteen inches long.

The mainland of Florida is less salubrious than the islands, but no portion of this coast, nor of the flat border which sweeps from Maryland to Texas, is quite free from malaria. All the inhabitants of this region, whether black or white, are liable to be prostrated by the ever-present fever and ague, to say nothing of the plagues of cholera and yellow fever that come and go suddenly like storms, prostrating the population and cutting gaps in it like hurricanes in woods.

The world, we are told, was made especially for man, a presumption not supported by all the facts. A numerous class of men are painfully astonished whenever they find anything, living or dead, in all God's universe, which they cannot eat or render in some way what they call useful to themselves. They have precise dogmatic insight of the intentions of the Creator, and it is hardly possible to be guilty of irreverence in speaking of their God any more than of heathen idols. He is regarded as a civilized, law-abiding gentleman in favor either of a republican form of government or of a limited monarchy; believes in the literature and language of England; is a warm supporter of the English constitution and Sunday schools and missionary societies; and is as purely a manufactured article as any puppet of a half-penny theater.

With such views of the Creator it is, of course, not surprising that erroneous views should be entertained of the creation. To such properly trimmed people, the sheep, for example, is an easy problem—food and clothing "for us," eating grass and daisies white by divine appointment for this predestined purpose, on perceiving the demand for wool that would be occasioned by the eating of the apple in the Garden of Eden.

In the same pleasant plan, whales are storehouses of oil for us, to help out the stars in lighting our dark ways until the discovery of the Pennsylvania oil wells. Among plants, hemp, to say nothing of the cereals, is a case of evident destination for ships' rigging, wrapping packages, and hanging the wicked. Cotton is another plain case of clothing. Iron was made for hammers and ploughs, and lead for bullets; all intended for us. And so of other small handfuls of insignificant things.

But if we should ask these profound expositors of God's intentions, How about those man-eating animals—lions, tigers, alligators—which smack their lips over raw man? Or about those myriads of noxious insects that destroy labor and drink his blood? Doubtless man was intended for food and drink for all these? Oh, no! Not at all! These are unresolvable difficulties connected with Eden's apple and the Devil. Why does water drown its lord? Why do so many minerals poison him? Why are so many plants and fishes deadly enemies? Why is the lord of creation subjected to the same laws of life as his subjects? Oh, all these things are satanic, or in some way connected with the first garden.

Now, it never seems to occur to these farseeing teachers that Nature's object in making animals and plants might possibly be first of all the happiness of each one of them, not the creation of all for the happiness of one. Why should man value himself as more than a small part of the one great unit of creation? And what creature of all that the Lord has taken the pains to make is not essential to the completeness of that unit—the cosmos? The universe would be incomplete without man; but it would also be incomplete without the smallest transmicroscopic creature that dwells beyond our conceitful eyes and knowledge.

From the dust of the earth, from the common elementary fund, the Creator has made Homo sapiens. From the same material he has made every other creature, however noxious and insignificant to us. They are earth-born companions and our fellow mortals. The fearfully good, the orthodox, of this laborious patchwork of modern civilization cry "Heresy" on every one whose sympathies reach a single hair's breadth beyond the boundary epidermis of our own species.

Not content with taking all of earth, they also claim the celestial country as the only ones who possess the kind of souls for which that imponderable empire was planned.

This star, our own good earth, made many a successful journey around the heavens ere man was made, and whole kingdoms of creatures enjoyed existence and returned to dust ere man appeared to claim them. After human beings have also played their part in Creation's plan, they too may disappear without any general burning or extraordinary commotion whatever.

Plants are credited with but dim and uncertain sensation, and minerals with positively none at all. But why may not even a mineral arrangement of matter be endowed with sensation of a kind that we in our blind exclusive perfection can have no manner of communication with?

But I have wandered from my object. I stated a page or two back that man claimed the earth was made for him, and I was going to say that venomous beasts, thorny plants, and deadly diseases of certain parts of the earth prove that the whole world was not made for him. When an animal from a tropical climate is taken to high latitudes, it may perish of cold, and we say that such an animal was never intended for so severe a climate. But when man betakes himself to sickly parts of the tropics and perishes, he cannot see that he was never intended for such deadly climates. No, he will rather accuse the first mother of the cause of the difficulty, though she may never have seen a fever district; or will consider it a providential chastisement for some self-invented form of sin.

Furthermore, all uneatable and uncivilizable animals, and all plants which carry prickles, are deplorable evils which, according to closet researches of clergy, require the cleansing chemistry of universal planetary combustion. But more than aught else mankind requires burning, as being in great part wicked, and if that transmundane furnace can be so applied and regulated as to smelt and purify us into conformity with the rest of the terrestrial creation, then the tophetization of the erratic genus Homo were a consummation devoutly to be prayed for. But, glad to leave these ecclesiastical fires and blunders, I joyfully return to the immortal truth and immortal beauty of Nature.

HARRIET BEECHER STOWE

1811–1896

A s the Civil War began, Harriet Beecher Stowe was one of the nation's best-known writers, and many thought her book, *Uncle Tom's Cabin*, was one of the causes of the war, enflaming Northern passions against slavery. It seemed odd that after the Civil War, she came to Florida, one of the former Confederate states.

In Florida, she found a climate she loved, a place to write without interruption, a chance to help former slaves, and thought that she might be able to save her son, Frederick, who had been an alcoholic since he was a teenager.

She wrote to her brother, "My plan of going to Florida, as it lies in my mind, is not in any sense a mere worldly enterprise. I have for many years had a longing to be more immediately doing Christ's work on earth. My heart is with that poor people whose cause in words I have tried to plead, and who now, ignorant and docile, are just in that formative stage in which whoever seizes has them."

She began with an old cotton plantation known as Laurel Grove, on the banks of the St. Johns River near Jacksonville. She invested $10,000 in the plantation, just one of many sad ways she squandered the fortunes she made from writing. The plan called for the plantation to employ former slaves and turn Frederick into a sober cotton planter. Neither worked. The workers soon found that their boss was often in Jacksonville drinking, and production fell to laughable levels. The mission to save her son was a total failure. He abandoned Florida and went to sea, sailing around South America and on to California, where he vanished.

During the winter of 1866–1867, she came down to inspect her investment and realized it was a failure, but she was not ready to give up on Florida. She wrote to her brother, "We are now thinking seriously of a place in Mandarin much more beautiful than any other in the vicinity." The house on the banks of the St. Johns River contained date palms, an olive tree, and an orange grove with 115 trees on 30 acres. She purchased the property and built a school for former slaves. It functioned as a community center, Sunday school, church, as well as a school. It drew both whites and former slaves, who turned out for classes offered by Mrs. Stowe in a variety of subjects such as singing and sewing.

Stowe wrote, "The house looked so pretty, and quiet, and restful, the day was so calm and lovely, it seemed as though I had passed away from all trouble, and was looking back upon you all from a secure resting-place. Mr. Stowe is very happy here, and is constantly saying how pleasant it is, and how glad he is that he is here. He is so much improved in health that already he is able to take a considerable walk every day. We are all well, contented, and happy, and we have six birds, two dogs, and a pony."

She was the most famous Florida resident, and her home soon became a tourist attraction. The St. Johns River was a major thoroughfare for ships carrying everything from tourists to lumber, and every captain passing by would point out the Stowe home. There was more excitement for the passengers when they saw Mrs. Stowe on the dock or on her front porch. She even became an official tourist attraction, mentioned in such guidebooks as *Appleton's Illustrated Handbook of American Winter Resorts* and Sidney Lanier's *Florida: Its Scenery, Climate, and History, etc.* Some were suspicious that she sought the limelight, sending her daughters out to stand on the dock as the ships sailed past.

Harper's Weekly sent a writer to do a story about Stowe's life in Florida. The writer found Stowe "besieged by hundreds of visitors, who do not seem to understand that she is not an exhibition." Stowe was more than just something to see along the way; she was the reason many people came, not only to the dock at Mandarin, but to Florida. The chance to escape the freezing northern weather and see one of the great celebrities of the century proved to be a successful formula. In one year, 14,000 people sailed past the Stowe home, an amazing number in a state with just 200,000 residents.

Stowe usually came down at the end of the year and remained until May, although there was a notable exception in 1874 when her brother, the eminent preacher Henry Ward Beecher, was caught in a sex scandal and came down three months early to escape the scandal.

Stowe began writing a series of letters and sketches to the *Christian Union*, the journal started by her brother, and *Hearth and Home*, a magazine for women. The columns discussed life in Florida and even offered tips for buying land. They proved so popular that in 1873, they were published in a book, *Palmetto Leaves*, which became a best seller. It also contained a plea for rights for the freed slaves. She said that the future of the Southern states "must depend, on a large degree, to the right treatment and education of the Negro population." The honest description of life, as well as practical advice, brought even more tourists, and in 1878 a large pier was erected in front of the Stowe home, stretching 556 feet into deep water, allowing four steamships to dock at the same time. Stowe's home became the first tourist attraction in Florida.

Her visits to Florida stopped in 1884. The house is gone, but one of the buildings she built is still there, in what is now suburban Jacksonville.

Buying Land in Florida
An excerpt from *Palmetto Leaves*
by Harriet Beecher Stowe

We have before us a neat little pile of what we call "Palmetto letters," responses to our papers from all States in the Union. Our knowledge of geography has really been quite brightened by the effort to find out where all our correspondents are living. Nothing could more mark the exceptional severity of the recent winter than the bursts of enthusiasm with which the tidings of flowers and open-air freedom in Florida have come to those struggling through snow-drifts and hailstorms in the more ungenial parts of our Union. Florida seems to have risen before their vision as the hymn sings of better shores—

"On Jordan's stormy banks I stand,
And cast a wistful eye
To Canaan's fair and happy land."

Consequently, the letters of inquiry have come in showers. What is the price of land? Where shall we go? How shall we get there? &c.

We have before advertised you, O beloved unknown! who write, that your letters are welcome, ofttimes cheering, amusing, and undeniably nice letters; yet we cannot pledge ourselves to answer, except in the gross, and through "The Christian Union." The last inquiry is from three brothers, who want to settle and have homes together at the South. They ask, "Is there government land that can be had in Florida?" Yes, there is a plenty of it; yet, as Florida is the oldest settled State in the Union, and has always been a sort of bone for which adventurers have wrangled, the best land in it has been probably taken up. We do not profess to be land-agents; and we speak only for the tract of land lying on the St. John's River, between Mandarin and Jacksonville, when we say that there are thousands of acres of good land, near to a market, near to a great river on which three or four steamboats are daily plying, that can be had for five dollars per acre, and for even less than that. Fine, handsome building lots in the neighborhood of Jacksonville are rising in value, commanding much higher prices than the mere productive value of the land. In other words, men pay for advantages, for society, for facilities afforded by settlements.

Now, for the benefit of those who are seriously thinking of coming to Florida, we have taken some pains to get the practical experience of men who are now working the land, as to what it will do. On the 2d of May, we accepted the invitation of Col. Hardee to visit his pioneer nursery, now in the fourth year of its existence. Mr. Hardee is an enthusiast in his business; and it is a department where we are delighted to see enthusiasm. The close of the war found him, as he said, miserably poor. But, brave and undiscouraged, he retained his former slaves as free laborers; took a tract of land about a mile and a half from Jacksonville; put up a house; cleared, planted, ploughed, and digged: and, in the course of four years, results are beginning to tell handsomely, as they always do for energy and industry. He showed us through his grounds, where everything was growing at the rate things do grow here in the month of May. Two things Mr. Hardee seems to have demonstrated: first, that strawberry-culture may be a success in Florida; and, second, that certain varieties of Northern apples and pears may be raised here. We arrived in Florida in the middle of January; and one of the party who spent a night at the St. James was surprised by seeing a peck of fresh, ripe strawberries brought in. They were from Mr. Hardee's nursery, and grown in the open air; and he informed us that they had, during all the winter, a daily supply of the fruit, sufficient for a large family, and a considerable overplus for the market. The month of May, however, is the height of the season; and they were picking, they informed us, at the rate of eighty quarts per day.

In regard to apples and pears, Mr. Hardee's method is to graft them upon the native hawthorn; and the results are really quite wonderful. Mr. Hardee was so complaisant as to cut and present to us a handsome cluster of red Astrachan apples about the size of large hickorynuts, the result of the second year from the graft. Several varieties of pears had made a truly astonishing growth, and promise to fruit, in time, abundantly. A large peach-orchard presented a show of peaches, some of the size of a butternut, and some of a walnut. Concerning one which he called the Japan peach, he had sanguine hope of ripe fruit in ten days. We were not absolute in the faith as to the exact date, but believe that there will undoubtedly be ripe peaches there before the month of May is out. Mr. Hardee is particularly in favor of cultivating fruit in partially-shaded ground. Most of these growths we speak of were under the shade of large live oaks; but when he took us into the wild forest, and showed us peach, orange, and lemon trees set to struggle for existence on the same footing, and with only the same advantages, as the wild denizens of the forest, we rather demurred. Was not this pushing theory to extremes?

Col. Hardee has two or three native seedling peaches grown in Florida, of which he speaks highly,—Mrs. Thompson's Golden Free, which commences ripening in June, and continues till the first of August; the "Cracker Cart," very large, weighing sometimes thirteen ounces; the Cling Yellow; and the Japan, very small and sweet, ripening in May.

Besides these, Mr. Hardee has experimented largely in vines, in which he gives preference to the Isabella, Hartford Prolific, and Concord.

He is also giving attention to roses and ornamental shrubbery. What makes the inception of such nurseries as Mr. Hardee's a matter of congratulation is that they furnish to purchasers things that have been proved suited to the climate and soil of Florida. Peach-trees, roses, and grapes, sent from the North, bring here the habit of their Northern growth, which often makes them worthless. With a singular stubbornness, they adhere to the times and seasons to which they have been accustomed farther North. We set a peach-orchard of some four hundred trees which we obtained from a nursery in Georgia. We suspect now, that, having a press of orders, our nurseryman simply sent us a packet of trees from some Northern nursery. The consequence is, that year after year, when all nature about them is bursting into leaf and blossom, when peaches of good size gem the boughs of Florida trees, our peach-orchard stands sullen and leafless; nor will it start bud or blossom till the time for peaches to start in New York. The same has been our trouble with some fine varieties of roses which we took from our Northern grounds. As yet, they are hardly worth the ground they occupy; and whether they ever will do anything is a matter of doubt. Meanwhile we have only to ride a little way into the pine-woods to see around many a rustic cabin a perfect blaze of crimson roses and cluster roses, foaming over the fences in cascades of flowers. These are Florida roses, born and bred; and this is the way they do with not one tithe of the work and care that we have expended on our poor Northern exiles. Mr. Hardee, therefore, in attempting the pioneer nursery of Florida, is doing a good thing for every newcomer; and we wish him all success. As a parting present, we received a fine summer squash, which, for the first of May, one must admit is good growth.

JOHN GREENLEAF WHITTIER

1807–1892

HARRIETT BEECHER STOWE rightfully receives much of the credit for writing the words that stirred the nation to the horrors of slavery with *Uncle Tom's Cabin.* But another writer, poet John Greenleaf Whittier, also played a role with his words, a poem that was widely circulated by anti-slavery forces beginning in 1845.

The poem told the dramatic story of Captain Jonathan Walker, who moved to Pensacola in 1837. His neighbors immediately noticed that he treated slaves and free blacks with respect, a trait almost unknown in the slave-holding state. Of the 50,000 people living in Florida, nearly half were slaves, and Florida was playing a major role in slave trading business. After 1808, it was illegal to bring slaves into the United States, but that did not stop determined slave traders, who could easily sneak ashore along the Panhandle coast of Florida and from there take their illegal cargo to be auctioned to the highest bidder. The federal government was virtually powerless to patrol the coast with its hundreds of miles of shoreline and hundreds of inlets.

By 1841, Jonathan Walker had had enough of slavery and was determined not to raise his children where there was slavery. He left for Massachusetts, but returned to Pensacola aboard his ship. His visit changed his life. He encountered seven slaves, whom he had worked with when he lived in Pensacola and who now begged him to sail them to freedom in the Bahamas.

Walker agreed, and he and the seven slaves left Pensacola in his small boat. Almost immediately, search parties were dispatched to look for the escaped slaves. It was not just a question of the missing seven: If their escape was successful, it might encourage other slaves to escape.

The journey lasted far longer than Walker had expected, and after fourteen days, Walker was suffering from sunstroke and his passengers could not navigate the ship. They were spotted by two sloops and taken to Key West, where Walker was arrested and charged with aiding the escape of the slaves. All eight sailed to Pensacola, where the slaves were returned to their masters and Walker was taken to jail.

A federal jury found him guilty of slave stealing, fined him $150, and added a bizarre penalty that led to the Whittier poem and created a storm in the North. The federal judge ordered Walker to be branded with the initials "S S" for slave stealer. It was such an unusual punishment that a brand had to be made.

The sentence was carried out beginning with Walker being placed in stocks and pelted with eggs and fruit for one hour. Then he was taken into the courtroom where a small fire was built to heat the brand. As the federal judge watched, the local sheriff heated the brand and held it to Walker's palm for fifteen to twenty seconds. After the branding he was served with more charges and fined $595.05, which was raised by abolitionists in the North.

When he returned to the North, he was proclaimed a hero.

John Greenleaf Whittier—he originally wrote under the name John G. Whittier—first encountered anti-slavery leader William Lloyd Garrison in 1826 when Garrison published a poem by Whittier, who was then a teenager. In 1833 Garrison published Whittier's first antislavery pamphlet "Justice and Expediency." Whittier spent the following two decades as a leading voice in the anti-slavery movement. He was a founding member of the American Anti-Slavery Society, and not only wrote anti-slavery articles, but also anti-slavery poems.

In 1845, he wrote "The Branded Hand," which was distributed throughout the North. Anti-slave leaders distributed thousands of copies of the poem—many with the words "Read and Circulate" at the top to encourage even larger distribution.

The Branded Hand

by John Greenleaf Whittier

Welcome home again, brave seaman! with thy thoughtful brow
    and gray,
And the old heroic spirit of our earlier, better day;
With that front of calm endurance, on whose steady nerve in vain
Pressed the iron of the prison, smote the fiery shafts of pain.

Is the tyrant's brand upon thee? Did the brutal cravens aim
To make God's truth thy falsehood, His holiest work thy shame?
When, all blood-quenched, from the torture the iron was with
    drawn,
How laughed their evil angel the baffled fools to scorn!

They change to wrong the duty which God hath written out
On the great heart of humanity, too legible for doubt!
They, the loathsome moral lepers, blotched from footsole up to
    crown,
Give to shame what God hath given unto honor and renown!

Why, that brand is highest honor! than its traces never yet
Upon old armorial hatchments was a prouder blazon set;
And thy unborn generations, as they tread our rocky strand,
Shall tell with pride the story of their father's branded hand!

As the Templar home was welcome, bearing back from Syrian wars
The scars of Arab lances and of Paynim scimitars,
The pallor of the prison, and the shackle's crimson span,
So we meet thee, so we greet thee, truest friend of God and man.

He suffered for the ransom of the dear Redeemer's grave,
Thou for His living presence in the bound and bleeding slave;
He for a soil no longer by the feet of angels trod,
Thou for the true Shechinah, the present home of God.

For, while the jurist, sitting with the slave-whip o'er him swung,
From the tortured truths of freedom the lie of slavery wrung,
And the solemn priest to Moloch, on each God-deserted shrine,
Broke the bondman's heart for bread, poured the bondman's blood
        for wine;

While the multitude in blindness to a far-off Saviour knelt,
And spurned, the while, the temple where a present Saviour dwelt;
Thou beheld'st Him in the task-field, in the prison shadows dim,
And thy mercy to the bondman, it was mercy unto Him!

In thy lone and long night-watches, sky above and wave below,
Thou didst learn a higher wisdom than the babbling schoolmen
        know;
God's stars and silence taught thee, as His angels only can,
That the one sole sacred thing beneath the cope of heaven is Man!

That he who treads profanely on the scrolls of law and creed,
In the depth of God's great goodness may find mercy in his need;
But woe to him who crushes the soul with chain and rod,
And herds with lower natures the awful form of God!

Then lift that manly right-hand, bold ploughman of the wave!
Its branded palm shall prophesy, "Salvation to the Slave!"
Hold up its fire-wrought language, that whoso reads may feel
His heart swell strong within him, his sinews change to steel.

Hold it up before our sunshine, up against our Northern air;
Ho! men of Massachusetts, for the love of God, look there!
Take it henceforth for your standard, like the Bruce's heart of yore,
In the dark strife closing round ye, let that hand be seen before!

And the masters of the slave-land shall tremble at that sign,
When it points its finger Southward along the Puritan line
Can the craft of State avail them? Can a Christless church with
        stand,
In the van of Freedom's onset, the coming of that hand?

FREDERICK REMINGTON

1861–1909

B Y THE MID 1890s, Frederick Remington was running out of frontier. The census of 1890 determined that the West was settled, leaving southwest Florida as the final frontier. With the end of the Western frontier came the end of the things Remington cherished and had captured so brilliantly in his words, drawings, and statues.

After 1894, Remington made no Western excursions, but his search for the frontier, cowboys, and adventure was not over. In 1895, *Harper's Weekly* sent Remington to southwest Florida to capture this last frontier in pictures and words. He found the frontier and the cowboys, but it was far different from the West he had loved.

Southwest Florida was lightly populated and every bit as wild as the far West. It remained a frontier almost until World War II. In 1937, a cattleman drove a herd of cattle 160 miles without encountering any fences or people.

Remington went to Punta Gorda and Arcadia and invited his close friend, Owen Wister, the author of the Western classic *The Virginian,* to join him. He promised Wister, "Bear, tarpon, red snapper, ducks, birds of paradise" if he came. And he told him there would be "curious cowboys who shoot up the railroad trains."

Remington, whose work had glorified the Western cowboys, was not impressed with the Florida version. When he first saw them, he wrote: "Two very emaciated Texas ponies pattered down the street; bearing wild-looking individuals, . . . [with] hanging hair and drooping hats and generally bedraggled appearance. . . ." The two cowboys tied up their horses, entered a saloon, and were drunk within fifteen minutes. He found the Florida cowboys slovenly, drunken, dishonest, and unromantic—they did not even wear cowboy boots, but instead wore the shoes of a farmer.

He did find many of the things he had found in the West: cattle stealing, gunfire, and a propensity by law enforcement to look the other way. One cowboy was shot while trying to rebrand a stolen steer, but the coroner's jury decided he had died when he fell on the horns of the steer.

It wasn't just the cowboys who disappointed Remington. He even found fault with the cows. Cattle were first brought over by the Spanish, beginning in the 1500s. The Florida cows were scrawny when compared to the magnificent animals that roamed the West.

Remington also discovered tarpon fishing in the Gulf of Mexico, but again he was disappointed, not finding tarpon, and advising his readers to sell their fishing gear and buy a shotgun to hunt ducks.

Despite his views, he was back a year later to begin coverage of the growing crisis in Cuba. He and veteran reporter Richard Harding Davis stopped in Key West en route to Cuba—Davis would provide the words, Remington the drawings. They were on assignment for William Randolph Hearst's *New York Journal*, which was leading the call for a war with Spain.

They were stuck in Key West as Spain erected a blockade around its possession. They tried to use Hearst's power boat to outrun the blockade, but ran into foul weather and turned back. (Author Stephen Crane was stranded in Jacksonville, and when he attempted to sail he also encountered foul weather, which nearly took his life.)

Finally after several weeks, they were able to book passage on a commercial ship. It could not have been soon enough for Remington, who hated Key West. He said the "sun makes men sweat and wish to God they were somewhere else."

He may have hated Key West, which he called a "dusty smelly bit of sandy coral," but he came back as the war came closer, joining scores of other journalists who were waiting to cover the first American war in a third of a century.

He made it to Cuba, but found little to write about. In one of the most famous exchanges in journalism, he wired Hearst, "Everything is quiet. There is no trouble. There will be no war. I wish to return." Hearst replied, "Please remain. You furnish the pictures and I'll furnish the war."

Hearst was right. His constant drumbeat for war with Spain, combined with the explosion of the U.S.S. *Maine*, led to war and sent Remington to Tampa, where he joined thousands of troops preparing to embark for Cuba. He stayed at the Tampa Bay Hotel, the finest in town and home to dozens of reporters, generals, and those seeking to do business with the Army. As with Key West, he was not impressed with Tampa, saying it was "chiefly composed of derelict houses drifting on an ocean of sand." His drawings captured the military buildup in Tampa, displaying a complete range—officers, animals, and enlisted men.

Finally, he sailed for Cuba aboard the headquarters ship but did not like war. He came down with yellow fever and was repulsed by the dead bodies. "From now on I mean to paint fruits and flowers," he wrote.

Cracker Cowboys of Florida

In *Harper's Weekly,* 1895

by Frederick Remington

One can thresh the straw of history until he is well worn out, and also is running some risk of wearing others out, who may have to listen, so I will waive the telling of who the first cowboy was, even if I knew; but the last one who has come down under my observation lives down in Florida, and the way it happened was this: I was sitting in a "sto'un'," as the "Crackers" say, waiting for the clerk to load some "number eights," when my friend said, "Look at the cowboys!" This immediately caught my interest. With me cowboys are what gems and porcelain are to some others. Two very emaciated Texas ponies pattered down the street, bearing wild-looking individuals, whose hanging hair and drooping hats and generally bedraggled appearance would remind you at once of the Spanish-moss which hangs so quietly and helplessly to the limbs of the oaks out in the swamps. There was none of the bilious fierceness and rearing plunge which I had associated with my friends out West, but as a fox-terrier is to a yellow cur, so were these last. They had on about four dollars worth of clothes between them, and rode McClellan saddles, with saddlebags, and guns tied on before. The only things they did which were conventional were to tie their ponies up by the head in brutal disregard, and then get drunk in about fifteen minutes. I could see that in this case, while some of the tail feathers were the same, they would easily classify as new birds.

"And so you have cowboys down here," I said to the man who ran the meat-market.

He picked up a tiny piece of raw liver out of the meshes of his long black beard, tilted his big black hat, shoved his arms into his white apron front, and said,

"Gawd! Yes, stranger; I was once one myself."

The plot thickened so fast that I was losing much, so I became more deliberate. "Do the boys come into town often?" I inquired further.

"Oh, yes, mos' every little spell," replied the butcher, as he reached behind his weighing scales and picked up a double-barreled shot gun, sawed off, "We-uns are expectin' of they-uns to-day." And he broke the barrels and took out the shells to examine them.

"Do they come shooting?" I interposed.

He shut the gun with a snap. "We split even, stranger."

Seeing that the butcher was a fragile piece of bric-a-brac, and that I might need him for future study, I bethought me of the banker down the street. Bankers are bound to be broad-gauged, intelligent, and conservative, so I would go to him and get at the ancient history of his neck of the woods. I introduced myself, and was invited behind the counter. The look of things reminded me of one of those great green terraces which covered fortifications and ugly cannon. It was boards and wire screen in front, but behind it were shot-guns and six-shooters hung in the handiest way, on sort of disappearing gun-carriage arrangement. Shortly one of the cowboys of the street scene floundered in. He was two-thirds drunk, with brutal shifty eyes and a flabby lower lip.

"I want twenty dollars on the old man. Ken I have it?"

I rather expected that the ban would go into "action front," but the clerk said, "Certainly," and completed this rather odd financial transaction, whereat the bull-hunter stumbled out.

"Who is the old man in this case?' I ventured.

"Oh, it's his boss, old Colonel Zuigg, of Crow City. I gave some money to some of his boys some weeks ago, and when the colonel was down here I asked him if he wanted the boys to draw against him in that way, and he said, "Yes, for a small amount; they will steal a cow or two, and pay me that way."

Here was something tangible.

"What happens when a man steals another man's brand in this country?"

"He mustn't get caught; that's all. They all do it, but they never bring their troubles to court. They just shoot it out there in the brush. The last time old Colonel Zuigg brought Zorn Zuidden in here and had him indicted for stealing cattle, said Zorn: "Now see here, old man Zuigg, what do you want for to go and git me arrested for? I have stole thousands of cattle and put your mark and brand on 'em, and jes because I have stole a couple of hundred from you, you go and get me indicted. You jes better go and get that whole deal prossed;" and it was done.

The argument was perfect.

"From that I should imagine that the cow-people have no more idea of law than the 'gray apes,' " I commented.

"Yes, that's about it. Old Colonel Zuigg was a judge for a spell, till some feller filled him with buckshot, and he had to resign; and I remember he decided a case against me once. I was hot about it, and the old colonel he saw I was. Says he, 'Now yer mad, ain't you?' And I allowed I was. 'Well,' says he, 'You hain't got no call to get mad. I have decided the last eight cases in yer favor, and you kin't have it go yer way all the time; it wouldn't look right,' and I had to be satisfied."

The courts in that locality were but the faint and sickly flame of a taper offered at the shrine of justice which was traditional only, it seemed. Moral forces having ceased to operate, the large owners began to brand everything in sight, never realizing they were sowing the wind. This action naturally demoralized the cowboys, who shortly began to brand a little on their own account—and then the deluge. The rights of property having been destroyed, the large owners put strong outfits in the field, composed of desperate men armed to the teeth, and what happens in the lonely pine woods no one knows but the desperadoes themselves, albeit some of them never come back to the little fringe of settlements. The winter visitor from the North kicks up the jack snipe along the beach or tarponizes in the estuaries of the Gulf, and when he comes to the hotel for dinner he eats Chicago dressed beef, but, out in the wilderness low-browed cow-folks shoot and stab each other for possession of scrawny creatures not fit for pointer dog to mess on. One cannot but feel the force of Buckle's law of "the physical aspects of nature" in this sad country. Flat and sandy with miles on miles of straight pine timber, each tree an exact duplicate of its neighbor tree, and underneath the scrub palmettos, the twisted brakes and hammocks, and the gnarled water-oaks festooned with the sad gray Spanish moss—truly not a country for a high spirited race or moral giants.

The land gives only a tough wiregrass, and the poor little cattle, no bigger than a donkey, wander half starved and horribly emaciated in search of it. There used to be a trade with Cuba, but now that has gone; and beyond the supplying of Key West and the small fringe of settlements they have no market. How well the cowboys serve their masters I can only guess, since the big owners do not dare go into the woods, or even to their own doors at night, and they do not keep a light burning in the houses. One, indeed, attempted to assert his rights, but some one pumped sixteen buckshot into him as he bent over a spring to drink, and he left the country. They do tell of a late encounter between two rival foremen, who rode on to each other in the woods, and drawing, fired, and both were found stretched dying under the palmettos, one calling deliriously the name of his boss. The unknown reaches of the Everglades lie just below, and with a half-hour's start a man who knew the country would be safe from pursuit, even if it were attempted; and as one man cheerfully confided to me, "A boat don't leave no trail, stranger."

That might makes right, and that they steal by wholesale, any cattle hunter will admit; and why they brand at all I can not see, since one boy tried to make it plain to me, as he shifted his body in drunken abandon and grabbed my pencil and a sheet of wrapping-paper: "See yer; ye see that?" And he drew a circle O and then another ring around it. "That brand ain't no good. Well then—" And again his knotted and dirty fingers essayed the brand. He laboriously drew upon it and made a brand, which of course destroyed the former brand. "Then here," he continued, as he drew 13, "all ye've got ter do is this— 3 1 3" I gasped in amazement, not at his cleverness as a brand destroyer, but at his honest abandon. With a horrible operatic laugh, such as is painted in "the Cossack's Answer," he again laboriously drew a crossed circle, and then added some marks. And again breaking into his devil's "ha, ha!" said, "Make the damned thing whirl."

I did not protest. He would have shot me for that. But I did wish he was living in the northwest quarter of New Mexico, where Mr. Cooper and Dan could throw their eyes over the trail of his pony. Of course each man has adjusted himself to this lawless rustling, and only calculates that he can steal as much as his opponent. It is rarely that their affairs are brought to court, but when they are, the men come en masse to the room, armed.

There is also a noticeable absence of negroes among them, as they still retain some *ante bellum* theories, and it is only very lately that they have "reconstructed." Their general ignorance is "miracalous," and quite satisfying to an outside man. Some whom I met did not even know where the Texas was which furnished them their ponies. The railroads of Florida have had their ups and downs with them in a petty way on account of the running over their cattle by the trains; and then some long-haired old Cracker drops into the nearest station with his gun and pistol, and wants the telegraph operator to settle immediately on the basis of the Cracker's claim for damages, which is always absurdly high. At first the railroads demurred, but the cowboys lined up in the "bresh" on some dark night and pumped Winchesters into the train in a highly picturesque way. The trainmen at once recognized the force of the Cracker's view on cattle killing, but it took some considerable "potting" at the more conservative superintendents before the latter could bestir themselves and invent a "cow-attorney," as the company adjuster is called, who now settles with the bashmen as best he can. Certainly no worse people ever lived since the big killing up Muscleshell way, and the romance is taken out of it by the cowardly assassination which is the practice. They are well paid for their desperate work, and always eat fresh beef or "razor-backs," and deer which they kill in the woods. The heat, the poor grass, their brutality, and the pest of the flies kill their ponies, and, as a rule, they lack dash and are indifferent riders, but they are picturesque in their unkempt, almost unearthly wildness. A strange effect is added by their use of large, fierce cur-dogs, one of which accompanies each cattle-hunter, and is taught to pursue cattle, and to even take them by the nose, which is another instance of their brutality. Still, as they have only a couple of horses apiece, it saves them much extra running.

These men do not use the rope, unless to noose a pony in a corral, but work their cattle in strong log corrals, which are made at about a day's march apart all through the woods. Indeed, ropes are hardly necessary, since the cattle are so small and thin that two men can successfully "wrestle" a three-year-old. A man goes into the corral, grabs a cow by one horn, and throwing his other arm over her back, waits until some other man takes her hind leg, whereat causes some very entertaining Greco-Roman style.

When the cow is successful, she finds her audience of Cracker cowboys sitting on the fence awaiting another opening, and gasping for breath. The best bull will go over three hundred pounds, while I have seen a yearling at a hundred and fifty—if you, O knights of the riata, can imagine it! Still, it is desperate work. Some of the men are so reckless and active that they do not hesitate to encounter a wild bull in the open. The cattle are as wild as deer, they race off at scent; and when "rounded up" many will not drive, whereupon these are promptly shot. It frequently happens when the herd is being driven quietly along a bull will turn on the drivers, charging at once. Then there is a scamper and great shooting. The bulls often become so maddened in these forays that they drop and die in their tracks, for which strange fact no one can account, but as a rule they are too scrawny and mean to make their handling difficult.

So this is the Cracker cowboy, whose chief interest would be found in the tales of some bushwhacking enterprise, which I very much fear would be a one-sided story, and not worth the telling. At best they must be revolting, having no note of the savage encounters which used to characterize the easy days in West Texas and New Mexico, when every man tossed his life away in the crackle of his own revolver. The moon shows pale through the leafy canopy on their evening fires, and the mists, the miasma, and the mosquitoes settle over their dreary camp talk. In place of the wild stampede, there is only the bellowing in the pens, and instead of the plains shaking under the dusty air as the bedizened vaqueros plough their fiery broncos through the milling herds, the cattle-hunter wends his lonely way through the ooze and rank grass, while the dreary pine trunks line up and shut the view.

(Historians agree that Colonel Zuigg was Ziba King (1838–1901), a cattle king of DeSoto County, and Zorn Zuidden was Morgan Bonaparte "Bone" Mizell (1863–1921), the legendary cowhunter.)

JAMES WELDON JOHNSON

1871–1938

THE YEAR AFTER slavery ended, James Johnson arrived in Jacksonville from the Bahamas, where a hurricane had ruined his sponge fishing business. He took a job as a waiter at the St. James Hotel, the grandest hotel in Florida, and was soon promoted to head waiter, a significant job for an African American at that time, and one that allowed him some financial security. Jacksonville was different from other Southern towns; it was a vacation center for wealthy Northerners who came each winter expecting quality service, usually provided by African Americans. The Northerners could provide significant tips, and their attitudes toward blacks, while still racist, were far better than that of most of the Southern whites.

Five years later, James Weldon Johnson, was born. He had advantages other African Americans did not; his mother, a school teacher, taught him at home, then enrolled him at the prestigious all-black Stanton School. He attended Atlanta University, then returned to the Stanton School as principal at the age of 23. The next year he launched the *Daily American*, a newspaper devoted to the black community. The newspaper struggled financially and survived less than a year. It was, he wrote, "my first taste of defeat in public life . . ." The paper may have been a financial failure, but it brought Johnson to the attention of the African-American leaders throughout the nation, including Booker T. Washington and W. E. B. DuBois.

He studied law with a white lawyer, although it seemed as though he was wasting his time—no African American had been admitted to the Florida Bar since the end of Reconstruction. To the surprise of many, Johnson joined the bar and built a successful practice while remaining principal at Stanton. Two incidents may have convinced Johnson that it was time to leave Jacksonville. In 1901, a massive fire swept through the city. The African-American section was particularly hard hit because the fire department did not provide services to blacks and the Stanton School went up in flames.

One of those who came to Jacksonville to report on the fire was a fair-skinned African American who wanted to interview Johnson. When they went to a nearby park to talk, an angry mob with bloodhounds attacked them because they believed Johnson was talking with a white woman. The mob dragged him to police headquarters, where he received an apology when the situation became clear. He realized that in the segregated South, even a leading African American could be beaten in a public park.

He moved to New York where he and his brother became famous for their musical compositions, and he became a leader in the Harlem Renaissance movement. President Theodore Roosevelt named him a United States consul to Venezuela and later Nicaragua, where he completed his only novel, *The Autobiography of an Ex-Colored Man*.

As director of the National Association for the Advancement of Colored People, he increased membership but failed to secure passage of legislation to make life better for African Americans. He left the NAACP for a faculty post at Fisk College in Tennessee.

He gained worldwide fame but is best known for a poem he wrote while at Stanton. In 1900, the school was about to observe Abraham Lincoln's birthday, and Booker T. Washington accepted an invitation to speak there. To introduce Washington, Johnson wanted the school's 500 students to do something memorable. He wrote a poem titled "Lift Every Voice and Sing." Five years later, his brother, John, put music to the poem and in 1919 the NAACP named it "The Negro National Anthem."

The song became a staple at gatherings of African Americans, pasted into the back of church hymnals, and nearly a century later recorded by such artists as Anita Baker, Stephanie Mills, Dionne Warwick, and Stevie Wonder. At the 2009 inauguration for President Barack Obama, the former president of the Southern Christian Leadership Conference, Joseph Lowery, read part of the poem during his benediction.

Lift Every Voice and Sing

by James Weldon Johnson

Lift every voice and sing till earth and heaven ring,
Ring with the harmonies of liberty;
Let our rejoicing rise, high as the listening skies,
Let it resound loud as the rolling sea.
Sing a song full of the faith that the dark past has taught us,
Sing a song full of the hope that the present has brought us;
Facing the rising sun of our new day begun,
Let us march on till victory is won.

Stony the road we trod, bitter the chastening rod,
Felt in the days when hope unborn had died;
Yet with a steady beat, have not our weary feet,
Come to the place for which our fathers sighed?
We have come, over a way that which tears has been watered,
We have come, treading our path through the blood of the slaughtered;
Out of the gloomy past, till now we stand at last,
Where the white gleam of our bright star is cast.

God of our weary years, God of our silent tears,
Thou Who has brought us thus far on the way;
Thou Who hast by Thy might, led us into the light,
Keep us forever in the path, we pray.
Lest our feet stray from the places our God, where me met Thee.
Lest our hearts, drunk with the wine of the world, we forget Thee.
Shadowed beneath Thy hand, may we forever stand,
True to our God, true to our native land.

JULES VERNE

1828–1905

FRENCHMAN JULES VERNE was about one hundred years and one hundred miles off, but his fantasy of a spacecraft leaving Florida for the moon became a reality. Verne created the science fiction writing genre and brought worldwide attention to a little-known state and an almost unknown town, Tampa.

Jules Verne studied law but was drawn to writing. Increasingly, he neglected his law studies to write, leading his father to cut him off financially. He struggled, but by the time he was in his thirties, he produced a remarkable string of best sellers that are still in print nearly 150 years later: *Journey to the Center of the Earth*, *From the Earth to the Moon*, *Twenty Thousand Leagues Under the Sea*, and *Around the World in Eighty Days*.

Each has sold millions of copies and been made into successful movies. *From the Earth to the Moon* remains the most amazing, not only because of its success in the 1860s, but because of the research Verne did. Writers still wonder at the similarities between his moon launch and the actual event a century later.

For his research, Verne consulted the handful of available books about Florida and shared his research with his readers. In *From the Earth to the Moon*, Verne's missile launch is underwritten by a Baltimore gun club, which has to select a site. The competition is between Texas and Florida—very much as it would be in the twentieth century, when Florida was chosen over Texas.

In his book, Verne tells the story of the selection process, which drew nationwide interest. Gun club members traveled from Baltimore to New Orleans, then by ship to Tampa.

> When the decision was arrived at by the Gun Club, to the disparagement of Texas, every one in America, where reading is a universal acquirement, set to work to study the geography of Florida. Never before had there been such a sale for works like *Bartram's Travels in Florida*, *Roman's Natural History of East and West Florida*, *William's Territory of Florida*, and *Cleland on the Cultivation of the Sugar-Cane in Florida*.

Verne liberally borrowed from the descriptions in these texts. In Verne's book, a location near Tampa Town is chosen. Although his description is generally accurate, he does place the site at 1,800 feet above sea level, nearly five times higher than the actual highest point in the state. When the real launch site was selected a century later, it was on the east coast of Florida so that spacecraft would not be launched over populous areas in case of a crash or explosion.

His book includes an attack by the Seminole Indians against the moon travelers, but the first space men push on with their project. Verne's research on Indians, however, focused on tribes in the West. He had herds of buffalo wandering around Tampa. The construction of the launch site keeps the Indians at bay in Verne's telling.

Not only was Florida the site of the real moon launch in 1969, both Verne and NASA decided on a three-member crew for the journey. Verne calls his the device used to launch the spacecraft the *Columbiad,* and the Apollo 11 command module was named *Columbia.* The men aboard Verne's spacecraft were Ardan, Barbicane, and Nicholl, while the three astronauts on the Apollo 8—the first to travel around the moon—were Anders, Borman and Lovell. Both Verne's craft and NASA's returned to earth, crashing down in the Pacific and being fished out by a U.S. Navy ship.

As the astronauts of Apollo 11—the first to land on the moon—sped homeward on July 23, 1969, Mission Commander Neil Armstrong said, "A hundred years ago, Jules Verne wrote a book about a voyage to the Moon. His spaceship, *Columbia* [sic], took off from Florida and landed in the Pacific Ocean after completing a trip to the Moon. It seems appropriate to us to share with you some of the reflections of the crew as the modern-day *Columbia* completes its rendezvous with the planet Earth and the same Pacific Ocean tomorrow."

Verne came to the United States in 1867, two years after the publication of his book, but did not come to Florida.

Florida and Texas

An excerpt from *From the Earth to the Moon*
by Jules Verne

One question yet remained to be decided; it was necessary to choose a favorable spot for the experiment. According to the advice of the Observatory of Cambridge, the gun must be fired perpendicularly to the plane of the horizon, that is to say, toward the zenith. Now the moon does not traverse the zenith, except in places situated between 0° and 28° of latitude. It became, then, necessary to determine exactly that spot on the globe where the immense Columbiad should be cast.

On the 20th of October, at a general meeting of the Gun Club, Barbicane produced a magnificent map of the United States. "Gentlemen," said he, in opening the discussion, "I presume that we are all agreed that this experiment cannot and ought not to be tried anywhere but within the limits of the soil of the Union. Now, by good fortune, certain frontiers of the United States extend downward as far as the 28th parallel of the north latitude. If you will cast your eye over this map, you will see that we have at our disposal the whole of the southern portion of Texas and Florida."

It was finally agreed, then, that the Columbiad must be cast on the soil of either Texas or Florida. The result, however, of this decision was to create a rivalry entirely without precedent between the different towns of these two States.

The 28th parallel, on reaching the American coast, traverses the peninsula of Florida, dividing it into two nearly equal portions. Then, plunging into the Gulf of Mexico, it subtends the arc formed by the coast of Alabama, Mississippi, and Louisiana; then skirting Texas, off which it cuts an angle, it continues its course over Mexico, crosses the Sonora, Old California, and loses itself in the Pacific Ocean. It was, therefore, only those portions of Texas and Florida which were situated below this parallel which came within the prescribed conditions of latitude.

Florida, in its southern part, reckons no cities of importance; it is simply studded with forts raised against the roving Indians. One solitary town, Tampa Town, was able to put in a claim in favor of its situation.

In Texas, on the contrary, the towns are much more numerous and important. Corpus Christi, in the county of Nueces, and all the cities situated on the Rio Bravo, Laredo, Comalites, San Ignacio on the Web, Rio Grande City on the Starr, Edinburgh in the Hidalgo, Santa Rita, Elpanda, Brownsville in the Cameron, formed an imposing league against the pretensions of Florida. So, scarcely was the decision known, when the Texan and Floridan deputies arrived at Baltimorc in an incredibly short space of time. From that very moment President Barbicane and the influential members of the Gun Club were besieged day and night by formidable claims. If seven cities of Greece contended for the honor of having given birth to a Homer, here were two entire States threatening to come to blows about the question of a cannon.

The rival parties promenaded the streets with arms in their hands; and at every occasion of their meeting a collision was to be apprehended which might have been attended with disastrous results. Happily the prudence and address of President Barbicane averted the danger. These personal demonstrations found a division in the newspapers of the different States. The New York *Herald* and the *Tribune* supported Texas, while the *Times* and the *American Review* espoused the cause of the Floridan deputies. The members of the Gun Club could not decide to which to give the preference.

Texas produced its array of twenty-six counties; Florida replied that twelve counties were better than twenty-six in a country only one-sixth part of the size.

Texas plumed itself upon its 330,000 natives; Florida, with a far smaller territory, boasted of being much more densely populated with 56,000.

The Texans, through the columns of the *Herald,* claimed that some regard should be had to a State which grew the best cotton in all America, produced the best green oak for the service of the navy, and contained the finest oil, besides iron mines, in which the yield was fifty per cent of pure metal.

To this the *American Review* replied that the soil of Florida, although not equally rich, afforded the best conditions for the moulding and casting of the Columbiad, consisting as it did of sand and argillaceous earth.

"That may be all very well," replied the Texans; "but you must first get to this country. Now the communications with Florida are difficult, while the coast of Texas offers the bay of Galveston, which possesses a circumference of fourteen leagues, and is capable of containing the navies of the entire world!"

"A pretty notion truly," replied the papers in the interest of Florida, "that of Galveston Bay *below the 29th parallel!* Have we not got the bay of Espiritu Santo, opening precisely upon *the 28th degree,* and by which ships can reach Tampa Town by direct route?"

"A fine bay! Half choked with sand!"

"Choked yourselves!" returned the others.

Thus the war went on for several days, when Florida endeavored to draw her adversary away on to fresh ground; and one morning the *Times* hinted that, the enterprise being essentially American, it ought not to be attempted upon other than purely American territory.

To these words Texas retorted, "American! are we not as much so as you? Were not Texas and Florida both incorporated into the Union in 1845?"

"Undoubtedly," replied the *Times;* "but we have belonged to the Americans ever since 1820."

"Yes!" returned the *Tribune;* "after having been Spaniards or English for two hundred years, you were sold to the United States for five million dollars!"

"Well! and why need we blush for that? Was not Louisiana bought from Napoleon in 1803 at the price of sixteen million dollars?"

"Scandalous!" roared the Texan deputies. "A wretched little strip of country like Florida to dare to compare itself to Texas, who, in place of selling herself, asserted her own independence, drove out the Mexicans in March 2, 1846, and declared herself a federal republic after the victory gained by Samuel Houston on the banks of the San Jacinto, over the troops of Santa Annal—a country, in fine, which voluntarily annexed itself to the United States of America!"

"Yes; because it was afraid of the Mexicans!" replied Florida.

"Afraid!" From this moment the state of things became intolerable. A sanguinary encounter seemed daily imminent between the two parties in the streets of Baltimore. It became necessary to keep an eye upon the deputies.

President Barbicane knew not which way to look. Notes, documents, letters full of menaces showered down upon his house. Which side ought he to take? As regarded the appropriation of the soil, the facility of communication, the rapidity of transport, the claims of both States were evenly balanced. As for political prepossessions, they had nothing to do with the question.

This dead block had existed for some little time, when Barbicane resolved to get rid of it at once. He called a meeting of his colleagues, and laid before them a proposition which, it will be seen, was profoundly sagacious.

"On carefully considering," he said, "what is going on now between Florida and Texas, it is clear that the same difficulties will recur with all the towns of the favored State. The rivalry will descend from State to city, and so on downward. Now Texas possesses eleven towns within the prescribed conditions, which will further dispute the honor and create us new enemies, while Florida has only one. I go in, therefore, for Florida and Tampa Town."

This decision, on being made known, utterly crushed the Texan deputies. Seized with an indescribable fury, they addressed threatening letters to the different members of the Gun Club by name. The magistrates had but one course to take, and they took it. They chartered a special train, forced the Texans into it whether they would or no; and they quitted the city with a speed of thirty miles an hour.

Quickly, however, as they were dispatched, they found time to hurl one last and bitter sarcasm at their adversaries.

Alluding to the extent of Florida, a mere peninsula confined between two seas, they pretended that it could never sustain the shock of the discharge, and that it would "bust up" at the very first shot.

"Very well, let it bust up!" replied the Floridans, with a brevity of the days of ancient Sparta.

STEPHEN CRANE

1871–1900

STAID JACKSONVILLE HAD suddenly become the center of excitement. It was 1896, and there was a great deal to be excited about. The city had become a tourist mecca, thanks to its warm weather and the arrival of oil king Henry Flagler a decade earlier. In the winter months, thousands of wealthy Northerners flocked to the town, creating their own social structure and bringing the small city national attention.

In 1896, it was not only the tourists who brought attention to Jacksonville, but those whose interest was not social but military: men and women seeking to play a role in the war with Cuba. The city was teeming with journalists, spies, and those who saw a chance to make their fortune in running guns to Cuba.

One of those in town was Stephen Crane, who had become famous for his Civil War book, *The Red Badge of Courage*, and was on assignment to go to Cuba and cover the Cuban revolution against Spanish rule, which threatened to bring the United States into the conflict.

Crane had become an overnight sensation with the publication of *The Red Badge of Courage*, praised for a realistic portrayal of war and death, even though Crane was born six years after the war ended. It was serialized in newspapers throughout the nation, then combined into a best-selling book.

The book was serialized by Irving Bacheller, who came up with the idea of providing newspapers with great literature offered in installments. Not only did Bacheller introduce Crane to Americans, he brought them Joseph Conrad, Arthur Conan Doyle, and Rudyard Kipling. He decided not just to syndicate existing works, but to use well-known writers to cover the news. He sent Crane to Cuba by way of Jacksonville.

Crane checked in at the St. James Hotel, the finest in Florida and the first in the state to have electricity. Huau's cigar store on Main Street was the center of Cuban activity, and on any day, Cuban leaders José Martí and José Alejandro Huau might show up, along with secret agents for the Spanish government, journalists, and Pinkerton agents who could be working for Spain or the United States. Also present were the gunrunners, who made contact at the cigar store to arrange for deliveries to the revolutionaries.

The gunrunning was illegal, which seemed to make it all the more exciting. Although it was illegal, the gunrunning ships sat in the Jacksonville harbor for all to see.

Crane registered under an alias, Samuel Carleton, which allowed him to move about without being a celebrity, but he soon found that getting to Cuba was difficult. There were plenty of gunrunners in Jacksonville ready to take a chance to make money, but carrying live passengers in violation of neutrality laws was different. As Crane and other reporters sought the ship that would carry them to Cuba, they spent their days and nights in local bars. For Crane, that meant the seedy waterfront saloons where he downed drink after drink.

The Spanish spies were so obvious that the *Daily Florida Citizen* reported that Crane (Carleton) and two other men were "being closely watched by Spanish spies." Carleton was mistakenly identified as a former soldier who was helping the rebels with tactics and maneuvers. Crane also became a regular in the local brothels, where business was booming. To one madam, Cora Taylor, he inscribed a book:

> Brevity is an element
> That enters importantly
> Into all pleasures of
> Life and this is what
> Makes pleasure sad
> And so there is no
> Pleasure but only sadness

The relationship between Cora and Crane turned into more than a business arrangement. Friends thought she had fallen in love with him, especially after she learned his real identity.

It began to appear as though 1896 would end with Crane still waiting in Jacksonville. But on the last day of the year, the cargo ship *Commodore* finally received clearance to carry Crane and guns to Cuba. Spanish spies were watching as the cargo was loaded, including forty bundles of rifles and more than 200,000 shells.

From the beginning, luck was not with the *Commodore*. Two miles off shore, she struck a sandbar and had to wait for help to escape. Once at sea, she ran into foul weather, which violently rocked the ship, leaving everyone except Crane and the captain terribly seasick. Things became worse: the pumps failed and the passengers formed a human bucket brigade to try to keep the ankle-deep water from rising more. As the water continued to rise, they attempted to build a huge fire to create enough power in the boilers to reach land, but that failed.

The ship was about thirteen miles off the coast of Florida, about a hundred miles south of Jacksonville, when she began to sink. Crew members launched the three lifeboats, a difficult task that at times seemed impossible. There was confusion and some panic as crew members and passengers filled the three boats, leaving Crane, the captain, and a few others to seek safety in a small dinghy. Crane began 1897 in a tiny dinghy in rough seas.

The next morning, one of the lifeboats reached the Florida coast, followed two hours later by a second, but when the third boat arrived, it was empty. Word of the sinking reached Jacksonville, but the stories were conflicting and no one knew for sure what Crane's fate had been.

They finally washed ashore near Daytona Beach, although one member from their dinghy drowned near the end. Crane sent telegrams to let people know he was safe, including his Jacksonville companion, Cora. Four days later he returned to the St. James, and, wearing the same clothes as when he left, he walked into the lobby to a large crowd gathered there. Crane's survival was front page news throughout the country, including in *The New York Times*.

Crane initially wrote a thousand-word story about his ordeal, then began writing the long story generally known as "The Open Boat," though officially titled "The Open Boat: A Tale Intended To Be After the Fact. Being the Experience of Four Men from the Sunk Steamer Commodore." Working in Jacksonville was hopeless. He was too well known and the distractions, including Cora, could not be overcome. He scrapped plans for Cuba and headed for New York, writing along the way. A month later, *Scribner's Magazine* published his story, and one of the nation's best-known writers became even better known.

The Open Boat

by Stephen Crane

None of them knew the color of the sky. Their eyes glanced level, and were fastened upon the waves that swept toward them. These waves were the hue of slate, save for the tops, which were of foaming white, and all of the men knew the colors of the sea. The horizon narrowed and widened and dipped and rose, and at all times its edge was jagged with waves that seemed thrust up in points like rocks.

Many a man ought to have a bath-tub larger than the boat which here rode upon the sea. These waves were most wrongfully and barbarously abrupt and tall, and each froth-top was a problem in small-boat navigation.

The cook squatted in the bottom, and looked with both eyes at the six inches of gunwale which separated him from the ocean. His sleeves were rolled over his fat forearms, and the two flaps of his unbuttoned vest dangled as he bent to bail out the boat. Often he said: "Gawd! that was a narrow clip." As he remarked it he invariably gazed eastward over the broken sea.

The oiler, steering with one of the two oars in the boat, sometimes raised himself suddenly to keep clear of water that swirled in over the stern. It was a thin little oar, and it seemed often ready to snap.

The correspondent, pulling at the other oar, watched the waves and wondered why he was there.

The injured captain, lying in the bow, was at this time buried in that profound dejection and indifference which comes, temporarily at least, to even the bravest and most enduring when, willy-nilly, the firm fails, the army loses, the ship goes down. The mind of the master of a vessel is rooted deep in the timbers of her, though he command for a day or a decade; and this captain had on him the stern impression of a scene in the grays of dawn of seven turned faces, and later a stump of a topmast with a white ball on it, that slashed to and fro at the waves, went low and lower, and down. Thereafter there was something strange in his voice. Although steady, it was deep with mourning, and of a quality beyond oration or tears.

"Keep'er a little more south, Billie," said he.

"A little more south, sir," said the oiler in the stern.

A seat in this boat was not unlike a seat upon a bucking bronco, and, by the same token, a bronco is not much smaller. The craft pranced and reared and plunged like an animal. As each wave came, and she rose for it, she seemed like a horse making at a fence outrageously high. The manner of her scramble over these walls of water is a mystic thing, and, moreover, at the top of them were ordinarily these problems in white water, the foam racing down from the summit of each wave, requiring a new leap, and a leap from the air. Then, after scornfully bumping a crest, she would slide and race and splash down a long incline, and arrive bobbing and nodding in front of the next menace.

A singular disadvantage of the sea lies in the fact that, after successfully surmounting one wave, you discover that there is another behind it, just as important and just as nervously anxious to do something effective in the way of swamping boats. In a ten-foot dinghy one can get an idea of the resources of the sea in the line of waves that is not probable to the average experience, which is never at sea in a dinghy. As each slaty wall of water approached, it shut all else from the view of the men in the boat, and it was not difficult to imagine that this particular wave was the final outburst of the ocean, the last effort of the grim water. There was a terrible grace in the move of the waves, and they came in silence, save for the snarling of the crests.

In the wan light the faces of the men must have been gray. Their eyes must have glinted in strange ways as they gazed steadily astern. Viewed from a balcony, the whole thing would, doubtless, have been weirdly picturesque. But the men in the boat had no time to see it, and if they had had leisure, there were other things to occupy their minds. The sun swung steadily up the sky, and they knew it was broad day because the color of the sea changed from slate to emerald-green streaked with amber lights, and the foam was like tumbling snow. The process of the breaking day was unknown to them. They were aware only of this effect upon the color of the waves that rolled toward them.

In disjointed sentences the cook and the correspondent argued as to the difference between a life-saving station and a house of refuge. The cook had said: "There's a house of refuge just north of the Mosquito Inlet Light, and as soon as they see us they'll come off in their boat and pick us up."

"As soon as who see us?" said the correspondent.

"The crew," said the cook.

"Houses of refuge don't have crews," said the correspondent. "As I understand them, they are only places where clothes and grub are stored for the benefit of shipwrecked people. They don't carry crews."

"Oh, yes, they do," said the cook.

"No, they don't," said the correspondent.

"Well, we're not there yet, anyhow," said the oiler in the stern.

"Well," said the cook, "perhaps it's not a house of refuge that I'm thinking of as being near Mosquito Inlet Light; perhaps it's a life-saving station."

"We're not there yet," said the oiler in the stern.

II

As the boat bounced from the top of each wave the wind tore through the hair of the hatless men, and as the craft plopped her stern down again the spray slashed past them. The crest of each of these waves was a hill, from the top of which the men surveyed for a moment a broad, tumultuous expanse, shining and wind-driven. It was probably splendid, it was probably glorious, this play of the free sea, wild with lights of emerald and white and amber.

"Bully good thing it's an on-shore wind," said the cook. "If not, where would we be? Wouldn't have a show."

"That's right," said the correspondent.

The busy oiler nodded his assent.

Then the captain, in the bow, chuckled in a way that expressed humor, contempt, tragedy, all in one. "Do you think we've got much of a show now, boys?" said he.

Whereupon the three were silent, save for a trifle of hemming and hawing. To express any particular optimism at this time they felt to be childish and stupid, but they all doubtless possessed this sense of the situation in their minds. A young man thinks doggedly at such times. On the other hand, the ethics of their condition was decidedly against any open suggestion of hopelessness. So they were silent.

"Oh, well," said the captain, soothing his children, "we'll get ashore all right."

But there was that in his tone which made them think; so the oiler quoth, "Yes! if this wind holds."

The cook was bailing. "Yes! if we don't catch hell in the surf."

Canton-flannel gulls flew near and far. Sometimes they sat down on the sea, near patches of brown seaweed that rolled over the waves with a moment like carpets on a line in a gale. The birds sat comfortably in groups, and they were envied by some in the dinghy, for the wrath of the sea was no more to them than it was to a covey of prairie-chickens a thousand miles inland. Often they came very close and stared at the men with black, bead-like eyes. At these times they were uncanny and sinister in their unblinking scrutiny, and the men hooted angrily at them, telling them to be gone. One came, and evidently decided to alight on the top of the captain's head. The bird flew parallel to the boat, and did not circle, but made short sidelong jumps in the air in chicken fashion. His black eyes were wistfully fixed upon the captain's head. "Ugly brute," said the oiler to the bird. "You look as if you were made with a jack-knife." The cook and the correspondent swore darkly at the creature. The captain naturally wished to knick it away with the end of the heavy painter, but he did not dare do it, because anything resembling an emphatic gesture would have capsized this freighted boat; and so, with his open hand, the captain gently and carefully waved the gull away. After it had been discouraged from the pursuit the captain breathed easier on account of his hair, and others breathed easier because the bird struck their minds at this time as being somehow gruesome and ominous.

In the meantime the oiler and the correspondent rowed; and also they rowed. They sat together in the same seat, and each rowed an oar. Then the oiler took both oars; then the correspondent took both oars; then the oiler; then the correspondent. They rowed and they rowed. The very ticklish part of the business was when the time came for the reclining one in the stern to take his turn at the oars. By the very last star of truth, it is easier to steal eggs from under a hen than it was to change seats in the dinghy. First the man in the stern slid his hand along the thwart and moved with care, as if he were of Sèvres. Then the man in the rowing-seat slid his hand along the other thwart. It was all done with the most extraordinary care. As the two sidled past each other, the whole party kept watchful eyes on the coming wave, and the captain cried: "Look out, now! Steady, there!"

The brown mats of seaweed that appeared from time to time were like islands, bits of earth. They were traveling, apparently, neither one way nor the other. They were, to all intents, stationary. They informed the men in the boat that it was making progress slowly toward the land.

The captain, rearing cautiously in the bow after the dinghy soared on a great swell, said that he had seen the lighthouse at Mosquito Inlet. Presently the cook remarked that he had seen it. The correspondent was at the oars then, and for some reason he too wished to look at the lighthouse; but his back was toward the far shore, and the waves were important, and for some time he could not seize an opportunity to turn his head. But at last there came a wave more gentle than the others, and when at the crest of it he swiftly scoured the western horizon.

"See it?" said the captain.

"No," said the correspondent, slowly; "I didn't see anything."

"Look again," said the captain. He pointed. "It's exactly in that direction."

At the top of another wave the correspondent did as he was bid, and this time his eyes chanced on a small, still thing on the edge of the swaying horizon. It was precisely like the point of a pin. It took an anxious eye to find a lighthouse so tiny.

"Think we'll make it, Captain?"

"If this wind holds and the boat don't swamp, we can't do much else," said the captain.

The little boat, lifted by each towering sea and splashed viciously by the crests, made progress that in the absence of seaweed was not apparent to those in her. She seemed just a wee thing wallowing miraculously, top up, at the mercy of five oceans. Occasionally a great spread of water, like white flames, swarmed into her.

"Bail her, cook," said the captain, serenely.

"All right, Captain," said the cheerful cook.

III

It would be difficult to describe the subtle brotherhood of men that was here established on the seas. No one said that it was so. No one mentioned it. But it dwelt in the boat, and each man felt it warm him. They were a captain, an oiler, a cook, and a correspondent, and they were friends—friends in a more curiously iron-bound degree than may be common. The hurt captain, lying against the water-jar in the bow, spoke always in a low voice and calmly; but he could never command a more ready and swiftly obedient crew than the motley three of the dinghy. It was more than a mere recognition of what was best for the common safety. There was surely in it a quality that was personal and heartfelt. And after this devotion to the commander of the boat, there was this comradeship that the correspondent, for instance, who had been taught to be cynical of men, knew even at the time was the best experience of his life. But no one said that it was so. No one mentioned it.

"I wish we had a sail," remarked the captain. "We might try my overcoat on the end of an oar, and give you two boys a chance to rest." So the cook and the correspondent held the mast and spread wide the overcoat; the oiler steered; and the little boat made good way with her new rig. Sometimes the oiler had to scull sharply to keep a sea from breaking into the boat, but otherwise sailing was a success.

Meanwhile the lighthouse had been growing slowly larger. It had now almost assumed color, and appeared like a little gray shadow on the sky. The man at the oars could not be prevented from turning his head rather often to try for a glimpse of this little gray shadow.

At last, from the top of each wave, the men in the tossing boat could see land. Even as the lighthouse was an upright shadow on the sky, this land seemed but a long black shadow on the sea. It certainly was thinner than paper. "We must be about opposite New Smyrna," said the cook, who had coasted this shore often in schooners. "Captain, by the way, I believe they abandoned that life-saving station there about a year ago."

"Did they?" said the captain.

The wind slowly died away. The cook and the correspondent were not now obliged to slave in order to hold high the oar; but the waves continued their old impetuous swooping at the dinghy, and the little craft, no longer under way, struggled woundily over them.

The oiler or the correspondent took the oars again.

Shipwrecks are *apropos* of nothing. If men could only train for them and have them occur when the men had reached pink condition, there would be less drowning at sea. Of the four in the dinghy none had slept any time worth mentioning for two days and two nights previous to embarking in the dinghy, and in the excitement of clambering about the deck of a foundering ship they had also forgotten to eat heartily.

For these reasons, and for others, neither the oiler nor the correspondent was fond of rowing at this time. The correspondent wondered ingenuously how in the name of all that was sane could there be people who thought it amusing to row a boat. It was not an amusement; it was a diabolical punishment, and even a genius of mental aberrations could never conclude that it was anything but a horror to the muscles and a crime against the back. He mentioned to the boat in general how the amusement of rowing struck him, and the weary-faced oiler smiled in full sympathy.

Previously to the foundering, by the way, the oiler had worked double watch in the engine-room of the ship.

"Take her easy now, boys," said the captain. "Don't spend yourselves. If we have to run a surf you'll need all your strength, because we'll sure have to swim for it. Take your time."

Slowly the land arose from the sea. From a black line it became a line of black and a line of white—trees and sand. Finally the captain said that he could make out a house on the shore. "That's the house of refuge, sure," said the cook. "They'll see us before long, and come out after us."

The distant lighthouse reared high. "The keeper ought to be able to make us out now, if he's looking through a glass," said the captain. "He'll notify the life-saving people."

"None of those other boats could have got ashore to give word of the wreck," said the oiler, in a low voice, "else the lifeboat would be out hunting us."

Slowly and beautifully the land loomed out of the sea. The wind came again. It had veered from the northeast to the southeast. Finally a new sound struck the ears of the men in the boat. It was the low thunder of the surf on the shore. "We'll never be able to make the lighthouse now," said the captain. "Swing her head a little more north, Billie."

"A little more north, sir," said the oiler.

Whereupon the little boat turned her nose once more down the wind, and all but the oarsman watched the shore grow. Under the influence of this expansion doubt and direful apprehension were leaving the minds of the men. The management of the boat was still most absorbing, but it could not prevent a quiet cheerfulness. In an hour, perhaps, they would be ashore.

Their backbones had become thoroughly used to balancing in the boat, and they now rode this wild colt of a dinghy like circus men. The correspondent thought that he had been drenched to the skin, but happening to feel in the top pocket of his coat, he found therein eight cigars. Four of them were soaked with seawater; four were perfectly scatheless. After a search, somebody produced three dry matches; and thereupon the four waifs rode in their little boat and, with an assurance of an impending rescue shining in their eyes, puffed at the big cigars, and judged well and ill of all men. Everybody took a drink of water.

IV

"Cook," remarked the captain, "there don't seem to be any signs of life about your house of refuge."

"No," replied the cook. "Funny they don't see us!"

A broad stretch of lowly coast lay before the eyes of the men. It was of low dunes topped with dark vegetation. The roar of the surf was plain, and sometimes they could see the white lip of a wave as it spun up the beach. A tiny house was blocked out black upon the sky. Southward, the slim lighthouse lifted its little gray length.

Tide, wind, and waves were swinging the dinghy northward. "Funny they don't see us," said the men.

The surf's roar was here dulled, but its tone was nevertheless thunderous and mighty. As the boat swam over the great rollers the men sat listening to this roar. "We'll swamp sure," said everybody.

It is fair to say here that there was not a life-saving station within twenty miles in either direction; but the men did not know this fact, and in consequence they made dark and opprobrious remarks concerning the eyesight of the nation's lifesavers. Four scowling men sat in the dinghy, and surpassed records in the invention of epithets.

"Funny they don't see us."

The light-heartedness of a former time had completely faded. To their sharpened minds it was easy to conjure pictures of all kinds of incompetency and blindness and, indeed, cowardice. There was the shore of the populous land, and it was bitter and bitter to them that from it came no sign.

"Well," said the captain, ultimately, "I suppose we'll have to make a try for ourselves. If we stay out here too long, we'll none of us have strength left to swim after the boat swamps."

And so the oiler, who was at the oars, turned the boat straight for the shore. There was a sudden tightening of muscles. There was some thinking.

"If we don't all get ashore," said the captain—"if we don't all get ashore, I suppose you fellows know where to send news of my finish?"

They then briefly exchanged some addresses and admonitions. As for the reflections of the men, there was a great deal of rage in them. Perchance they might be formulated thus: "If I am going to be drowned—if I am going to be drowned—if I am going to be drowned, why, in the name of the seven mad gods who rule the sea, was I allowed to come thus far and contemplate sand and trees? Was I brought here merely to have my nose dragged away as I was about to nibble the sacred cheese of life? It is preposterous! If this old ninny-woman, Fate, cannot do better than this, she should be deprived of the management of men's fortunes. She is an old hen who knows not her intention. If she has decided to drown me, why did she not do it in the beginning, and save me all this trouble? The whole affair is absurd. . . . But no; she cannot mean to drown me. She dare not drown me. She cannot drown me. Not after all this work!" Afterward the man might have had an impulse to shake his fist at the clouds. "Just you drown me, now, and then hear what I call you!"

The billows that came at this time were more formidable. They seemed always just about to break and roll over the little boat in turmoil of foam. There was a preparatory and long growl in the speech of them. No mind unused to the sea would have concluded that the dinghy could ascend these sheer heights in time. The shore was still afar. The oiler was a wily surfman.

"Boys," he said swiftly, "she won't live three minutes more, and we're too far out to swim. Shall I take her to sea again, Captain?"

"Yes; go ahead!" said the captain.

This oiler, by a series of quick miracles and fast and steady oarsmanship, turned the boat in the middle of the surf and took her safely to sea again.

There was a considerable silence as the boat bumped over the furrowed sea to deeper water. Then somebody in gloom spoke: "Well, anyhow, they must have seen us from the shore by now."

The gulls went in slanting flight up the wind toward the gray, desolate east. A squall, marked by dingy clouds, and clouds brick-red, like smoke from a burning building, appeared from the southeast.

"What do you think of those life-saving people? Ain't they peaches?"

"Funny they haven't seen us."

"Maybe they think we're out here for sport! Maybe they think we're fishin.' Maybe they think we're damned fools."

It was a long afternoon. A changed tide tried to force them southward, but wind and wave said northward. Far ahead, where coast-line, sea, and sky formed their mighty angle, there were little dots which seemed to indicate a city on the shore.

"St. Augustine?"

The captain shook his head. "Too near Mosquito Inlet."

And the oiler rowed, and then the correspondent rowed; then the oiler rowed. It was a weary business. The human back can become the seat of more aches and pains than are registered in books for the composite anatomy of a regiment. It is a limited area; but it can become the theater of innumerable muscular conflicts, tangles, wrenches, knots, and other comforts.

"Did you ever like to row, Billie?" asked the correspondent.

"No," said the oiler, "hang it!"

When one exchanged the rowing-seat for a place in the bottom of the boat, he suffered a bodily depression that caused him to be careless of everything save an obligation to wiggle one finger. There was cold sea-water swashing to and fro in the boat, and he lay in it. His head, pillowed on a thwart, was within an inch of the swirl of a wave-crest, and sometimes a particularly obstreperous sea came inboard and drenched him once more. But these matters did not annoy him. It is almost certain that if the boat had capsized he would have tumbled comfortably out upon the ocean as if he felt sure that it was a great, soft mattress.

"Look! There's a man on the shore!"

"Where?"

"There! See 'im? See 'im?"

"Yes, sure! He's walking along."

"Now he's stopped. Look! He's facing us!"

"He's waving at us!"

"So he is! By thunder!"

"Ah, now we're all right! Now we're all right! There'll be a boat out here for us in half an hour."

"He's going on. He's running. He's going up to that house there."

The remote beach seemed lower than the sea, and it required a searching glance to discern the little black figure. The captain saw a floating stick, and they rowed to it. A bath towel was by some weird chance in the boat, and tying this on the stick, the captain waved it. The oarsman did not dare turn his head, so he was obliged to ask questions.

"What's he doing now?"

"He's standing still again. He's looking, I think. . . . There he goes again toward the house. . . . Now he's stopped again."

"Is he waving at us?"

"No, not now; he was though."

"Look! There comes another man!"

"He's running."

"Look at him go, would you!"

"Why, he's on a bicycle. Now he's met the other man. They're both waving at us. Look!"

"There comes something up the beach."

"What the devil is that thing?"

"Why, it looks like a boat."

"Why, certainly, it's a boat."

"No; it's on wheels."

"Yes, so it is. Well, that must be the life-boat. They drag them along shore on a wagon."

"That's the life-boat, sure."

"No, by——, it's—it's an omnibus."

"I tell you it's a life-boat."

"It is not! It's an omnibus. I can see it plain. See? One of these big hotel omnibuses."

"By thunder, you're right. It's an omnibus, sure as fate. What do you suppose they are doing with an omnibus? Maybe they are going around collecting the life-crew, hey?"

"That's it, likely. Look! There's a fellow waving a little black flag. He's standing on the steps of the omnibus. There come those other two fellows. Now they're all talking together. Look at the fellow with the flag. Maybe he ain't waving it!"

"That ain't a flag, is it? That's his coat. Why, certainly, that's his coat."

"So it is; it's his coat. He's taken it off and is waving it around his head. But would you look at him swing it!"

"Oh, say, there isn't any life-saving station there. That's just a winter-resort hotel omnibus that has brought over some of the boarders to see us drown."

"What's that idiot with the coat mean? What's he signaling, anyhow?"

"It looks as if he were trying to tell us to go north. There must be a life-saving station up there."

"No; he thinks we're fishing. Just giving us a merry hand. See? Ah, there, Willie!"

"Well, I wish I could make something out of those signals. What do you suppose he means?"

"He don't mean anything; he's just playing."

"Well, if he'd just signal us to try the surf again, or to go to sea and wait, or go north, or go south, or go to hell, there would be some reason in it. But look at him! He just stands there and keeps his coat revolving like a wheel. The ass!"

"There come more people."

"Now there's quite a mob. Look! Isn't that a boat?"

"Where? Oh, I see where you mean. No, that's no boat."

"That fellow is still waving his coat."

"He must think we like to see him do that. Why don't he quit it? It don't mean anything."

"I don't know. I think he is trying to make us go north. It must be that there's a life-saving station there somewhere."

"Say, he ain't tired yet. Look at 'im wave!"

"Wonder how long he can keep that up. He's been revolving his coat ever since he caught sight of us. He's an idiot. Why aren't they getting men to bring a boat out? A fishing-boat, one of those big yawls, could come out here all right. Why don't he do something?"

"Oh, it's all right now."

"They'll have a boat out here for us in less than no time, now that they've seen us."

A faint yellow tone came into the sky over the low land. The shadows on the sea slowly deepened. The wind bore coldness with it, and the men began to shiver.

"Holy smoke!" said one, allowing his voice to express his impious mood, "if we keep on monkeying out here! If we've got to flounder out here all night!"

"Oh, we'll never have to stay here all night! Don't you worry. They've seen us now, and it won't be long before they'll come chasing out after us."

The shore grew dusky. The man waving a coat blended gradually into this gloom, and it swallowed in the same manner the omnibus and the group of people. The spray, when it dashed uproariously over the side, made the voyagers shrink and swear like men who were being branded.

"I'd like to catch the chump who waved the coat. I feel like soaking him one, just for luck."

"Why? What did he do?"

"Oh, nothing, but then he seemed so damned cheerful."

In the meantime the oiler rowed, and then the correspondent

rowed, and then the oiler rowed. Gray-faced and bowed forward, they mechanically, turn by turn, plied the leaden oars. The form of the lighthouse had vanished from the southern horizon, but finally a pale star appeared, just lifting from the sea. The streaked saffron in the west passed before the all-merging darkness, and the sea to the east was black. The land had vanished, and was expressed only by the low and drear thunder of the surf.

"If I am going to be drowned, if I am going to be drowned, if I am going to be drowned, why, in the name of the seven mad gods who rule the sea, was I allowed to come thus far and contemplate sand and trees? Was I brought here merely to have my nose dragged away as I was about to nibble the sacred cheese of life?"

The patient captain, drooped over the water-jar, was sometimes obliged to speak to the oarsman.

"Keep her head up! Keep her head up!"

"Keep her head up, sir." The voices were weary and low.

This was surely a quiet evening. All save the oarsman lay heavily and listlessly in the boat's bottom. As for him, his eyes were just capable of noting the tall black waves that swept forward in a most sinister silence, save for an occasional subdued growl of a crest.

The cook's head was on a thwart, and he looked without interest at the water under his nose. He was deep in other scenes. Finally he spoke. "Billie," he murmured dreamfully, "what kind of pie do you like best?"

V

"Pie!" said the oiler and the correspondent, agitatedly. "Don't talk about those things, blast you!"

"Well," said the cook, "I was just thinking about ham sandwiches, and—"

A night on the sea in an open boat is a long night. As darkness settled finally, the shine of the light, lifting from the sea in the south, changed to full gold. On the northern horizon a new light appeared, a small bluish gleam on the edge of the waters. These two lights were the furniture of the world. Otherwise there was nothing but waves.

Two men huddled in the stern, and distances were so magnificent in the dinghy that the rower was enabled to keep his feet partly warm by thrusting them under his companions. Their legs indeed extended far under the rowing-seat until they touched the feet of the captain forward. Sometimes, despite the efforts of the tired oarsman, a wave came piling into the boat, an icy wave of the night, and the chilling water soaked them anew. They would twist their bodies for a moment and groan, and sleep the dead sleep once more, while the water in the boat gurgled about them as the craft rocked.

The plan of the oiler and the correspondent was for one to row until he lost the ability, and then arouse the other from his sea-water couch in the bottom of the boat.

The oiler plied the oars until his head drooped forward and the overpowering sleep blinded him; and he rowed yet afterward. Then he touched a man in the bottom of the boat, and called his name. 'Will you spell me for a little while?" he said meekly.

"Sure, Billie," said the correspondent, awaking and dragging himself to a sitting position. They exchanged places carefully, and the oiler, cuddling down in the sea-water at the cook's side, seemed to go to sleep instantly. The particular violence of the sea had ceased. The waves came without snarling. The obligation of the man at the oars was to keep the boat headed so that the tilt of the rollers would not capsize her, and to preserve her from filling when the crests rushed past. The black waves were silent and hard to be seen in the darkness. Often one was almost upon the boat before the oarsman was aware.

In a low voice the correspondent addressed the captain. He was not sure that the captain was awake, although this iron man seemed to be always awake. "Captain, shall I keep her making for that light north, sir?"

The same steady voice answered him. "Yes. Keep it about two points off the port bow."

The cook had tied a life-belt around himself in order to get even the warmth which this clumsy cork contrivance could donate, and he seemed almost stove-like when a rower, whose teeth invariably chattered wildly as soon as he ceased his labor, dropped down to sleep.

The correspondent, as he rowed, looked down at the two men sleeping under foot. The cook's arm was around the oiler's shoulders, and, with their fragmentary clothing and haggard faces, they were the babes of the sea—a grotesque rendering of the old babes in the wood.

Later he must have grown stupid at his work, for suddenly there was a growling of water, and a crest came with a roar and a swash into the boat, and it was a wonder that it did not set the cook afloat in his life-belt. The cook continued to sleep, but the oiler sat up, blinking his eyes and shaking with the new cold.

"Oh, I'm awful sorry, Billie" said the correspondent, contritely.

"That's all right, old boy," said the oiler, and lay down again and was asleep.

Presently it seemed that even the captain dozed, and the correspondent thought that he was the one man afloat on all the oceans. The wind had a voice as it came over the waves, and it was sadder than the end. There was a long, loud swishing astern of the boat, and a gleaming trail of phosphorescence, like blue flame, was furrowed on the black waters. It might have been made by a monstrous knife.

Then there came a stillness, while the correspondent breathed with the open mouth and looked at the sea.

Suddenly there was another swish and another long flash of bluish light, and this time it was alongside the boat, and might almost have been reached with an oar. The correspondent saw an enormous fin speed like a shadow through the water, hurling the crystalline spray and leaving the long glowing trail.

The correspondent looked over his shoulder at the captain. His face was hidden, and he seemed to be asleep. He looked at the babes of the sea. They certainly were asleep. So, being bereft of sympathy, he leaned a little way to one side and swore softly into the sea.

But the thing did not then leave the vicinity of the boat. Ahead or astern, on one side or the other, at intervals long or short, fled the long sparkling streak, and there was to be heard the whiroo of the dark fin. The speed and power of the thing was greatly to be admired. It cut the water like a gigantic and keen projectile.

The presence of this biding thing did not affect the man with the same horror that it would if he had been a picnicker. He simply looked at the sea dully and swore in an undertone.

Nevertheless, it is true that he did not wish to be alone with the thing. He wished one of his companions to awake by chance and keep him company with it. But the captain hung motionless over the water-jar, and the oiler and the cook in the bottom of the boat were plunged in slumber.

VI

"If I am going to be drowned, if I am going to be drowned, if I am going to be drowned, why, in the name of the seven mad gods who rule the sea, was I allowed to come thus far and contemplate sand and trees?"

During this dismal night, it may be remarked that a man would conclude that it was really the intention of the seven mad gods to drown him, despite the abominable injustice of it. For it was certainly an abominable injustice to drown a man who had worked so hard, so hard. The man felt it would be a crime most unnatural. Other people had drowned at sea since galleys swarmed with painted sails, but still—

When it occurs to a man that nature does not regard him as important, and that she feels she would not maim the universe by disposing of him, he at first wishes to throw bricks at the temple, and he hates deeply the fact that there are no bricks and no temples. Any visible expression of nature would surely be pelleted with his jeers.

Then, if there be no tangible thing to hoot, he feels, perhaps, the desire to confront a personification and indulge in pleas, bowed to one knee, and with hands supplicant, saying, "Yes, but I love myself."

A high cold star on a winter's night is the word he feels that she says to him. Thereafter he knows the pathos of his situation.

The men in the dinghy had not discussed these matters, but each had, no doubt, reflected upon them in silence and according to his mind. There was seldom any expression upon their faces save the general one of complete weariness. Speech was devoted to the business of the boat.

To chime the notes of his emotion, a verse mysteriously entered the correspondent's head. He had even forgotten that he had forgotten this verse, but it suddenly was in his mind:

A soldier of the Legion lay dying in Algiers;
There was lack of woman's nursing, there was dearth of
woman's tears;
But a comrade stood beside him, and he took that comrade's
hand,
And he said, "I never more shall see my own, my native land."

In his childhood the correspondent had been made acquainted with the fact that a soldier of the Legion lay dying in Algiers, but he had never regarded it as important. Myriads of his school-fellows had informed him of the soldier's plight, but the dinning had naturally ended by making him perfectly indifferent. He had never considered it his affair that a soldier of the Legion lay dying in Algiers, nor had it appeared to him as a matter for sorrow. It was less to him than breaking of a pencil's point.

Now, however, it quaintly came to him as a human, living thing. It was no longer merely a picture of a few throes in the breast of a poet, meanwhile drinking tea and warming his feet at the grate; it was an actuality—stern, mournful, and fine.

The correspondent plainly saw the soldier. He lay on the sand with his feet out straight and still. While his pale left hand was upon his chest in an attempt to thwart the going of his life, the blood came between his fingers. In the far Algerian distance, a city of low square forms was set against a sky that was faint with the last sunset hues. The correspondent, plying the oars and dreaming of the slow and slower movements of the lips of soldier, was moved by a profound

and perfectly impersonal comprehension. He was sorry for the soldier of the Legion who lay dying in Algiers.

The thing which had followed the boat and waited had evidently
grown bored at the delay. There was no longer to be heard the slash of
the cutwater, and there was no longer the flame of the long trail. The
light in the north still glimmered, but it was apparently no nearer to
the boat. Sometimes the boom of the surf rang in the correspondent's
ears, and he turned the craft seaward then and rowed harder. Southward, some one had evidently built a watch-fire on the beach. It was
too low and too far to be seen, but it made a shimmering, roseate
reflection upon the bluff back of it, and this could be discerned from
the boat. The wind came stronger, and sometimes a wave suddenly
raged out like a mountain-cat, and there was to be seen the sheen and
sparkle of a broken crest.

The captain, in the bow, moved on his water-jar and sat erect.
"Pretty long night," he observed to the correspondent. He looked at
the shore. "Those life-saving people take their time."

"Did you see that shark playing around?"

"Yes, I saw him. He was a big fellow, all right."

"Wish I had known you were awake."

Later the correspondent spoke into the bottom of the boat.

"Billie!" There was a slow and gradual disentanglement. "Billie,
will you spell me?"

"Sure," said the oiler.

As soon as the correspondent touched the cold, comfortable sea-
water in the bottom of the boat and had huddled close to the cook's
life-belt he was deep in sleep, despite the fact that his teeth played
all the popular airs. This sleep was so good to him that it was but a

moment before he heard a voice call his name in a tone that demonstrated the last stages of exhaustion. "Will you spell me?"

"Sure, Billie."

The light in the north had mysteriously vanished, but the correspondent took his course from the wide-awake captain.

Later in the night they took the boat farther out to sea, and the captain directed the cook to take one oar at the stern and keep the boat facing the seas. He was to call out if he should hear the thunder of the surf. This plan enabled the oiler and the correspondent to get respite together. "We'll give those boys a chance to get into shape again," said the captain. They curled down and, after a few preliminary chatterings and trembles, slept once more the dead sleep. Neither knew they had bequeathed to the cook the company of another shark, or perhaps the same shark.

As the boat caroused on the waves, spray occasionally bumped over the side and gave them a fresh soaking, but this had no power to break their repose. The ominous slash of the wind and the water affected them as it would have affected mummies.

"Boys," said the cook, with the notes of every reluctance in his voice, "she's drifted in pretty close. I guess one of you had better take her to sea again." The correspondent, aroused, heard the crash of the toppled crests.

As he was rowing, the captain gave him some whisky and water, and this steadied the chills out of him. "If I ever get ashore and anybody shows me even a photograph of an oar—"

At last there was a short conversation.

"Billie! . . . Billie, will you spell me?"

"Sure," said the oiler.

VII

When the correspondent again opened his eyes, the sea and the sky were each of the gray hue of the dawning. Later, carmine and gold was painted upon the waters. The morning appeared finally, in its splendor, with a sky of pure blue, and the sunlight flamed on the tips of the waves.

On the distant dunes were set many little black cottages, and a tall white windmill reared above them. No man, nor dog, nor bicycle appeared on the beach. The cottages might have formed a deserted village.

The voyagers scanned the shore. A conference was held in the boat. "Well," said the captain, "if no help is coming, we might better try a run through the surf right away. If we stay out here much longer we will be too weak to do anything for ourselves at all." The others silently acquiesced in this reasoning. The boat was headed for the beach. The correspondent wondered if none ever ascended the tall wind-tower, and if then they never looked seaward. This tower was a giant, standing with its back to the plight of the ants. It represented in a degree, to the correspondent, the serenity of nature amid the struggles of the individual nature in the wind, and nature in the vision of men. She did not seem cruel to him then, nor beneficent, nor treacherous, nor wise. But she was indifferent, flatly indifferent. It is, perhaps, plausible that a man in this situation, impressed with the unconcern of the universe, should see the innumerable flaws of his life and have them taste wickedly in his mind and wish for another chance. A distinction between right and wrong seems absurdly clear to him, then, in this new ignorance of the grave edge, and he understands that if he were given another opportunity he would mend his

conduct and his words, and be better and brighter during an introduction or at a tea.

"Now, boys," said the captain, "she is going to swamp sure. All
we can do is to work her in as far as possible, and then when she
swamps, pile out and scramble for the beach. Keep cool now, and
don't jump until she swamps sure."

The oiler took the oars. Over his shoulders he scanned the surf.
"Captain," he said, "I think I'd better bring her about, and keep her
head-on to the seas, and back her in."

"All right, Billie," said the captain. "Back her in." The oiler swung
the boat then, and, seated in the stern, the cook and the correspondent were obliged to look over their shoulders to contemplate the
lonely and indifferent shore.

The monstrous inshore rollers heaved the boat high until the
men were again enabled to see the white sheets of water scudding
up the slanted beach. "We won't get in very close," said the captain.
Each time a man could wrest his attention from the rollers, he turned
his glance toward the shore, and in the expression of the eyes during
this contemplation there was a singular quality. The correspondent,
observing the others, knew that they were not afraid, but the full
meaning of their glances was shrouded.

As for himself, he was too tired to grapple fundamentally with
the fact. He tried to coerce his mind into thinking of it, but the mind
was dominated at this time by the muscles, and the muscles said they
did not care. It merely occurred to him that if he should drown it
would be a shame.

There were no hurried words, no pallor, no plain agitation. The
men simply looked at the shore. "Now, remember to get well clear of

the boat when you jump," said the captain.

Seaward the crest of a roller suddenly fell with a thunderous crash, and the long white comber came roaring down upon the boat.

"Steady now," said the captain. The men were silent. They turned their eyes from the shore to the comber and waited. The boat slid up the incline, leaped at the furious top, bounced over it, and swung down the long back of the wave. Some water had been shipped, and the cook bailed it out.

But the next crest crashed also. The tumbling, boiling flood of white water caught the boat and whirled it almost perpendicular. Water swarmed in from all sides. The correspondent had his hands on the gunwale at this time, and when the water entered at that place he swiftly withdrew his fingers, as if he objected to wetting them.

The little boat, drunken with this weight of water, reeled and snuggled deeper into the sea.

"Bail her out, cook! Bail her out!" said the captain.

"All right, Captain," said the cook.

"Now, boys, the next one will do for us sure," said the oiler. "Mind to jump clear of the boat."

The third wave moved forward, huge, furious, implacable. It fairly swallowed the dinghy, and almost simultaneously the men tumbled into the sea. A piece of life-belt had lain in the bottom of the boat, and as the correspondent went overboard he held this to his chest with his left hand.

The January water was icy, and he reflected immediately that it was colder than he had expected to find it off the coast of Florida. This appeared to his dazed mind as a fact important enough to be noted at the time. The coldness of the water was sad; it was tragic. This fact was somehow mixed and confused with his opinion of his own situation so that it seemed almost a proper reason for tears. The water was cold.

When he came to the surface he was conscious of little but the noisy water. Afterward he saw his companions in the sea. The oiler was ahead in the race. He was swimming strongly and rapidly. Off to the correspondent's left, the cook's great white and corked back bulged out of the water; and in the rear the captain was hanging with his one good hand to the keel of the overturned dinghy.

There is a certain immovable quality to a shore, and the correspondent wondered at it amid the confusion of the sea.

It seemed also very attractive; but the correspondent knew that it was a long journey, and he paddled leisurely. The piece of life-preserver lay under him, and sometimes he whirled down the incline of a wave as if he were on a hand-sled.

But finally he arrived at a place in the sea where travel was beset with difficulty. He did not pause swimming to inquire what manner of current had caught him, but there his progress ceased. The shore was set before him like a bit of scenery on a stage, and he looked at it, and understood with his eyes each detail of it.

As the cook passed, much farther to the left, the captain was calling to him. "Turn over on your back, cook! Turn over on your back and use the oar."

"All right, sir." The cook turned on his back, and paddling with an oar, went ahead as if he were a canoe.

Presently the boat also passed to the left of the correspondent, with the captain clinging with one hand to the keel. He would have appeared like a man raising himself to look over a board fence if it were not for the extraordinary gymnastics of the boat. The correspondent marveled that the captain could still hold to it.

They passed on nearer to shore—the oiler, the cook, the captain—and following them went the water-jar, bouncing gaily over the seas.

The correspondent remained in the grip of this strange new enemy, a current. The shore, with its white slope of sand and its green bluff, topped with little silent cottages, was spread like a picture before him. It was very near to him then, but he was impressed as one who, in a gallery, looks at a scene from Brittany or Algiers.

He thought: "I am going to drown? Can it be possible? Can it be possible? Can it be possible?" Perhaps an individual must consider his own death to be the final phenomenon of nature.

But later a wave perhaps whirled him out of this small deadly current, for he found suddenly that he could again make progress toward the shore. Later still he was aware that the captain, clinging with one hand to the keel of the dinghy, had his face turned away from the shore and toward him, and was calling his name. "Come to the boat! Come to the boat!"

In his struggle to reach the captain and the boat, he reflected that when one gets properly wearied drowning must really be a comfortable arrangement—a cessation of hostilities accompanied by a large degree of relief; and he was glad of it, for the main thing in his mind for some moments had been horror of the temporary agony; he did not wish to be hurt.

Presently he saw a man running along the shore. He was undressing with most remarkable speed. Coat, trousers, shirt, everything flew magically off him.

"Come to the boat!" called the captain.

"All right, Captain." As the correspondent paddled, he saw the captain let himself down to bottom and leave the boat. Then the correspondent performed his one little marvel of the voyage. A large wave caught him and flung him with ease and supreme speed completely over the boat and far beyond it. It struck him even then as an event in gymnastics and a true miracle of the sea. An overturned boat in the surf is not a plaything to a swimming man.

The correspondent arrived in water that reached only to his waist, but his condition did not enable him to stand for more than a moment. Each wave knocked him into a heap, and the undertow pulled at him.

Then he saw the man who had been running and undressing, and undressing and running, come bounding into the water. He dragged ashore the cook, and then waded toward the captain; but the captain waved him away and sent him to the correspondent. He was naked—naked as a tree in winter; but a halo was about his head, and he shone like a saint. He gave a strong pull, and a long drag, and a bully heave at the correspondent's hand. The correspondent, schooled in the minor formula said, "Thanks, old man." But suddenly the man cried, 'What's that?" He pointed a swift finger. The correspondent said, "Go."

In the shallows, face downward, lay the oiler. His forehead touched sand that was periodically, between each wave, clear of the sea.

The correspondent did not know all that transpired afterward. When he achieved safe ground he fell, striking the sand with each particular part of his body. It was as if he had dropped from a roof, but the thud was grateful to him.

It seems that instantly the beach was populated with men with blankets, clothes, and flasks, and women with coffee-pots and all the remedies sacred to their minds. The welcome of the land to the men from the sea was warm and generous; but a still and dripping shape was carried slowly up the beach, and the land's welcome for it could only be the different and sinister hospitality of the grave.

When it came night, the white waves paced to and fro in the moonlight, and the wind brought the sound of the great sea's voice to the men on shore, and they felt that they could then be interpreters.

DAMON RUNYON

1880–1946

As Damon Runyon lay dying alone in his New York hotel room, he was thinking about Florida. At one time, he had captured the characters who populated Miami, but in his final days, he was thinking about the all-white house he had built on Hibiscus Island off Miami for his wife, and what would become of it when he died.

Runyon was a newspaperman and short story writer who populated his writing with characters real and imagined, who caught the attention of the nation. He started his career in Denver, then moved to New York in 1910, where he covered sports for the *New York American*. It was Runyon who nicknamed boxer James J. Braddock "Cinderella Man."

In Texas one year to cover spring training, he met the Mexican bandit-turned-revolutionary Pancho Villa and later joined the American expedition seeking to find Villa in Mexico. While there, he met Patrice Amati del Grande, a child he helped financially to gain an education.

At the time, Runyon was married to Ellen Runyon, whose drinking became worse and worse during their twenty-year marriage, probably at least partially caused by Runyon's frequent absences and his many affairs. She died in 1932.

Patrice Amati del Grande moved from Mexico to New York and looked up her friend Runyon. He had promised that if she came to the United States, he would help her find a job. She was twenty-six years younger than Runyon, but the two married the same year his estranged wife died.

Runyon began visiting Miami in the 1920s, when the town was wide open, featuring a land boom, gangsters, an abundant supply of illegal liquor—and the horse racing Runyon loved. His distinctive writing style featured his own fractured version of English: head became noggin, a knife was a shiv, a pineapple was a grenade, and a roscoe or equalizer was a gun.

One of his Miami friends was Al Capone, who purchased a mansion on Palm Island in 1928. Runyon and Capone could be seen together frequently, and in 1929 Runyon acted as a press agent for the gangster. The Stribling-Sharkey fight was set for Miami Beach, and reporters from all the major newspapers were coming to Miami. Capone wanted to throw a large party for the reporters and asked Runyon to help spread the word. Runyon, working through boxing promoter Nat Fleischer, rounded up sixty journalists for Capone. At the Capone home, the journalists, including Runyon, were searched for weapons, then allowed to go wherever they wanted. One of the journalists—no one ever knew exactly who—stole a diamond ring from Mrs. Capone's bedroom. The guilty journalist escaped, but the incident did not hurt Runyon's friendship with Capone.

Runyon was a regular at the Miami race tracks, Hialeah and Tropical, where he had a habit of putting two dollars on each horse, then bragging to friends about picking the winner. He lost staggering sums on raising and betting on horses. One of his stories, "Pick the Winner," takes place at a south Florida race track, and parts of the story appear in the musical *Guys and Dolls*. It was Runyon who wrote the classic line, "The race is not always to the swift, nor the battle to the strong, but that's how the smart money bets."

He built a magnificent home for his new wife on Hibiscus Island, located between Miami and Miami Beach on one of the several excusive islands and near the island where Al Capone lived. His health began to decline and in 1944 he underwent surgery to remove his voice box, the consequences of heavy smoking. Unable to speak, he began to communicate by memo and moved from Miami to a New York hotel, while his wife stayed behind in their Miami mansion. She left him for a younger man, but it was clear that Runyon still loved her. After their divorce in 1946, he rewrote his will but still gave her a large portion of his estate. His will gave her the Miami house and an interest in his writings, which turned out to be incredibly valuable. *Guys and Dolls* became a play after his death and has produced millions of dollars over the years.

Several Runyon stories, including "Palm Beach Santa Claus" and two other stories, were published in *Runyon à la Carte*, published three years after he died.

Palm Beach Santa Claus
by Damon Runyon

It is the afternoon of a hot day in the city of West Palm Beach, Florida, and a guy by the name of Fatso Zimpf is standing on a street corner thinking of very little and throwing so much shade that a couple
of small stove lids are sitting on the curb at his feet keeping cool, for
this Fatso weighs three hundred pounds if he weighs a carat and as
he is only about five feet eight inches tall he is really quite a tub of
blubber and casts a very wide shadow.

At that, he is somewhat undernourished at this time and in fact is
maybe fifteen or twenty pounds underweight as he does not partake
of food for two days, and if the small stove lids know how hungry he
is the chances are they will not be sitting so close to him. To tell the
truth, Fatso is so hungry that his stomach is wondering if his throat is
on a vacation and what is more he does not have as much as one thin
dime in his pants pockets to relieve his predicament.

This Fatso is a horse player by trade and he is en route to Miami
to participate in the winter meetings at Tropical Park and Hialeah,
and he leaves New York City with just enough money to get him as
far as West Palm Beach by bus, but with nothing over for food and
drink on the journey. However, he does not regret having to leave
the bus at West Palm Beach as his strength is slowly dwindling from
hunger and he figures he may be able to get something to eat there.
Besides, the bus people are talking of charging him excess fare because it seems that Fatso laps over on both sides in one seat so much
that they claim it is just the same as if he has three seats, and other

passengers are complaining and the journey is by no means a pleasure trip for Fatso.

Well, while Fatso is standing there on the corner all of a sudden a big red roadster pulls up in the street in front of him with a good-looking tanned young guy in a sport shirt driving it and a skinny Judy sitting in the seat next to him and the skinny Judy motions for Fatso to come out to the car.

At first Fatso does not pay any attention to her because he does not wish to move around and take his shade away from the small stove lids, as he can see that they are very comfortable, and when it comes to children no kinder-hearted guy than Fatso ever lived no matter if they are slightly colored children. In fact, Fatso is enduring no little suffering from the heat, standing there just because he is too kind-hearted to move.

The skinny Judy in the roadster keeps motioning to him and then she cries "Hey, you!" in a loud tone so finally Fatso goes out in the street to the car figuring that maybe she wishes to ask him the way to some place although of course Fatso does not know the way to any place in these parts, and he can see that she is not a bad-looking Judy, though not young, and that she has yellow hair tied back with a fancy handkerchief and a blue sweater and blue slacks and a lot of bracelets on her arms and rings on her fingers.

Fatso can see that this is a party who must be in the money and he can also see that she has hard blue eyes and a bossy way about her because as he goes up to the side of the car with the small stove lids following in his shade she speaks to him in a voice that seems to scratch on her tonsils coming up, as follows: "Look here," she says, "are you out of a job?"

Now this Fatso is always very courteous to all female characters even when he can see that they are nothing but mountain lions and he bows and says:

"Well," he says, "not to give you a short answer, ma'am, but who wants to know?"

"I do," the skinny Judy says. "I'm Mrs. Manwaring Mimm."

"I am Elmore Zimpf," Fatso says; though up to this time he never before mentions his first name in public for fear of arousing criticism.

"Never mind who you are," Mrs. Mimm says. "Do you want a job or are you on relief?"

Naturally, Fatso does not want a job, for jobs are what he is keeping away from all his life and furthermore he does not care for Mrs. Mimm's manner and he is about to back away from this situation when he gets to thinking how hungry he is. So he asks her what kind of a job she is thinking of and she says to him like this:

"I want you for my Santa Claus," she says. "I am giving my annual Christmas Eve party at my place in Palm Beach tomorrow night and as soon as I see you I say to the count here that you are the very one for my Santa Claus. My Santa Claus suit will just fit you," she says. "We always have to stuff it up with pillows for my butler Sparks and he never looks natural."

At this Fatso remembers that Christmas is indeed close at hand and naturally this makes him think of Mindy's restaurant on Broadway and the way they cook turkey there with dressing and cranberry sauce and with mashed potatoes and turnips or maybe baked squash to come along and thinking of these matters causes him to sigh heavily and to forget where he is for the moment until he is aroused by hearing the young guy driving the car speak as follows:

"This fat bum is dead from the neck up, Margaret," he says. "You better find someone else."

"No," she says, "I must have this one. Why, Gregorio, he will be a sensational Santa Claus. See here," she says to Fatso, "I will give you fifty dollars."

Well, on hearing the young guy speak of him as a fat bum, Fatso's thoughts return to West Palm Beach at once and he takes a good look at the young guy and he can now see that he has a piece of a mustache on his upper lip and that there is something about him that is quite familiar.

However, Fatso cannot place him as anybody he knows so he figures it is just the type that makes him seem familiar because of course there are thousands of good-looking tanned young guys with pieces of mustaches on their upper lips running around Florida at this season of the year, but he is greatly displeased with this particular young guy for calling him a fat bum.

In fact, Fatso is insulted because while he does not mind being called fat or even a bum he does not care to be called both at the same time because it sounds unrefined. He is figuring that maybe it will be an excellent idea to reach over and tag this young guy one on the chops, when he remembers hearing Mrs. Mimm mention fifty dollars.

So he takes this matter up with her to make certain his ears do not deceive him and sure enough she is willing to give him half a C to be her Santa Claus with two boffoes in advance so he can get across Lake Worth to an address she gives him without walking, provided he will proceed there at once, and Fatso accepts these terms and dismisses the small stove lids from his shade with a nickel apiece and the chances are they figure he is Santa Claus already.

Now this is how Fatso Zimpf comes to be at Pink Waters which is the name of Mrs. Manwaring Mimm's estate in Palm Beach and this estate is about the size of Central Park and faces on the ocean and has many palm trees and fountains and statuary and a swimming pool and a house that reminds Fatso of Rockefeller Center, and with enough servants running around to form a union.

Fatso reports to the butler Sparks and it turns out that this Sparks is very glad to see him when he learns that Fatso is to be Santa Claus because it seems that Sparks always considers it most undignified for a high-class butler to go around being Santa Claus with pillows stuffed down his pants.

Furthermore, it turns out that Sparks is a horse player at heart and when he finds that Fatso is familiar with the gee-gees he becomes very friendly to be sure and supplies him with plenty of information and scandal about one and all in the best circles of Palm Beach and several surrounding spots.

He explains to Fatso that Pink Waters is one of the biggest estates in these parts and that Mrs. Manwaring Mimm is richer than six feet down in Iowa, with money that she gets off her papa, who makes it out of the oil dodge years back, and that she marries anytime she feels like it and that she feels like it three times so far and is now feeling like it again. In fact, Sparks tells Fatso that she is now feeling like marrying a young guy by the name of Johnny Relf who also has plenty of dough or will have when his parents kindly pass away.

Sparks says that personally he does not approve of this marriage because there is a slight disparity in age between the parties concerned. He says Johnny is only in his middle twenties and not too bright for his years, at that, while Mrs. Mimm is two face-liftings old that he knows of, but he says she is such a determined character that he does not think it advisable for him to mention his disapproval of her plan.

Then Fatso remembers the young guy in the roadster with Mrs. Mimm and he asks Sparks is this the party she is going to marry and Sparks says:

"Oh, no," he says. "That is Count Gregorio Ferrone of an old Italian noble family. Mrs. Mimm meets him in New York last summer and brings him here to Pink Waters as a houseguest. I understand," Sparks says, "that he is about to contract a marriage that will be most advantageous to him. I do not think," he says, "that the count is in funds to any extent."

"He is very impolite," Fatso says. "He does not talk much like a foreigner to me. He calls me a fat bum without any accent. Personally," Fatso says, "I mark him N.G."

"Well," Sparks says, "to tell you the truth I second the motion. The count is indeed a little brusque at times, especially," he says, "with the servants. He claims he lives in this country off and on for years so perhaps he loses his accent. Mrs. Mimm does not really seem to know much about him."

Then Sparks tells Fatso that he is not expected to do anything at all until it comes time for him to be Santa Claus the next night so Fatso wanders around and about and admires the sights and scenes of Palm Beach and finally he strolls along the ocean sands and there in a lonely spot what does he behold but a beautiful young Judy of maybe eighteen crying as if her heart will break.

Now if there is one thing Fatso cannot stand it is the sight of a female character in distress, so he steps up to her and taps her on the shoulder and says to her like this:

"Little miss," he says, "are you in trouble?"

"Yes, I am," she says, "who are you?"

"Why," Fatso says, "I am Santa Claus."

"Oh, no," she says. "There is no Santa Claus. I know it better now than anybody else in this world. Anyway," she says, "if you are Santa Claus where are your whiskers?"

Then Fatso explains about how he is to be Santa Claus for Mrs. Mimm the next night and as soon as he mentions Mrs. Mimm's name the beautiful young Judy starts crying harder than ever.

"Mrs. Mimm is the whole trouble," she says. "Mrs. Mimm steals my Johnny away from me and now I must marry Count Gregorio. I hate him even if he is a count. Mrs. Mimm is an old thing and I want my Johnny."

She continues her crying and Fatso stands there putting two and two together and he can see that he comes upon another angle of the situation that Sparks the butler describes to him.

"Tut-tut," he says. "They tell me Johnny is a lightweight. Dry your tears and think no more of the matter."

Well, at this she stops crying and gazes at Fatso who observes that her eyes are a soft brown and he also observes that she has a shape that is worthy of mention, for Fatso is very observing even if he is fat, and finally she says:

"Of course Johnny is a lightweight," she says. "Everybody knows that. In fact," she says, "everybody knows he is a complete nitwit, but," she says, "what difference does that make? I love him. He is awfully good-looking and lots of fun. I love him a zillion dollars' worth.

If you are Santa Claus," she says, "you give me my Johnny for *my* Christmas present instead of the speedboat my papa is getting me. I want my Johnny. I hope Mrs. Mimm drops dead."

Now there are more tears and Fatso keeps patting her on the shoulder and saying now, now, now, and there, there, there, and finally she quiets down and he is able to get a better idea of her story.

It is a simple love story such as Fatso often hears before, because a fat guy is always hearing love stories though he never has any to tell himself.

It seems that she and this Johnny have a big quarrel one night in New York because she wishes to go to the Stork Club and he wishes to go to El Morocco and harsh words are exchanged and they part in bitter anger and the next thing she knows he is in Palm Beach and Mrs. Mimm is taking dead aim at him and then this Count Gregorio Ferrone comes along and her papa and mama decide that it will be a great idea for her to marry him and give them excuse to have a villa in Italy.

Well, it seems that she agrees to do same while she is still sored up at Johnny but when her papa and mama take her to their own home in Palm Beach for the winter and she learns the situation between Johnny and Mrs. Mimm is quite serious, she regrets her decision and spends all her time wandering along the sands by herself.

In fact, she says if Fatso does not happen along this particular day the chances are her remainders will now be floating out to sea, because she learns from a jeweler on Worth Avenue that Johnny just buys a square-cut diamond ring the size of a bath rug and that she knows it must be Mrs. Mimm's Christmas present and to tell the truth she hears that Mrs. Mimm picks it out herself and tips the jeweler off to promote Johnny into buying this ring. Furthermore, she hears that Mrs. Mimm is going to announce her engagement to Johnny at the Christmas party.

"And," she says, "I will have to be there to hear it because Count Gregorio is her houseguest and my papa and mama are going and it will be considered very peculiar if I fail to be present. Anyway," she says, "I will hate to have anyone know I am so downcast about Johnny and why I am telling you I cannot think except you are fat and have a kind face."

By this time Fatso is becoming somewhat impatient with tears, so he changes the subject and asks her who she is and she says her name is Betty Lou Marvel and that her papa is nobody but Junius X. Marvel, the big automobile guy.

She says everybody in Palm Beach is afraid of Mrs. Mimm because she can think up very strange things to say about anybody she does not like and that nobody dare stay away from her parties if they are invited, specially her Christmas party. Betty Lou says it is years since anybody has a private Christmas in Palm Beach because Mrs. Mimm makes them bring all their presents to her party and has them given away there by her own Santa Claus and Betty Lou says she is glad they cannot take her speedboat there, and so is Fatso when he comes to think it over.

"Well, little miss," Fatso finally says, "kindly give Count Gregorio no more thought. I am personally giving him much consideration ever since he calls me a fat bum and I will take care of him. But," he says, "I do not see what I can do about your Johnny and Mrs. Mimm and if he is such a numskull as to prefer her to you maybe you are better off without him. Merry Christmas, little miss," he says.

"Merry Christmas, Santa Claus," Betty Lou says, and then Fatso goes on strolling along the sands wishing he is younger and two hundred pounds lighter.

Well, it comes on Christmas Eve and Pink Waters is all lighted up like Palisades Park with a Christmas tree as tall as a church steeple in the middle of the patio and all the fountains going with colored lights squirting on the water and two orchestras playing one after the other and long tables spread out in the open. In fact, it is as beautiful a scene as anybody could wish to see and very Christmasy-looking except it is quite hot.

When the guests are assembling, Fatso is taken in his Santa Claus suit into the library of the house which opens out into the patio by Sparks the butler and given a little final coaching there.

It seems that the first part of the party is for the neighbors' children and the second part is for the grown-ups, male and female, and on the Christmas tree in the patio and stacked up at the foot of the tree are many packages containing the presents for the little ones and Sparks explains that it is the duty of Fatso as Santa Claus to distribute these packages.

On a table in the library is a pile of small packages and Sparks says that after he distributes the packages to the children in the patio, Fatso is to return to the library and put these small packages in his Santa Claus bag and go out and stand under the tree again and take the small packages out of the bag one by one and call off the names written on them and hand them out to the parties they are meant for.

"You will be very careful with these small packages," Sparks says. "They contain presents from husbands to their ever-loving wives and vice versa and from one sweet pea to another, and so forth and so on.

The chances are there are many valuable gewgaws in these packages," he says.

Then Sparks leaves Fatso alone in the library while he goes out to see if everything is ready for the appearance of Santa Claus and Fatso can observe him through the tall French window that opens on the patio, bustling about through the gay scene, and with nothing else to do until Sparks's return, Fatso takes to examining the small packages and thinking to himself that if he has the money the contents represent the chances are he will be able to retire from horse playing and perhaps find some beautiful young Judy like Betty Lou to love him.

He observes Betty Lou in the patio with the young guy that he now knows as Count Gregorio and he can see that she seems somewhat depressed and then he notices Mrs. Mimm with a tall blond young guy at her heels that he figures must be the Johnny Relf that Betty Lou is crying about and Fatso thinks to himself that from his looks this Johnny must indeed be something of a waste ball.

Finally Sparks returns and says everything is all set and out into the patio goes Fatso jingling a lot of sleigh bells and beaming on one and all and the orchestras play and the little children let out shrill cries of joy. There is no doubt but what Fatso is a wonderful success as Santa Claus with the little children and many of them wish to shake hands with him but after an hour of standing under the tree picking up packages and calling off names, Fatso commences to get a little weary.

Moreover, he commences to get a trifle vexed with the little ones, especially when some of them insist on pulling his whiskers and small boys start kicking him on the ankles to see if he is alive and by and by Fatso is thinking that maybe President Roosevelt is right about the redistribution of wealth.

In fact, Fatso becomes so vexed that he takes to quietly stepping on a few little toesies here and there accidentally on purpose and the childish cries of pain are enough to break anybody's heart and probably many of these children stop believing in Santa Claus.

Well, he finally gets rid of all the little children and they are taken away by their nurses and only the grown-ups are left and it is a gay gathering to be sure with one and all in evening dress and drinking champagne and dancing, and Fatso retires to the library again and when Sparks comes in to help him load up with the small packages, Fatso says to him like this:

"Sparksy," he says, "who is the most jealous married guy present at this party?"

"Why," Sparks says, "that is an easy one. The most jealous married guy at this party or anywhere else in the world is undoubtedly old Joel Brokebaugh. He is an old walrus who is married to a young mouse, and," Sparks says, "he thinks that every guy who says good morning to Mrs. Brokebaugh is after her, although," he says, "this idea will make you laugh yourself sick when you see her.

"She is undoubtedly a very low score for looks," Sparks says.

"Furthermore," he says, "she has no more spirit than a gooseberry. Old Brokebaugh is so stingy he will not let her buy a new hat or a new dress more than once every few years although he has millions. He does not wish her to dress up for fear some guy may notice her. Personally," Sparks says, "I think old Brokebaugh is touched in the wind for figuring anybody else will ever want his wife, but he has a violent temper and often causes scenes and some say he even carries a pistol in his pocket at all times."

"Brokebaugh, eh?" Fatso says.

"Yes," Sparks says. "They are sitting together under the coconut palm by the big fountain, though why they come to a Christmas party nobody knows because they never give each other anything in the way of presents and take no part in the festivities. Everybody feels sorry for Mrs. Brokebaugh, but," Sparks says, "I say what she needs is some spunk."

Well, Fatso again goes out into the patio with his bag full of the small packages and by this time what with the champagne and the dancing and the spirit of the occasion and this and that, everybody is in a lively mood and they give Fatso a big cheer and no one is any gayer than Mrs. Mimm.

In fact, she is practically hilarious and she gives Fatso a large smile as he goes past her and he can see that she is pleased with his efforts and he can also see that she still has this Johnny with her and that Johnny looks no brighter than before, if as bright, and then Fatso spots the couple Sparks speaks of under the coconut palm and he is somewhat surprised to note that Sparks slightly overrates Mrs. Brokebaugh's appearance.

Even from a distance Fatso can see that she is a zero for looks but he can also see that the old guy with her seems to be about as described by Sparks, only more so. He is a tall, thin old guy with a red face and a bald head and eyes like a shark and Fatso observes that the servants tiptoe going past him.

Well, Fatso gets under the tree and starts calling out names once more and giving out packages and there is now great excitement and many oohs and ahs in female voices on all sides and finally he gets down to just a few packages and calls out the name of Johnny Relf and right away afterward the name of Miss Betty Lou Marvel and in fact Fatso calls them so close together that they meet under the tree though all they do is exchange cruel glances.

Fatso does not say anything whatever to this Johnny as he gives him his package, because Fatso feels that he already does enough talking in words of one syllable to the children, but when Miss Betty Lou steps up he gives her a smile and says:

"Merry Christmas, little miss."

"Merry Christmas, Santa Claus," she says, "but I still do not believe in you."

Then she starts walking away opening her package as she goes and all of a sudden she lets out a cry and starts running toward Johnny Relf but by now Johnny opens his own package, too, and starts running toward Betty Lou.

So they meet practically head-on and start taking holds on each other in the presence of one and all, because it seems that Betty Lou's present is a large square-cut diamond ring with a card in the box which states that it is to my beloved from Johnny and that his present is a pair of big black pearl studs with a card saying they are with all my heart to Johnny from Betty Lou.

Of course nobody bothers to look into the matter at the moment, but when somebody does so later on it is considered something of a coincidence that the writing on the two cards is exactly the same and not very neat, but one and all figure it is just an act of Providence and let it go at that, especially as an act of Providence is regarded as quite a compliment to Palm Beach.

In fact, at this particular moment nobody is paying much attention to anything much but the great happiness of Betty Lou and Johnny, except Mrs. Mimm and she is watching Fatso with keen interest, though Fatso is unaware of her attention as he walks over to where Mrs. Brokebaugh is sitting and hands her a package instead of calling out her name.

Then Fatso returns to the house figuring to get his Santa Claus suit off and collect his wages from Sparks and vanish from these parts before anybody learns that he writes these cards when he is alone in the library and swaps them for cards that will give the ring to Mrs. Mimm from Johnny and the black pearls to Johnny from Mrs. Mimm, in both cases with love.

While he is walking through a long hallway, all of a sudden Fatso gets a feeling that he is being followed, and looking around he observes Mrs. Mimm close behind him. There is something about Mrs. Mimm that causes Fatso to walk a little faster and then he notes that Mrs. Mimm is walking quite a little faster than he is.

So Fatso dodges into an open doorway that he hopes and trusts may lead him elsewhere but he forgets that when he goes through doors it is usually advisable for him to turn sideways because of his great width. He goes at this door frontways and the next thing he knows there he is stuck right in the middle of the doorway and then he becomes conscious of great discomfort to the southward as it seems that Mrs. Mimm is forgetting she is a lady and is kicking him severely and it also seems that these evening shoes that the Judys wear nowadays with their bare toes sticking out in front are capable of inflicting greater pain when used for kicking than just ordinary shoes.

In the meantime, it appears that there is some commotion in the patio because Mrs. Brokebaugh is so startled at getting any Christmas present at all that she cannot open the package Fatso gives her so old Mr. Brokebaugh opens it for her and finds a gold vanity case with a card that reads as follows:

"To my sweetest sweet from Gregorio."

Well, of course old Mr. Brokebaugh has no way of knowing that this is Count Gregorio's present to Betty Lou and that Fatso does not even change the card but only rubs out Betty Lou's name on it and puts down Mrs. Brokebaugh's, though naturally old Mr. Brokebaugh knows who Gregorio is.

In fact, he can see Gregorio at this very moment standing near by feeling of his little mustache and looking greatly bewildered at the scene that is still going on at intervals, between Betty Lou and Johnny, and all of a sudden old Mr. Brokebaugh lets out a yell and jumps up and pulls a pistol out of his pocket and starts full tilt at the count speaking in a loud tone, as follows:

"So," he says, "you are making a play for my wife, are you, scoundrel?"

Well, of course Count Gregorio has no idea what old Mr. Brokebaugh is talking about, but he has eyes in his head and he can see that Mr. Brokebaugh is making a dead set for him and that he is hotter than a firecracker and he can also see the pistol and from the way the count turns and starts running it is plain to be seen that whatever he may be, he is no sucker.

He knocks over three debutantes and a banker worth ten million dollars making for the patio wall and trying to keep trees and bushes between him and Mr. Brokebaugh as he goes and all this time old Mr. Brokebaugh is running after him and with surprising speed for a guy his age and waving the pistol and requesting the count to stand still and be shot.

He never gets a really fair crack at the count except when Gregorio is going over the wall and then old Mr. Brokebaugh lets fly twice and misses both times and the sound of this shooting probably saves Fatso many more contusions as it brings Mrs. Mimm running into the patio to find out what is going on and in her absence Fatso wiggles on through the doorway.

So Fatso shakes the sands of Palm Beach from his feet regretting only that he never gets a chance to ask Betty Lou if she now believes in Santa Claus and he goes on down to Miami and a year later he relates the above circumstances to me one day when we are sitting in the rocking chairs on the veranda of the Hotel McAllister hoping to catch somebody going to the races with a couple of spare seats in their car, for things are by no means dinkum with Fatso and me at the moment.

"You see," Fatso says, "tomorrow is Christmas again and this is what reminds me of these matters at this time."

"So it is, Fatso," I say. "It is strange how time flies. But, Fatso," I say, "are you not most severe on Count Gregorio in not only knocking him out of a chance to pick up a few boffoes by marriage but in almost getting him plugged by a jealous husband?"

"No," Fatso says. "By no means. You must always remember he calls me a fat bum. Besides," he says, "old Brokebaugh just spares me the humiliation of denouncing Gregorio as a former busboy in Vincenti's wop restaurant in West Fiftieth Street and still wanted for robbing the damper of thirty-six dollars.

"I will never forgive myself if I am compelled to holler copper on anybody whatsoever," Fatso says, "but," he says, "of course I will do so as a last resort to prevent Gregorio from marrying Betty Lou. It comes to me all of a sudden why his face is familiar when I am strolling on the sands the time I meet Betty Lou. I never forget a face."

Well, at this moment a big limousine stops in front of the hotel and a small-sized lively Judy all dressed up and sparkling with jewelry hops out of the car and runs up the veranda steps with three good-looking tanned young guys with little mustaches running after her and she is laughing and gay and looks like plenty in the bank, and I am greatly surprised when she skips up to Fatso and gives him a pat on the arm and says like this:

"Merry Christmas, Santa Claus!"

Then she is gone as quick as she comes and the young guys with her and she is still laughing and Fatso is gazing at a fifty-dollar note in his hand with great pleasure and he says:

"She is from Palm Beach," he says. "Anytime anybody from Palm Beach recognizes me they stake me to something because they remember that Mrs. Mimm never pays me the fifty she promises me for being her Santa Claus. I understand," Fatso says, "that it is a public scandal in Palm Beach."

"Is this one Betty Lou?" I ask.

"Oh, no," Fatso says. "She is Mrs. Brokebaugh. I recall now I hear that ever since she gets the Christmas present that she thinks to this very day is from Count Gregorio, she decides she is a natural-born charmer and blossoms out into a life of gaiety, and," Fatso says, "they tell me her husband cannot do a thing about it. Well, Merry Christmas to you."

"Merry Christmas, Fatso," I say.

ZORA NEALE HURSTON
1891–1960

Throughout her life, Zora Neale Hurston always came back to Florida. It was more than home; it was her sanctuary. She became world-famous, but she drew her strength and inspiration from Florida. "I've got the map of Florida on my tongue."

She was only a child when her family moved from Alabama to Eatonville, a small community on the outskirts of Orlando. After the Civil War, scores of African-American communities sprung up, but only a handful, including Eatonville, survived into the twentieth century. She had a hardscrabble childhood; her mother died when she was young, and her father pulled her out of school when she was just thirteen to care for other children, including her seven brothers and sisters. A job as a maid in a white household rescued her from a life of deprivation. Her employer gave her a book—her first—and arranged for her to attend high school, then go to Howard University, where she helped found the school's newspaper. After three years of study, she received a scholarship to Barnard College, becoming the school's only African-American student. Her long journey finally brought her a degree in anthropology and graduate study at Columbia.

Her time in New York coincided with the Harlem Renaissance as the growing African-American community in New York exploded with music, literature, and art. Her short story "Spunk" appeared in *The New Negro*, an anthology of writing by African Americans.

In 1929, she moved to Eau Gallie, Florida, a coastal community about an hour's drive from Eatonville. She rented a small cottage and went to work on her book *Mules and Men*, which was finally published to wide acclaim in 1935. She wrote more short stories and tried unsuccessfully to collaborate on a play with Langston Hughes.

In 1937 the girl from Eatonville won a Guggenheim Fellowship to study in Jamaica and Haiti, leading to her finest novel, *Their Eyes Were Watching God*. During the Great Depression she worked for the Works Progress Administration, touring Florida to contribute to a guidebook about the state and conducting interviews with former slaves. In 1934 she created a drama program at Bethune-Cookman College in Daytona Beach.

Her fame was spreading, and she wrote for such publications as *The Saturday Evening Post*. During the 1940s and 1950s, her reputation faded, and her books, which once seemed to capture life in the African-American community, drew criticism for their portrayal of blacks, especially the speech patterns.

Her personal life was also faltering. There were a couple of marriages, one lasting a few years, the other a few months. In 1948, a mother accused Hurston of molesting her mentally retarded ten-year-old son in New York. Although cases such as this involving juveniles were sealed, a court employee leaked the information to two African-American newspapers, which wasted no time in publicizing the case. The *Afro-American* did not even bother to interview Hurston and slanted the story to make Hurston appear guilty. The boy had mental problems, and his mother may have played a role in encouraging the charges. The accusations came although Hurston's passport proved that she had been in Honduras when the alleged molestation took place. Cleared when the boy admitted that he had made up the charges, her reputation was still in tatters. As often happens, the public was ready to believe the worst.

By the late 1950s she was all but forgotten, with most of her books out of print. She went through a series of jobs, scratching constantly for money. In 1956 she was evicted from a cottage in Eau Gallie, then landed a job as a librarian at Patrick Air Force Base in Cocoa Beach. Things went well at first, but the she became involved in a controversy in which a white supervisor was fired. Months later, she was fired by her white supervisor, William McKay, who said she was "too well-educated for the job." A job teaching at Lincoln Academy in Fort Pierce also ended badly, and she eventually found work again as a maid.

In 1958 she suffered a series of strokes and was admitted to the St. Lucie County Welfare Home, where she died in 1960. A friend saved her manuscripts from destruction after her death.

She died alone and forgotten, and it was fifteen years before her reputation revived. In 1975, another prominent African-American writer, Alice Walker, wrote a magazine article praising Hurston's work. It led to her books being reprinted and caused Walker to take care of a long neglected task. Walker searched for and found Hurston's gravesite in Fort Pierce, Florida, and placed a tombstone there. Hurston's reputation has revived and each year her hometown of Eatonville celebrates her with a festival.

Hurston's works of fiction featured real people and real situations. She also wrote nonfiction stories and articles, including one of the first examinations of the riot and killings on election day in the tiny crossroads of Ocoee, Florida, in 1920. At the time, the incident received little notice, but Hurston brought it to national attention. There were similar riots across the country beginning in 1919, in what became known as "Red Summer." When Julius Perry tried to vote, the violence came to Ocoee.

The Ocoee Riot

by Zora Neale Hurston

This happened on election day, November 2, 1920. Though the catastrophe took place in Ocoee, and it is always spoken of as the Ocoee Riot, witnesses both white and Negro state that it was not the regular population of Ocoee which participated in the affair. It is said that the majority of whites of the community deplored it at the time and have refused to accept full responsibility for it since.

According to witnesses, the racial disorder began in Winter Garden, a citrus town about three miles from Ocoee. There had been very lively electioneering during the Harding campaign, and the Negroes who were traditional Republicans were turning out in mass at the polls. Some of the poor whites who are traditional Democrats resented this under the heading that the Negroes were voting jobs away from the local people. It was decided with a great deal of heat to prevent the blacks from voting, which was done. Over in Ocoee, the blacks and the whites were turning out to the polls with great enthusiasm and no trouble was contemplated. In the afternoon, however, many of the whites of Winter Garden came on over to Ocoee celebrating election day. Seeing the Ocoee Negroes swarming to the polls, they began to urge the Ocoee whites to stop them, citing the evil happenings of the Reconstruction. Finally the Negroes were being pushed and shoved at the polls. Then they were ordered away, but some of them persisted.

The first act of physical violence occurred when Mose Norman came up to the polls to vote in defiance of the warning for Negroes to keep away. He was struck and driven off. But he did not let the matter drop so easily. He got into his automobile and drove to Orlando, the County seat to see one Mr. Cheney, a well-known lawyer there and told him what was happening. He advised Mose Norman that the men who were interfering with the voting were doing so illegally and that it was a very serious matter indeed. He instructed Mose to return to Ocoee and to take the names of all the Negroes who had been denied their constitutional right to vote, and some say he advised Norman to also take the names of the whites who were violating the polls. Mose Norman returned to Ocoee and parked his car on the main street of the town near the place of polling and got out. While he was away from the car, some of the disorderly whites from Winter Garden went to the car and searched it and found a shotgun under the seat. When he returned to the car, he was set upon and driven off.

His speedy foot work was the only thing that saved him from serious injury. When this got around, the Negroes generally stayed away from the polling place and began to leave town for the day. Two or three more were hustled and beaten, however, during the afternoon. Then the white mobs began to parade up and down the streets and grew more disorderly and unmanageable. Towards sundown, it was suggested that they go over to Mose Norman's house and give him a good beating for his officiousness and for being a smart-aleck. But some one going around the lake had seen him visiting July Perry, a very prosperous Negro farmer and contractor and they decided, come nightfall, they would go to the home of Perry and drag Mose out and chastise him.

In the meantime, The Black Dispatch (grapevine) had published all that was happening and most of the Negroes had left town or hidden out in the orange groves. July Perry armed himself and prepared to defend himself and his home. His friends all took to the woods and groves and left him to his courage. Even his sons hid out with the rest. His wife and daughter alone remained in the house with him. Perhaps they were afraid to leave the shelter of the house. Terrible rumors were about. Two of the three churches had been burned. The whole Negro settlement was being assaulted. It was cried that Langmaid, a Negro carpenter, had been beaten and castrated. But one thing was certain: Mose Norman, who had been the match to touch off the explosion, could not be found. He had thoroughly absented himself from the vicinity. When asked by some of the Negroes why he had had the gun under the seat of his car, he explained that he was doing some clearing out at Tildenville for Mr. Saddler, and always had his gun handy for a little hunting. At any rate, no Negro except

July Perry had maintained his former address. So night dusted down on Ocoee, with the mobs seeking blood and ashes and July Perry standing his lone watch over his rights to life and property.

The night color gave courage to many men who had been diffident during the day hours. Fire was set to whole rows of Negro houses and the wretches who had thought to hide by crawling under these buildings were shot or shot at as they fled from the flames. In that way Maggie Genlack and her daughter were killed and their bodies left and partially burned by the flames that consumed their former home. The daughter was far advanced in pregnancy and so felt unequal to flight since there was no conveyance that she could get. Her mother would not leave her alone as all the others vanished out of the quarters. They took counsel together and the old woman and her pregnant daughter crept under the house to escape the notice of the mob. Roosevelt Barton died of fire and gunshot wounds when the barn of July Perry was put to flames. He had thought that that would be a good hiding place, but when the fury of the crowd swept over the Perry place, the barn was fired and when Roosevelt tried to rush out he was driven back by a bullet to die in the fire. But this only happened after a pitched battle had been fought at Perry's house, with July Perry against the mob.

He loaded his high powered rifle and waited, at the same time unwilling to believe that the white people with whom he had worked and associated so long would permit the irresponsibles from Winter Garden to harm him or his things. Nevertheless he waited ready to do that which becomes a man. He could not know that the mob was not seeking him at all, that they had come there because they thought that Mose Norman was hiding about the place. Perhaps if the mob had not been so sure that Mose was there that it was unnecessary to ask, all might have been different. They might have called out to him and he might have assured them by word of mouth or invited them in to see for themselves. They did not know that Norman had only spent a few minutes at the Perry home and then fled away to the groves. So they there outside began the assault upon the front of the house to gain entrance and Perry defended his door with all that he could command. He was effective. The mob was forced to retreat, and considered what was best to do. It was decided that while some kept up the harassment at the front, others would force an entrance through the back. Never had any of the mob suspected that Perry was alone in the house. They thought from the steady fire that several Negroes were at bay in there. It was Sam Salsbury who took a running start and kicked the back door open. Perry had not expected this, but he whirled at once and began to shoot at the gaping mouth of the door. His daughter, terrified at this new danger, tried to run out of the door and was shot in the shoulder by her father who had not expected her to run into the line of fire. But the next bullet struck Sam Salsbury in the arm and the rear attackers retreated. But not before Elmer McDonald and a man named Overberry had lost their lives. The council decided that reinforcements were necessary to take the place so the whole fighting force withdrew. Some phoned to Orlando to friends to come and help. Some phoned to Apopka and to other points. Some went in cars to bring help. So there was a lull in the fighting for two or three hours.

July Perry had not gone unhurt. A bullet or two had hit him. So in the lull his wife persuaded him to leave. He was weak from his hurts so she lent her strength to get him away from the house and far down into the cane patch where they felt he would not be found. When the reinforced mob came back the doors were open and the searchers found only Perry's wounded daughter there. They did nothing to harm her but began an intensive hunt for Perry. It was around dawn when they found him weak and helpless in his hiding place and he was removed to the jail in Orlando. It was after sunup when the mob stormed the jail and dragged him out and tied him to the back of a car and killed him and left his body swinging to a telephone post beside the highway.

That was the end of what happened in Ocoee on election day, 1920.

RING LARDNER

1885–1933

By 1926, RING Lardner—he hated his real name, Ringgold, and shortened it—was one of the best-known writers in America, and a regular fixture in Florida. Both Lardner and Florida were undergoing booms at the time. Lardner wrote a popular newspaper column, articles for major magazines, and screenplays for movies. In Florida, land prices seemed to increase every day, often doubling and tripling within days.

Lardner once wrote that he had three goals: seeing plenty of baseball, writing for magazines, and producing a successful play. He excelled in all three.

After graduating from high school, Lardner enrolled in engineering school in Chicago, but he hated engineering and his grades were miserable. He dropped out and took a job as a bookkeeper for a gas company.

A stroke of luck landed him a job as a sports reporter for a newspaper in South Bend, Indiana, where he got the opportunity to see plenty of baseball. In 1907, the White Sox played in the World Series and he took his vacation to attend. He met a sports writer for *The Chicago Inter-Ocean,* once a major newspaper, but on the decline. But for Lardner it was a chance to cover his first love, major league baseball.

He moved to Boston, then St. Louis, and then landed one of the top sports jobs in the country, columnist for the *Chicago Tribune.* He loved the dialogue the players used, often ungrammatical and loaded with slang. Sometimes his column was just exchanges between players, and sometimes he created fictional baseball players. The readers loved it, and it led to magazine articles for the *Saturday Evening Post,* then the nation's leading magazine.

The magazine articles led to books and a job with a newspaper syndicate in New York.

It was spring training that first brought Lardner to Florida and led to some of his best-known work and his first movie. The movie was *The New Klondike,* one of the last of the silent movies. It was filmed in Florida against the backdrop of the state's booming economy.

The movie involves a baseball pitcher who convinces his teammates to invest in Florida land, only to end up being swindled into buying swampland. The pitcher loses the money, but makes it all back and repays the players. *The New York Times* review noted, "The wild scramble for Florida real estate is served up in a fairly humorous light."

Lardner often featured Florida in his spring training articles for the 135 newspapers his column reached, as well as in his major magazine articles, and in his books. While he became famous for his baseball stories, two of his best-known works have nothing to do with baseball and are set in Florida. In "The Golden Honeymoon" Lardner has fun with the Florida vacation. A couple comes to Florida to celebrate their 50th anniversary, and the story is not only funny but presents an accurate view of Florida vacations in the 1920s.

"Gullible's Travels," written in 1916, deals with another vacation, this one by a Midwestern couple who visit Palm Beach, lured by the high-society image of the resort and what they think will be reasonable prices. In many ways the story reflects experiences Lardner himself had while traveling around the state.

On a visit to St. Augustine, Lardner wandered the streets and went to the Ponce de Leon Hotel, the massive structure built by oil king Henry Flagler, just as his characters in "Gullible's Travels" do. In real life, Lardner spent time looking at the murals in the hotel. "We had to stand in front o' them for a couple hours and try to keep awake," he writes. Although the Royal Poinciana Hotel in Palm Beach advertises daily rates of $17, the couple soon finds out that is just the beginning of the spending. The Royal Poinciana was the grandest hotel in town and one Lardner stayed at frequently. In the story, his character points out that the dining room was so large, "From one end of it to the other is a toll call."

If 1926 was the year Lardner achieved his greatest success, it also brought the worst news—his health was declining at a rapid rate. He learned he had tuberculosis, combined with a heart problem probably made worse by too much drinking. He stopped writing his column in 1927, although he was able to write a successful play, *June Moon*, in 1929. In 1931 he went to Arizona in the hope of improving his health, but while he felt better temporarily, he soon continued his decline. In 1933 he suffered a heart attack and died. He was just 48 years old.

Gullible's Travels
by Ring Lardner

I promised the Wife that if anybody ast me what kind of a time did I have at Palm Beach I'd say I had a swell time. And if they ast me who did we meet I'd tell 'em everybody that was worth meetin'. And if they ast me didn't the trip cost a lot I'd say Yes; but it was worth the money. I promised her I wouldn't spill none o' the real details. But if you can't break a promise you made to your own wife what kind of a promise can you break? Answer me that, Edgar.

I'm not one o' these kind o' people that'd keep a joke to themself just because the joke was on them. But they's plenty of our friends that I wouldn't have 'em hear about it for the world. I wouldn't tell you, only I know you're not the village gossip and won't crack it to anybody. Not even to your own Missus, see? I don't trust no women.

It was along last January when I and the Wife was both hit by the society bacillus. I think it was at the opera. You remember me tellin' you about us and the Hatches goin' to *Carmen* and then me takin' my Missus and her sister, Bess, and four of one suit named Bishop to see *The Three Kings?* Well, I'll own up that I enjoyed wearin' the soup and fish and minglin' amongst the high polloi and pretendin' we really was somebody. And I know my wife enjoyed it, too, though they was nothin' said between us at the time.

The next stage was where our friends wasn't good enough for us no more. We used to be tickled to death to spend an evenin' playin' rummy with the Hatches. But all of a sudden they didn't seem to be no fun in it and when Hatch'd call up we'd stall out of it. From the number o' times I told him that I or the Missus was tired out and goin' right to bed, he must of thought we'd got jobs as telephone linemen.

We quit attendin' pitcher shows because the rest o' the audience wasn't the kind o' people you'd care to mix with. We didn't go over to Ben's and dance because they wasn't no class to the crowd there. About once a week we'd beat it to one o' the good hotels downtown, all dressed up like a horse, and have our dinner with the rest o' the E-light. They wasn't nobody talked to us only the waiters, but we could look as much as we liked and it was sport tryin' to guess the names o' the gang at the next table.

Then we took to readin' the society news at breakfast. It used to be that I didn't waste time on nothin' but the market and sportin' pages, but now I pass 'em up and listen w'ile the Missus rattled off what was doin' on the Lake Shore Drive.

Every little w'ile we'd see where So-and-So was at Palm Beach or just goin' there or just comin' back: We got to kiddin' about it.

"Well," I'd say, "we'd better be startin' pretty soon or we'll miss the best part o' the season."

"Yes," the Wife'd say back, "we'd go right now if it wasn't for all them engagements next week."

We kidded and kidded till finally, one night, she forgot we was just kiddin'.

"You didn't take no vacation last summer," she says.

"No," says I. "They wasn't no chance to get away."

"But you promised me," she says, "that you'd take one this winter to make up for it."

"I know I did," I says; "but it'd be a sucker play to take a vacation in weather like this."

"The weather ain't like this everywheres," she says.

"You must of been goin' to night school," I says.

"Another thing you promised me," says she, "was that when you could afford it you'd take me on a real honeymoon trip to make up for the dinky one we had."

"That still goes," I says, "when I can afford it."

"You can afford it now," says she. "We don't owe nothin' and we got money in the bank."

"Yes," I says. "Pretty close to three hundred bucks."

"You forgot somethin'," she says. "You forgot them war babies."

Did I tell you about that? Last fall I done a little dabblin' in Crucial Steel and at this time I'm tellin' you about I still had a hold of it, but stood to pull down six hundred. Not bad, eh?

"It'd be a mistake to let loose now," I says.

"All right," she says. "Hold on, and I hope you lose every cent. You never did care nothin' for me."

Then we done a little spoonin' and then I ast her what was the big idear.

"We ain't swelled on ourself," she says; "but I know and you know that the friends we been associatin' with ain't in our class. They don't know how to dress and they can't talk about nothin' but their goldfish and their meat bills. They don't try to get nowheres, but all they do is play rummy and take in the Majestic. I and you like nice people and good music and things that's worth w'ile. It's a crime for us to be wastin' our time with riff and raff that'd run round barefooted if it wasn't for the police."

"I wouldn't say we'd wasted much time on 'em lately," I says.

"No," says she, "and I've had a better time these last three weeks than I ever had in my life."

"And you can keep right on havin' it," I says.

"I could have a whole lot better time, and you could, too," she says, "if we could get acquainted with some congenial people to go round with; people that's tastes is the same as ourn."

"If any o' them people calls up on the phone," I says, "I'll be as pleasant to 'em as I can."

"You're always too smart," says the Wife. "You don't never pay attention to no schemes o' mine."

"What's the scheme now?"

"You'll find fault with it because I thought it up," she says. "If it was your scheme you'd think it was grand."

"If it really was good you wouldn't be scared to spring it," I says.

"Will you promise to go through with it?" says she.

"If it ain't too ridic'lous," I told her.

"See! I knowed that'd be the way," she says.

"Don't talk crazy," I says. "Where'd we be if we'd went through with every plan you ever sprang?"

"Will you promise to listen to my side of it without actin' cute?" she says.

So I didn't see no harm in goin' that far.

"I want you to take me to Palm Beach," says she. "I want you to take a vacation, and that's where we'll spend it."

"And that ain't all we'd spend," I says.

"Remember your promise," says she.

So I shut up and listened.

The dope she give me was along these lines: We could get special round-trip rates on any o' the railroads and that part of it wouldn't cost nowheres near as much as a man'd naturally think. The hotel rates was pretty steep, but the meals was throwed in, and just imagine what them meals would be! And we'd be stayin' under the same roof with the Vanderbilts and Goulds, and eatin' at the same table, and probably, before we was there a week, callin' 'em Steve and Gus. They was dancin' every night and all the guests danced with each other, and how would it feel fox-trottin' with the president o' the B. & O., or the Delmonico girls from New York! And all Chicago society was down there, and when we met 'em we'd know 'em for life and have some real friends amongst 'em when we got back home.

That's how she had it figured and she must of been practisin' her speech, because it certainly did sound good to me. To make it short, I fell, and dated her up to meet me down-town the next day and call on the railroad bandits. The first one we seen admitted that his was the best route and that he wouldn't only soak us one hundred and forty-seven dollars and seventy cents to and from Palm Beach and back, includin' an apartment from here to Jacksonville and as many stop-overs as we wanted to make. He told us we wouldn't have to write for no hotel accommodations because the hotels had an agent right over on Madison Street that'd be glad to do everything to us.

So we says we'd be back later and then we beat it over to the Florida East Coast's local studio.

"How much for a double room by the week?" I ast the man.

"They ain't no weekly rates," he says. "By the day it'd be twelve dollars and up for two at the Breakers, and fourteen dollars and up at the Poinciana."

"I like the Breakers better," says I.

"You can't get in there," he says. "They're full for the season."

"That's a long spree," I says.

"Can we get in the other hotel?" ast the Wife.

"I can find out," says the man.

"We want a room with bath," says she.

"That'd be more," says he. "That'd be fifteen dollars or sixteen dollars and up."

"What do we want of a bath," I says, "with the whole Atlantic Ocean in the front yard?"

"I'm afraid you'd have trouble gettin' a bath," says the man. "The hotels is both o' them pretty well filled up on account o' the war in Europe."

"What's that got to do with it?" I ast him.

"A whole lot," he says. "The people that usually goes abroad is all down to Palm Beach this winter."

"I don't see why," I says. "If one o' them U-boats hit 'em they'd at least be gettin' their bath for nothin'."

We left him with the understandin' that he was to wire down there and find out what was the best they could give us. We called him up in a couple o' days and he told us we could have a double room, without no bath, at the Poinciana, beginnin' the fifteenth o' February. He didn't know just what the price would be.

Well, I fixed it up to take my vacation startin' the tenth, and sold out my Crucial Steel, and divided the spoils with the railroad company. We decided we'd stop off in St. Augustine two days, because the Missus found out somewheres that they might be two or three o' the Four Hundred lingerin' there, and we didn't want to miss nobody.

"Now," I says, "all we got to do is set round and wait for the tenth o' the month."

"Is that so!" says the Wife. "I suppose you're perfectly satisfied with your clo'es."

"I've got to be," I says, "unless the Salvation Army has somethin' that'll fit me."

"What's the matter with our charge account?" she says.

"I don't like to charge nothin'," I says, "when I know they ain't no chance of ever payin' for it."

"All right," she says, "then we're not goin' to Palm Beach. I'd rather stay home than go down there lookin' like general housework."

"Do you need clo'es yourself?" I ast her.

"I certainly do," she says. "About two hundred dollars' worth. But I got one hundred and fifty dollars o' my own."

"All right," I says. "I'll stand for the other fifty and then we're all set."

"No, we're not," she says. "That just fixes me. But I want you to look as good as I do."

"Nature'll see to that," I says.

But they was no arguin' with her. Our trip, she says, was an investment; it was goin' to get us in right with people worth w'ile. And we wouldn't have a chance in the world unless we looked the part.

So before the tenth come round, we was long two new evenin' gowns, two female sport suits, four or five pairs o' shoes, all colors, one Tuxedo dinner coat, three dress shirts, half a dozen other kinds o' shirts, two pairs o' transparent white trousers, one new business suit and Lord knows how much underwear and how many hats and stockin's. And I had till the fifteenth o' March to pay off the mortgage on the old homestead.

Just as we was gettin' ready to leave for the train the phone rung.

It was Mrs. Hatch and she wanted us to come over for a little rummy. I was shavin' and the Missus done the talkin'.

"What did you tell her?" I ast.

"I told her we was goin' away," says the Wife.

"I bet you forgot to mention where we was goin'," I says.

"Pay me," says she.

II

I thought we was in Venice when we woke up next mornin', but the porter says it was just Cairo, Illinois. The river'd went crazy and I bet they wasn't a room without a bath in that old burg.

As we set down in the diner for breakfast the train was goin' acrost the longest bridge I ever seen, and it looked like we was so near the water that you could reach right out and grab a handful. The Wife was a little wabbly.

"I wonder if it's really safe," she says.

"If the bridge stays up we're all right," says I.

"But the question is, Will it stay up?" she says.

"I wouldn't bet a nickel either way on a bridge," I says. "They're treacherous little devils. They'd cross you as quick as they'd cross this river."

"The trainmen must be nervous," she says. "Just see how we're draggin' along."

"They're givin' the fish a chance to get off en the track," I says. "It's against the law to spear fish with a cowcatcher this time o' year."

Well, the Wife was so nervous she couldn't eat nothin' but toast and coffee, so I figured I was justified in goin' to the prunes and steak and eggs.

After breakfast we went out in what they call the sun parlor. It was a glassed-in room on the tail-end o' the rear coach and it must of been a pleasant place to set and watch the scenery. But they was a gang o' missionaries or somethin' had all the seats and they never budged out o' them all day. Every time they'd come to a crossroads they'd toss a stack o' Bible studies out o' the back window for the southern heathen to pick up and read. I suppose they thought they was doin' a lot o' good for their fellow men, but their fellow passengers meanw'ile was gettin' the worst of it.

Speakin' o' the scenery, it certainly was somethin' grand. First we'd pass a few pine trees with fuzz on 'em and then a couple o' acres o' yellow mud. Then they'd be more pine trees and more fuzz and then more yellow mud. And after a w'ile we'd come to some pine trees with fuzz on 'em and then, if we watched close, we'd see some yellow mud.

Every few minutes the train'd stop and then start up again on low. That meant the engineer suspected he was comin' to a station and was scared that if he run too fast he wouldn't see it, and if he run past it without stoppin' the inhabitants wouldn't never forgive him. You see, they's a regular schedule o' duties that's followed out by the more prominent citizens down those parts. After their wife's attended to the chores and got the breakfast they roll out o' bed and put on their overalls and eat. Then they get on their horse or mule or cow or dog and ride down to the station and wait for the next train. When it comes they have a contest to see which can count the passengers first. The losers has to promise to work one day the followin' month. If one fella loses three times in the same month he generally always kills himself.

All the towns has got five or six private residences and seven or eight two-apartment buildin's and a grocery and a post-office. They told me that somebody in one o' them burgs, I forget which one, got a letter the day before we come through. It was misdirected, I guess.

The two-apartment buildin's is constructed on the ground floor, with a porch to divide one flat from the other. One's the housekeepin' side and the other's just a place for the husband and father to lay round in so's they won't be disturbed by watchin' the women work.

It was a blessin' to them boys when their states went dry. Just think what a strain it must of been to keep liftin' glasses and huntin' in their overalls for a dime!

In the afternoon the Missus went into our apartment and took a nap and I moseyed into the readin'-room and looked over some o' the comical magazines. They was a fat guy come in and set next to me. I'd heard him, in at lunch, tellin' the dinin'-car conductor what Wilson should of done, so I wasn't su'prised when he opened up on me.

"Tiresome trip," he says.

I didn't think it was worth w'ile arguin' with him.

"Must of been a lot o' rain through here," he says.

"Either that," says I, "or else the sprinklin' wagon run shy o' streets."

He laughed as much as it was worth.

"Where do you come from?" he ast me.

"Dear old Chicago," I says.

"I'm from St. Louis," he says.

"You're frank," says I.

"I'm really as much at home one place as another," he says. "The Wife likes to travel and why shouldn't I humor her?"

"I don't know," I says. "I haven't the pleasure."

"Seems like we're goin' all the w'ile," says he. "It's Hot Springs or New Orleans or Florida or Atlantic City or California or somewheres."

"Do you get passes?" I ast him.

"I guess I could if I wanted to," he says. "Some o' my best friends is way up in the railroad business."

"I got one like that," I says. "He generally stands on the fourth or fifth car behind the engine."

"Do you travel much?" he ast me.

"I don't live in St. Louis," says I.

"Is this your first trip south?" he ast.

"Oh, no," I says. "I live on Sixty-fifth Street."

"I meant, have you ever been down this way before?"

"Oh, yes," says I. "I come down every winter."

"Where do you go?" he ast.

That's what I was layin' for.

"Palm Beach," says I.

"I used to go there," he says. "But I've cut it out. It ain't like it used to be. They leave everybody in now."

"Yes," I says; "but a man don't have to mix up with 'em."

"You can't just ignore people that comes up and talks to you," he says.

"Are you bothered that way much?" I ast.

"It's what drove me away from Palm Beach," he says.

"How long since you been there?" I ast him.

"How long you been goin' there?" he says.

"Me?" says I. "Five years."

"We just missed each other," says he. "I quit six years ago this winter."

"Then it couldn't of been there I seen you," says I. "But I know I seen you somewheres before."

"It might of been most anywheres," he says. "They's few places I haven't been at."

"Maybe it was across the pond," says I.

"Very likely," he says. "But not since the war started. I been steerin' clear of Europe for two years."

"So have I, for longer'n that," I says.

"It's certainly an awful thing, this war," says he.

"I believe you're right," says I; "but I haven't heard nobody express it just that way before."

"I only hope," he says, "that we succeed in keepin' out of it."

"If we got in, would you go?" I ast him.

"Yes, sir," he says.

"You wouldn't beat me," says I. "I bet I'd reach Brazil as quick as you."

"Oh, I don't think they'd be any action in South America," he says. "We'd fight defensive at first and most of it would be along the Atlantic Coast."

"Then maybe we could get accommodations in Yellowstone Park," says I.

"They's no sense in this country gettin' involved," he says. "Wilson hasn't handled it right. He either ought to of went stronger or not so strong. He's wrote too many notes."

"You certainly get right to the root of a thing," says I. "You must of thought a good deal about it."

"I know the conditions pretty well," he says. "I know how far you can go with them people over there. I been amongst 'em a good part o' the time."

"I suppose," says I, "that a fella just naturally don't like to butt in. But if I was you I'd consider it my duty to romp down to Washington and give 'em all the information I had."

"Wilson picked his own advisers," says he. "Let him learn his lesson."

"That ain't hardly fair," I says. "Maybe you was out o' town, or your phone was busy or somethin'."

"I don't know Wilson nor he don't know me," he says.

"That oughtn't to stop you from helpin' him out," says I. "If you seen a man drownin' would you wait for some friend o' the both o' you to come along and make the introduction?"

"They ain't no comparison in them two cases," he says. "Wilson ain't never called on me for help."

"You don't know if he has or not," I says. "You don't stick in one place long enough for a man to reach you."

"My office in St. Louis always knows where I'm at," says he. "My stenographer can reach me any time within ten to twelve hours."

"I don't think it's right to have this country's whole future dependin' on a St. Louis stenographer," I says.

"That's nonsense!" says he. "I ain't makin' no claim that I could save or not save this country. But if I and Wilson was acquainted I might tell him some facts that'd help him out in his foreign policy."

"Well, then," I says, "it's up to you to get acquainted. I'd introduce you myself only I don't know your name."

"My name's Gould," says he; "but you're not acquainted with Wilson."

"I could be, easy," says I. "I could get on a train he was goin' somewheres on and then go and set beside him and begin to talk.

Lots o' people make friends that way."

It was gettin' along to'rd supper-time, so I excused myself and went back to the apartment. The Missus had woke up and wasn't feelin' good.

"What's the matter?" I ast her.

"This old train," she says. "I'll die if it don't stop goin' round them curves."

"As long as the track curves, the best thing the train can do is curve with it," I says. "You may die if it keeps curvin', but you'd die a whole lot sooner if it left the rails and went straight ahead."

"What you been doin'?" she ast me.

"Just talkin' to one o' the Goulds," I says.

"Gould!" she says. "What Gould?"

"Well," I says, "I didn't ask him his first name, but he's from St. Louis, so I suppose it's Ludwig or Heinie."

"Oh," she says, disgusted. "I thought you meant one o' the real ones."

"He's a real one, all right," says I. "He's so classy that he's passed up Palm Beach. He says it's gettin' too common."

"I don't believe it," says the Wife. "And besides, we don't have to mix up with everybody."

"He says they butt right in on you," I told her.

"They'll get a cold reception from me," she says.

But between the curves and the fear o' Palm Beach not bein' so exclusive as it used to be, she couldn't eat no supper, and I had another big meal.

The next mornin' we landed in Jacksonville three hours behind time and narrowly missed connections for St. Augustine by over an hour and a half. They wasn't another train till one-thirty in the afternoon, so we had some time to kill. I went shoppin' and bought a shave and five or six rickeys. The Wife helped herself to a chair in the writin'-room of one o' the hotels and told pretty near everybody in Chicago that she wished they was along with us, accompanied by a pitcher o' the Elks' Home or the Germania Club, or Trout Fishin' at Atlantic Beach.

W'ile I was gettin' my dime's worth in the tonsorial parlors, I happened to look up at a calendar on the wall, and noticed it was the twelfth o' February.

"How does it come that everything's open here to-day?" I says to the barber. "Don't you-all know it's Lincoln's birthday?"

"Is that so?" he says. "How old is he?"

III

We'd wired ahead for rooms at the Alcazar, and when we landed in St. Augustine they was a motor-bus from the hotel to meet us at the station.

"Southern hospitality," I says to the Wife, and we was both pleased till they relieved us o' four bits apiece for the ride.

Well, they hadn't neither one of us slept good the night before, w'ile we was joltin' through Georgia; so when I suggested a nap they wasn't no argument.

"But our clo'es ought to be pressed," says the Missus. "Call up the valet and have it done w'ile we sleep."

So I called up the valet, and sure enough, he come.

"Hello, George!" I says. "You see, we're goin' to lay down and take a nap, and we was wonderin' if you could crease up these two suits and have 'em back here by the time we want 'em."

"Certainly, sir," says he.

"And how much will it cost?" I ast him.

"One dollar a suit," he says.

"Are you on parole or haven't you never been caught?" says I.

"Yes, sir," he says, and smiled like it was a joke.

"Let's talk business, George," I says. "The tailor we go to on Sixty-third walks two blocks to get our clo'es, and two blocks to take 'em to his joint, and two blocks to bring 'em back, and he only soaks us thirty-five cents a suit."

"He gets poor pay and he does poor work," says the burglar. "When I press clo'es I press 'em right."

"Well," I says, "the tailor on Sixty-third satisfies us. Suppose you don't do your best this time, but just give us seventy cents' worth."

But they wasn't no chance for a bargain. He'd been in the business so long he'd become hardened and lost all regard for his fellow men.

The Missus slept, but I didn't. Instead, I done a few problems in arithmetic. Outside o' what she'd gave up for postcards and stamps in Jacksonville, I'd spent two bucks for our lunch, about two more for my shave and my refreshments, one for a rough ride in a bus, one more for gettin' our trunk and grips carried round, two for havin' the clo'es pressed, and about half a buck in tips to people that I wouldn't never see again. Somewheres near nine dollars a day, not countin' no hotel bill, and over two weeks of it yet to come!

Oh, you rummy game at home, at half a cent a point!

When our clo'es come back I woke her up and give her the figures.

"But to-day's an exception," she says. "After this our meals will be included in the hotel bill and we won't need to get our suits pressed only once a week and you'll be shavin' yourself and they won't be no bus fare when we're stayin' in one place. Besides, we can practise economy all spring and all summer."

"I guess we need the practise," I says.

"And if you're goin' to crab all the time about expenses," says she, "I'll wish we had of stayed home."

"That'll make it unanimous," says I.

Then she begin sobbin' about how I'd spoiled the trip and I had to promise I wouldn't think no more o' what we were spendin'. I might just as well of promised to not worry when the White Sox lost or when I'd forgot to come home to supper.

We went in the dinin'-room about six-thirty and was showed to a table where they was another couple settin'. They was husband and wife, I guess, but I don't know which was which. She was wieldin' the pencil and writin' down their order.

"I guess I'll have clams," he says.

"They disagreed with you last night," says she.

"All right," he says. "I won't try 'em. Give me cream-o'-tomato soup."

"You don't like tomatoes," she says.

"Well, I won't have no soup," says he. "A little o' the blue-fish."

"The blue-fish wasn't no good at noon," she says. "You better try the bass."

"All right, make it bass," he says. "And them sweet-breads and a little roast beef and sweet potatoes and peas and vanilla ice-cream and coffee."

"You wouldn't touch sweet-breads at home," says she, "and you can't tell what they'll be in a hotel."

"All right, cut out the sweet-breads," he says.

"I should think you'd have the stewed chicken," she says, "and leave out the roast beef."

"Stewed chicken it is," says he.

"Stewed chicken and mashed potatoes and string beans and buttered toast and coffee. Will that suit you?"

"Sure!" he says, and she give the slip to the waiter.

George looked at it long enough to of read it three times if he could of read it once and then went out in the kitchen and got a trayful o' whatever was handy.

But the poor guy didn't get more'n a taste of anything. She was watchin' him like a hawk, and no sooner would he delve into one victual than she'd yank the dish away from him and tell him to remember that health was more important than temporary happiness. I felt so sorry for him that I couldn't enjoy my own repast and I told the Wife that we'd have our breakfast apart from that stricken soul if I had to carry the case to old Al Cazar himself.

In the evenin' we strolled acrost the street to the Ponce—that's supposed to be even sweller yet than where we were stoppin' at. We walked all over the place without recognizin' nobody from our set. I finally warned the Missus that if we didn't duck back to our room I'd probably have a heart attack from excitement; but she'd read in her Florida guide that the decorations and pitchers was worth goin' miles to see, so we had to stand in front o' them for a couple hours and try to keep awake. Four or five o' them was thrillers, at that. Their names was Adventure, Discovery, Contest, and so on, but what they all should of been called was Lady Who Had Mislaid Her Clo'es.

The hotel's named after the fella that built it. He come from Spain and they say he was huntin' for some water that if he'd drunk it he'd feel young. I don't see myself how you could expect to feel young on water. But, anyway, he'd heard that this here kind o' water could be found in St. Augustine, and when he couldn't find it he went into the hotel business and got even with the United States by chargin' five dollars a day and up for a room.

Sunday mornin' we went in to breakfast early and I ast the head waiter if we could set at another table where they wasn't no convalescent and his mate. At the same time I give the said head waiter somethin' that spoke louder than words. We was showed to a place way acrost the room from where we'd been the night before. It was a table for six, but the other four didn't come into our life till that night at supper.

Meanw'ile we went sight-seein'. We visited Fort Marion, that'd be a great protection against the Germans, provided they fought with paper wads. We seen the city gate and the cathedral and the slave market, and then we took the boat over to Anastasia Island, that the ocean's on the other side of it. This trip made me homesick, because the people that was along with us on the boat looked just like the ones we'd often went with to Michigan City on the Fourth o' July. The boat landed on the bay side o' the island and from there we was drug over to the ocean side on a horse car, the horse walkin' to one side o' the car instead of in front, so's he wouldn't get ran over.

We stuck on the beach till dinner-time and then took the chariot back to the pavilion on the bay side, where a whole family served the meal and their pigs put on a cabaret. It was the best meal I had in dear old Dixie—fresh oysters and chicken and mashed potatoes and gravy and fish and pie. And they charged two bits a plate.

"Goodness gracious!" says the Missus, when I told her the price. "This is certainly reasonable. I wonder how it happens."

"Well," I says, "the family was probably washed up here by the tide and don't know they're in Florida."

When we got back to the hotel they was only just time to clean up and go down to supper. We hadn't no sooner got seated when our table companions breezed in. It was a man about forty-five, that looked like he'd made his money in express and general haulin', and he had his wife along and both their mother-in-laws. The shirt he had on was the one he'd started from home with, if he lived in Yokohama. His womenfolks wore mournin' with a touch o' gravy here and there.

"You order for us, Jake," says one o' the ladies.

So Jake grabbed the bill o' fare and his wife took the slip and pencil and waited for the dictation.

"Let's see," he says. "How about oyster cocktail?"

"Yes," says the three Mrs. Black.

"Four oyster cocktails, then," says Jake, "and four orders o' blue-points."

"The oysters is nice, too," says I. They all give me a cordial smile and the ice was broke.

"Everything's good here," says Jake.

"I bet you know," I says.

He seemed pleased at the compliment and went on dictatin'.

"Four chicken soups with rice," he says, "and four o' the blue-fish and four veal chops breaded and four roast chicken and four boiled potatoes—"

But it seemed his wife would rather have sweet potatoes.

"All right," says Jake; "four boiled potatoes and four sweets. And chicken salad and some o' that tapioca puddin' and ice-cream and tea. Is that satisfactory?"

"Fine!" says one o' the mother-in-laws.

"Are you goin' to stay long?" says Mrs. Jake to my Missus.

The party addressed didn't look very clubby, but she was too polite to pull the cut direct.

"We leave to-morrow night," she says. Nobody ast her where we was goin'. "We leave for Palm Beach," she says. "That's a nice place, I guess," says one of the old ones. "More people goes there than comes here. It ain't so expensive there, I guess."

"You're some guesser," says the Missus and freezes up.

I ast Jake if he'd been to Florida before. "No," he says; "this is our first trip, but we're makin' up for lost time. We're all they is to see and havin' everything the best."

"You're havin' everything, all right," I says, "but I don't know if it's the best or not. How long have you been here?"

"A week to-morrow," says he. "And we stay another week and then go to Ormond."

"Are you standin' the trip O. K.?" I ast him.

"Well," he says, "I don't feel quite as good as when we first come."

"Kind o' logy?" I says.

"Yes; kind o' heavy," says Jake.

"I know what you ought to do," says I. "You ought to go to a European plan hotel."

"Not while this war's on," he says, "and besides, my mother's a poor sailor."

"Yes," says his mother; "I'm a very poor sailor."

"Jake's mother can't stand the water," says Mrs. Jake.

So I begun to believe that Jake's wife's mother-in-law was a total failure as a jolly tar.

Social intercourse was put an end to when the waiter staggered in with their order and our'n. The Missus seemed to of lost her appetite and just set there lookin' grouchy and tappin' her fingers on the table-cloth and actin' like she was in a hurry to get away. I didn't eat much, neither. It was more fun watchin'.

"Well," I says, when we was out in the lobby, "we finally got acquainted with some real people."

"Real people!" says the Missus, curlin' her lip. "What did you talk to 'em for?"

"I couldn't resist," I says. "Anybody that'd order four oyster cocktails and four rounds o' blue-points is worth knowin'."

"Well," she says, "if they're there when we go in to-morrow mornin' we'll get our table changed again or you can eat with 'em alone."

But they was absent from the breakfast board.

"They're probably stayin' in bed to-day to get their clo'es washed," says the Missus.

"Or maybe they're sick," I says. "A change of oysters affects some people."

I was for goin' over to the island again and gettin' another o' them quarter banquets, but the program was for us to walk round town all mornin' and take a ride in the afternoon.

First, we went to St. George Street and visited the oldest house in the United States. Then we went to Hospital Street and seen the oldest house in the United States. Then we turned the corner and went down St. Francis Street and inspected the oldest house in the United States. Then we dropped into a soda fountain and I had an egg phosphate, made from the oldest egg in the Western Hemisphere. We passed up lunch and got into a carriage drawn by the oldest horse in Florida, and we rode through the country all afternoon and the driver told us some o' the oldest jokes in the book. He felt it was only fair to give his customers a good time when he was chargin' a dollar an hour, and he had his gags rehearsed so's he could tell the same one a thousand times and never change a word. And the horse knowed where the point come in every one and stopped to laugh.

We done our packin' before supper, and by the time we got to our table Jake and the mourners was through and gone. We didn't have to ask the waiter if they'd been there. He was perspirin' like an evangelist.

After supper we said good-by to the night clerk and twenty-two bucks. Then we bought ourself another ride in the motor-bus and landed at the station ten minutes before train-time; so we only had an hour to wait for the train.

Say, I don't know how many stations they is between New York and San Francisco, but they's twice as many between St. Augustine and Palm Beach. And our train stopped twice and started twice at every one. I give up tryin' to sleep and looked out the window, amusin' myself by readin' the names o' the different stops. The only one that expressed my sentiments was Eau Gallie. We was an hour and a half late pullin' out o' that joint and I figured we'd be two hours to the bad gettin' into our destination. But the guy that made out the time-table must of had the engineer down pat, because when we went acrost the bridge over Lake Worth and landed at the Poinciana depot, we was ten minutes ahead o' time.

They was about two dozen uniformed Ephs on the job to meet us. And when I seen 'em all grab for our baggage with one hand and hold the other out, face up, I knowed why they called it Palm Beach.

IV

The Poinciana station's a couple hundred yards from one end o' the hotel, and that means it's close to five miles from the clerk's desk. By the time we'd registered and been gave our key and marathoned another five miles or so to where our room was located at, I was about ready for the inquest. But the Missus was full o' pep and wild to get down to breakfast and look over our stable mates. She says we would eat without changin' our clo'es; people'd forgive us for not dressin' up on account o' just gettin' there. W'ile she was lookin' out the window at the royal palms and buzzards, I moseyed round the room inspectin' where the different doors led to. Pretty near the first one I opened went into a private bath.

"Here," I says; "they've give us the wrong room."

Then my wife seen it and begin to squeal.

"Goody!" she says. "We've got a bath! We've got a bath!"

"But," says I, "they promised we wouldn't have none. It must be a mistake."

"Never you mind about a mistake," she says. "This is our room and they can't chase us out of it."

"We'll chase ourself out," says I. "Rooms with a bath is fifteen and sixteen dollars and up. Rooms without no bath is bad enough."

"We'll keep this room or I won't stay here," she says.

"All right, you win," I says; but I didn't mean it.

I made her set in the lobby down-stairs w'ile I went to the clerk pretendin' that I had to see about our trunk.

"Say," I says to him, "you've made a bad mistake. You told your man in Chicago that we couldn't have no room with a bath, and now you've give us one."

"You're lucky," he says. "A party who had a bath ordered for these two weeks canceled their reservation and now you've got it."

"Lucky, am I?" I says. "And how much is the luck goin' to cost me?"

"It'll be seventeen dollars per day for that room," he says, and turned away to hide a blush.

I went back to the Wife.

"Do you know what we're payin' for that room?" I says. "We're payin' seventeen dollars."

"Well," she says, "our meals is throwed in."

"Yes," says I, "and the hotel furnishes a key."

"You promised in St. Augustine," she says, "that you wouldn't worry no more about expenses."

Well, rather than make a scene in front o' the bellhops and the few millionaires that was able to be about at that hour o' the mornin', I just says "All right!" and led her into the dinin'-room.

The head waiter met us at the door and turned us over to his assistant. Then some more assistants took hold of us one at a time and we was relayed to a beautiful spot next door to the kitchen and bounded on all sides by posts and pillars. It was all right for me, but a whole lot too private for the Missus; so I had to call the fella that had been our pacemaker on the last lap.

"We don't like this table," I says.

"It's the only one I can give you," he says.

I slipped him half a buck.

"Come to think of it," he says, "I believe they's one I forgot all about."

And he moved us way up near the middle o' the place.

Say, you ought to seen that dinin'-room! From one end of it to the other is a toll call, and if a man that was settin' at the table farthest from the kitchen ordered roast lamb he'd get mutton. At that, they was crowded for fair and it kept the head waiters hustlin' to find trough space for one and all.

It was round nine o'clock when we put in our modest order for orange juice, oatmeal, liver and bacon, and cakes and coffee, and a quarter to ten or so when our waiter returned from the nearest orange grove with Exhibit A. We amused ourself meanw'ile by givin' our neighbors the once over and wonderin' which o' them was goin' to pal with us. As far as I could tell from the glances we received, they wasn't no immediate danger of us bein' annoyed by attentions.

They was only a few womenfolks on deck and they was dressed pretty quiet; so quiet that the Missus was scared she'd shock 'em with the sport skirt she'd bought in Chi. Later on in the day, when the girls come out for their dress parade, the Missus' costume made about as much noise as eatin' marshmallows in a foundry.

After breakfast we went to the room for a change o' raiment. I put on my white trousers and wished to heaven that the sun'd go under a cloud till I got used to tellin' people without words just where my linen began and I left off. The rest o' my outfit was white shoes that hurt, and white sox, and a two-dollar silk shirt that showed up a zebra, and a red tie and a soft collar and a blue coat. The Missus wore a sport suit that I won't try and describe—you'll probably see it on her sometime in the next five years.

We went down-stairs again and out on the porch, where some o' the old birds was takin' a sun bath.

"Where now?" I says.

"The beach, o' course," says the Missus.

"Where is it at?" I ast her.

"I suppose," she says, "that we'll find it somewheres near the ocean."

"I don't believe you can stand this climate," says I.

"The ocean," she says, "must be down at the end o' that avenue, where most everybody seems to be headed."

"Havin' went to our room and back twice, I don't feel like another five-mile hike," I says.

"It ain't no five miles," she says; "but let's ride, anyway."

"Come on," says I, pointin' to a street-car that was standin' in the middle o' the avenue.

"Oh, no," she says. "I've watched and found out that the real people takes them funnylookin' wheel chairs."

I was wonderin' what she meant when one o' them pretty near run over us. It was part bicycle, part go-cart and part African. In the one we dodged they was room for one passenger, but some o' them carried two.

"I wonder what they'd soak us for the trip," I says.

"Not more'n a dime, I don't believe," says the Missus.

But when we'd hired one and been w'isked down under the palms and past the golf field to the bath-house, we was obliged to part with fifty cents legal and tender.

"I feel much refreshed," I says. "I believe when it comes time to go back I'll be able to walk."

The bath-house is acrost the street from the other hotel, the Breakers, that the man had told us was full for the season. Both buildin's fronts on the ocean; and, boy, it's some ocean! I bet they's fish in there that never seen each other!

"Oh, let's go bathin' right away!" says the Missus.

"Our suits is up to the other beanery," says I, and I was glad of it. They wasn't nothin' temptin' to me about them man-eatin' waves.

But the Wife's a persistent cuss.

"We won't go to-day," she says, "but we'll go in the bath-house and get some rooms for to-morrow."

The bath-house porch was a ringer for the Follies. Here and down on the beach was where you seen the costumes at this time o' day. I was so busy rubberin' that I passed the entrance door three times without noticin' it. From the top o' their heads to the bottom o' their feet the girls was a mess o' colors. They wasn't no two dressed alike and if anyone them had of walked down State Street we'd of had an epidemic o' stiff neck to contend with in Chi. Finally the Missus grabbed me and hauled me into the office.

"Two private rooms," she says to the clerk. "One lady and one gent."

"Five dollars a week apiece," he says. "But we're all filled up."

"You ought to be all locked up!" I says.

"Will you have anything open to-morrow?" ast the Missus.

"I think I can fix you then," he says.

"What do we get for the five?" I ast him.

"Private room and we take care o' your bathin' suit," says he.

"How much if you don't take care o' the suit?" I ast him. "My suit's been gettin' along fine with very little care."

"Five dollars a week apiece," he says, "and if you want the rooms you better take 'em, because they're in big demand."

By the time we'd closed this grand bargain, everybody'd moved offen the porch and down to the water, where a couple dozen o' them went in for a swim and the rest set and watched. They was a long row o' chairs on the beach for spectators and we was just goin' to flop into two o' them when another bandit come up and told us it'd cost a dime apiece per hour.

"We're goin' to be here two weeks," I says. "Will you sell us two chairs?"

He wasn't in no comical mood, so we sunk down on the sand and seen the show from there. We had plenty o' company that preferred these kind o' seats free to the chairs at ten cents a whack.

Besides the people that was in the water gettin' knocked down by the waves and pretendin' like they enjoyed it, about half o' the gang on the sand was wearin' bathin' suits just to be clubby. You could tell by lookin' at the suits that they hadn't never been wet and wasn't intended for no such ridic'lous purpose. I wisht I could describe 'em to you, but it'd take a female to do it right.

One little girl, either fourteen or twenty-four, had white silk slippers and sox that come pretty near up to her ankles, and from there to her knees it was just plain Nature. Northbound from her knees was a pair o' bicycle trousers that disappeared when they come to the bottom of her Mother Hubbard. This here garment was a thing without no neck or sleeves that begin bulgin' at the top and spread out gradual all the way down, like a croquette. To top her off, she had a jockey cap; and—believe me—I'd of played her mount across the board. They was plenty o' class in the field with her, but nothin' that approached her speed. Later on I seen her several times round the hotel, wearin' somethin' near the same outfit, without the jockey cap and with longer croquettes.

We set there in the sand till people begun to get up and leave. Then we trailed along back o' them to the Breakers' porch, where they was music to dance and stuff to inhale.

"We'll grab a table," I says to the Missus. "I'm dyin' o' thirst."

But I was allowed to keep on dyin' .

"I can serve you somethin' soft," says the waiter.

"I'll bet you can't!" I says.

"You ain't got no locker here?" he says.

"What do you mean—locker?" I ast him.

"It's the locker liquor law," he says. "We can serve you a drink if you own your own bottles."

"I'd just as soon own a bottle," I says. "I'll become the proprietor of a bottle o' beer."

"It'll take three or four hours to get it for you," he says, "and you'd have to order it through the order desk. If you're stoppin' at one o' the hotels and want a drink once in a w'ile, you better get busy and put in an order."

So I had to watch the Missus put away a glass of orange juice that cost forty cents and was just the same size as they give us for breakfast free for nothin'. And, not havin' had nothin' to make me forget that my feet hurt, I was obliged to pay another four bits for an Afromobile to cart us back to our own boardin' house.

"Well," says the Missus when we got there, "it's time to wash up and go to lunch."

"Wash up and go to lunch, then," I says "but I'm goin' to investigate this here locker liquor or liquor locker law."

So she got her key and beat it, and I limped to the bar.

"I want a highball," I says to the boy.

"What's your number?" says he.

"It varies," I says. "Sometimes I can hold twenty and sometimes four or five makes me sing."

"I mean, have you got a locker here?" he says.

"No; but I want to get one," says I.

"The gent over there to the desk will fix you," says he.

So over to the desk I went and ast for a locker.

"What do you drink?" ast the gent.

"I'm from Chicago," I says. "I drink bourbon."

"What's your name and room number?" he says, and I told him.

Then he ast me how often did I shave and what did I think o' the Kaiser and what my name was before I got married, and if I had any intentions of ever running an elevator. Finally he says I was all right.

"I'll order you some bourbon," he says. "Anything else?"

I was goin' to say no, but I happened to remember that the Wife generally always wants a bronix before dinner. So I had to also put in a bid for a bottle o' gin and bottles o' the Vermouth brothers, Tony and Pierre. It wasn't till later that I appreciated what a grand law this here law was. When I got my drinks I paid ten cents apiece for 'em for service, besides payin' for the bottles o' stuff to drink. And, besides that, about every third highball or bronix I ordered, the waiter'd bring back word that I was just out of ingredients and then they'd be another delay w'ile they sent to the garage for more. If they had that law all over the country they'd soon be an end o' drinkin', because everybody'd get so mad they'd kill each other.

My cross-examination had took quite a long time, but when I got to my room the Wife wasn't back from lunch yet and I had to cover the Marathon route all over again and look her up. We only had the one key to the room, and o' course couldn't expect no more'n that at the price.

The Missus had bought one o' the daily programs they get out and she knowed just what we had to do the rest o' the day.

"For the next couple hours," she says, "we can suit ourself."

"All right," says I. "It suits me to take off my shoes and lay down."

"I'll rest, too," she says; "but at half past four we have to be in the Cocoanut Grove for tea and dancin'. And then we come back to the room and dress for dinner. Then we eat and then we set around till the evenin' dance starts. Then we dance till we're ready for bed."

"Who do we dance all these dances with?" I ast her.

"With whoever we get acquainted with," she says.

"All right," says I; "but let's be careful."

Well, we took our nap and then we followed schedule and had our tea in the Cocoanut Grove. You know how I love tea! My feet was still achin' and the Missus couldn't talk me into no dance.

When we'd set there an hour and was saturated with tea, the Wife says it was time to go up and change into our Tuxedos. I was all in when we reached the room and willin' to even pass up supper and nestle in the hay, but I was informed that the biggest part o' the day's doin's was yet to come. So from six o'clock till after seven I wrestled with studs, and hooks and eyes that didn't act like they'd ever met before and wasn't anxious to get acquainted, and then down we went again to the dinin'-room.

"How about a little bronix before the feed?" I says.

"It would taste good," says the Missus. So I called Eph and give him the order. In somethin' less than half an hour he come back empty-handed.

"You ain't got no cocktail stuff," he says.

"I certainly have," says I. "I ordered it early this afternoon."

"Where at?" he ast me.

"Over in the bar," I says.

"Oh, the regular bar!" he says. "That don't count. You got to have stuff at the service bar to get it served in here."

"I ain't as thirsty as I thought I was," says I.

"Me, neither," says the Missus.

So we went ahead and ordered our meal, and w'ile we was waitin' for it a young couple come and took the other two chairs at our table. They didn't have to announce through a megaphone that they was honeymooners. It was wrote all over 'em. They was reachin' under the table for each other's hand every other minute, and when they wasn't doin' that they was smilin' at each other or gigglin' at nothin'. You couldn't feel that good and be payin' seventeen dollars a day for room and board unless you was just married or somethin'.

I thought at first their company'd be fun, but after a few meals it got like the southern cookin' and begun to undermine the health.

The conversation between they and us was what you could call limited. It took place the next day at lunch. The young husband thought he was about to take a bite o' the entry, which happened to be roast mutton with sirup; but he couldn't help from lookin' at her at the same time and his empty fork started for his face prongs up.

"Look out for your eye," I says.

He dropped the fork and they both blushed till you could see it right through the sunburn. Then they give me a Mexican look and our acquaintance was at an end.

This first night, when we was through eatin', we wandered out in the lobby and took seats where we could watch the passin' show. The men was all dressed like me, except I was up to date and had on a mushroom shirt, w'ile they was sportin' the old-fashioned concrete bosom. The women's dresses begun at the top with a belt, and some o' them stopped at the mezzanine floor, w'ile others went clear down to the basement and helped keep the rugs clean. They was one that must of thought it was the Fourth o' July. From the top of her head to where the top of her bathin' suit had left off, she was a red, red rose. From there to the top of her gown was white, and her gown, what they was of it—was blue.

"My!" says the Missus. "What stunnin' gowns!"

"Yes," I says; "and you could have one just like 'em if you'd take the shade offen the piano lamp at home and cut it down to the right size."

Round ten o'clock we wandered in the Palm Garden, where the dancin' had been renewed. The Wife wanted to plunge right in the mazes o' the foxy trot.

"I'll take some courage first," says I. Around then was when I found out that it cost you ten cents extra besides the tip to pay for a drink that you already owned in fee simple.

Well, I guess we must of danced about six dances together and had that many quarrels before she was ready to go to bed. And oh, how grand that old hay-pile felt when I finally bounced into it!

The next day we went to the ocean at the legal hour—half past eleven. I never had so much fun in my life. The surf was runnin' high, I heard 'em say; and I don't know which I'd rather do, go bathin' in the ocean at Palm Beach when the surf is runnin' high, or have a dentist get one o' my molars ready for a big inlay at a big outlay. Once in a w'ile I managed to not get throwed on my head when a wave hit me. As for swimmin', you had just as much chance as if you was at State and Madison at the noon hour. And before I'd been in a minute they was enough salt in my different features to keep the Blackstone hotel runnin' all through the onion season.

The Missus enjoyed it just as much as me. She tried to pretend at first, and when she got floored she'd give a squeal that was supposed to mean heavenly bliss. But after she'd been bruised from head to feet and her hair looked and felt like spinach with French dressin', and she'd drank all she could hold o' the Gulf Stream, she didn't resist none when I drug her in to shore and staggered with her up to our private rooms at five a week per each.

Without consultin' her, I went to the desk at the Casino and told 'em they could have them rooms back.

"All right," says the clerk, and turned our keys over to the next in line.

"How about a refund?" I ast him; but he was waitin' on somebody else.

After that we done our bathin' in the tub. But we was down to the beach every morning at eleven-thirty to watch the rest o' them get batted round.

And at half past twelve every day we'd follow the crowd to the Breakers' porch and dance together, the Missus and I. Then it'd be back to the other hostelry, sometimes limpin' and sometimes in an

Afromobile, and a drink or two in the Palm Garden before lunch. And after lunch we'd lay down; or we'd pay some Eph two or three dollars to pedal us through the windin' jungle trail, that was every bit as wild as the Art Institute; or we'd ferry acrost Lake Worth to West Palm Beach and take in a movie, or we'd stand in front o' the portable Fifth Avenue stores w'ile the Missus wished she could have this dress or that hat, or somethin' else that she wouldn't of looked at if she'd been home and in her right mind. But always at half past four we had to live up to the rules and be in the Cocoanut Grove for tea and some more foxy trottin'. And then it was dress for dinner, eat dinner, watch the parade and wind up the glorious day with more dancin'.

I bet you any amount you name that the Castles in their whole life haven't danced together as much as I and the Missus did at Palm Beach. I'd of gave five dollars if even one the waiters had took her off en my hands for one dance. But I knowed that if I made the offer public they'd of been a really serious quarrel between us instead o' just the minor brawls occasioned by steppin' on each other's feet.

She made a discovery one night. She found out that they was a place called the Beach Club where most o' the real people disappeared to every evenin' after dinner. She says we would have to go there too.

"But I ain't a member," I says.

"Then find out how you get to be one," she says.

So to the Beach Club I went and made inquiries.

"You'll have to be introduced by a guy that already belongs," says the man at the door.

"Who belongs?" I ast him.

"Hundreds o' people," he says. "Who do you know?"

"Two waiters, two barkeepers and one elevator boy," I says.

He laughed, but his laugh didn't get me no membership card and I had to dance three or four extra times the next day to square myself with the Missus.

She made another discovery and it cost me six bucks. She found out that, though the meals in the regular dinin'-room was included in the triflin' rates per day, the real people had at least two o' their meals in the garden grill and paid extra for 'em. We tried it for one meal and I must say I enjoyed it—all but the check.

"We can't keep up that clip," I says to her.

"We could," says she, "if you wasn't spendin' so much on your locker."

"The locker's a matter o' life and death," I says. "They ain't no man in the world that could dance as much with their own wife as I do and live without liquid stimulus."

When we'd been there four days she got to be on speakin' terms with the ladies' maid that hung round the lobby and helped put the costumes back on when they slipped off. From this here maid the Missus learned who was who, and the information was relayed to me as soon as they was a chance. We'd be settin' on the porch when I'd feel an elbow in my ribs all of a sudden. I'd look up at who was passin' and then try and pretend I was excited.

"Who is it?" I'd whisper.

"That's Mrs. Vandeventer," the Wife'd say. "Her husband's the biggest street-car conductor in Philadelphia."

Or somebody'd set beside us at the beach or in the Palm Garden and my ribs would be all battered up before the Missus was calm enough to tip me off.

"The Vincents," she'd say; "the canned prune people."

It was a little bit thrillin' at first to be rubbin' elbows with all them celeb's; but it got so finally that I could walk out o' the dinin'-room right behind Scotti, the opera singer, without forgettin' that my feet hurt.

The Washington's Birthday Ball brought 'em all together at once, and the Missus pointed out eight and nine at a time and got me so mixed up that I didn't know Pat Vanderbilt from Maggie Rockefeller. The only one you couldn't make no mistake about was a Russian count that you couldn't pronounce. He was buyin' bay mules or somethin' for the Russian government, and he was in ambush.

"They say he can't hardly speak a word of English," says the Missus.

"If I knowed the word for barber shop in Russia," says I, "I'd tell him they was one in this hotel."

V

In our mail box the next mornin' they was a notice that our first week was up and all we owed was one hundred and forty-six dollars and fifty cents. The bill for room and meals was one hundred and nineteen dollars. The rest was for gettin' clo'es pressed and keepin' the locker damp.

I didn't have no appetite for breakfast. I told the Wife I'd wait up in the room and for her to come when she got through. When she blew in I had my speech prepared.

"Look here," I says; "this is our eighth day in Palm Beach society. You're on speakin' terms with a maid and I've got acquainted with half a dozen o' the male hired help. It's cost us about a hundred and sixty-five dollars, includin' them private rooms down to the Casino and our Afromobile trips, and this and that. You know a whole lot o' swell people by sight, but you can't talk to 'em. It'd be just as much satisfaction and hundreds o' dollars cheaper to look up their names in the telephone directory at home; then phone to 'em and, when you got 'em, tell 'em it was the wrong number. That way, you'd get 'em to speak to you at least.

"As for sport," I says, "we don't play golf and we don't play tennis and we don't swim. We go through the same program o' doin' nothin' every day. We dance, but we don't never change partners. For twelve dollars I could buy a phonograph up home and I and you could trot round the livin'-room all evenin' without no danger o' havin' some o' them fancy birds cave our shins in. And we could have twice as much liquid refreshments up there at about a twentieth the cost.

"That Gould I met on the train comin' down," I says, "was a even bigger liar than I give him credit for. He says that when he was here people pestered him to death by comin' up and speakin' to him. We ain't had to dodge nobody or hide behind a cocoanut tree to remain exclusive. He says Palm Beach was too common for him. What he should of said was that it was too lonesome. If they was just one white man here that'd listen to my stuff I wouldn't have no kick. But it ain't no pleasure tellin' stories to the Ephs. They laugh whether it's good or not, and then want a dime for laughin'.

"As for our clo'es," I says, "they would be all right for a couple o' days' stay. But the dames round here, and the men, too, has somethin' different to put on for every mornin', afternoon and night. You've wore your two evenin' gowns so much that I just have to snap my finger at the hooks and they go and grab the right eyes.

"The meals would be grand," I says, "if the cook didn't keep gettin' mixed up and puttin' puddin' sauce on the meat and gravy on the pie.

"I'm glad we've been to Palm Beach," I says. "I wouldn't of missed it for nothin'. But the ocean won't be no different to-morrow than it was yesterday, and the same for the daily program. It don't even rain here, to give us a little variety.

"Now what do you say," I says, "to us just settlin' this bill, and whatever we owe since then, and beatin' it out o' here just as fast as we can go?"

The Missus didn't say nothin' for a w'ile. She was too busy cryin'. She knowed that what I'd said was the truth, but she wouldn't give up without a struggle.

"Just three more days," she says finally. "If we don't meet somebody worth meetin' in the next three days I'll go wherever you want to take me."

"All right," I says; "three more days it is. What's a little matter o' sixty dollars?"

Well, in them next two days and a half she done some desperate flirtin', but as it was all with women I didn't get jealous. She picked out some o' the E-light o' Chicago and tried every trick she could think up. She told 'em their noses was shiny and offered 'em her powder. She stepped on their white shoes just so's to get a chance to beg their pardon. She told 'em their clo'es was unhooked, and then unhooked 'em so's she could hook 'em up again. She tried to loan 'em her finger-nail tools. When she seen one fannin' herself she'd say: "Excuse me, Mrs. So-and-So; but we got the coolest room in the hotel, and I'd be glad to have you go up there and quit perspirin'." But not a rise did she get.

Not till the afternoon o' the third day o' grace. And I don't know if I ought to tell you this or not—only I'm sure you won't spill it nowheres. We'd went up in our room after lunch. I was tired out and she was discouraged. We'd set round for over an hour, not sayin' or doin' nothin'. I wanted to talk about the chance of us gettin' away the next mornin', but I didn't dast bring up the subject.

The Missus complained of it bein' hot and opened the door to leave the breeze go through. She was settin' in a chair near the doorway, pretendin' to read the *Palm Beach News*. All of a sudden she jumped up and kind o' hissed at me.

"What's the matter?" I says, springin' from the lounge.

"Come here!" she says, and went out the door into the hall.

I got there as fast as I could, thinkin' it was a rat or a fire. But the Missus just pointed to a lady walkin' away from us, six or seven doors down.

"It's Mrs. Potter," she says; "*the* Mrs. Potter from Chicago!"

"Oh!" I says, puttin' all the excitement I could into my voice.

And I was just startin' back into the room when I seen Mrs. Potter stop and turn round and come to'rd us. She stopped again maybe twenty feet from where the Missus was standin'.

"Are you on this floor?" she says.

The Missus shook like a leaf.

"Yes," says she, so low you couldn't hardly hear her.

"Please see that they's some towels put in 559," says the Mrs. Potter from Chicago.

VI

About five o'clock the Wife quieted down and I thought it was safe to talk to her. "I've been readin' in the guide about a pretty river trip," I says. "We can start from here on the boat to-morrow mornin'. They run to Fort Pierce to-morrow and stay there to-morrow night. The next day they go from Fort Pierce to Rockledge, and the day after that from Rockledge to Daytona. The fare's only five dollars apiece. And we can catch a north-bound train at Daytona."

"All right, I don't care," says the Missus.

So I left her and went down-stairs and acrost the street to ask Mr. Foster. Ask Mr. Foster happened to be a girl. She sold me the boat tickets and promised she would reserve a room with bath for us at Fort Pierce, where we was to spend the followin' night. I bet she knowed all the w'ile that rooms with a bath in Fort Pierce is scarcer than toes on a sturgeon.

I went back to the room and helped with the packin' in an advisory capacity. Neither one of us had the heart to dress for dinner. We ordered somethin' sent up and got soaked an extra dollar for service. But we was past carin' for a little thing like that.

At nine o'clock next mornin' the good ship *Constitution* stopped at the Poinciana dock w'ile we piled aboard. One bellhop was down to see us off and it cost me a quarter to get that much attention. Mrs. Potter must of overslept herself.

The boat was loaded to the guards and I ain't braggin' when I say that we was the bestlookin' people aboard. And as for manners, why, say, old Bill Sykes could of passed off for Henry Chesterfield in that gang! Each one o' them occupied three o' the deck chairs and sprayed orange juice all over their neighbors. We could of talked to plenty o' people here, all right; they were as clubby a gang as I ever seen. But I was afraid if I said somethin' they'd have to answer; and, with their mouths as full o' citrus fruit as they was, the results might of been fatal to my light suit.

We went up the lake to a canal and then through it to Indian River. The boat run aground every few minutes and had to be pried loose. About twelve o'clock a cullud gemman come up on deck and told us lunch was ready. At half past one he served it at a long family table in the cabin. As far as I was concerned, he might as well of left it on the stove. Even if you could of bit into the food, a glimpse of your fellow diners would of strangled your appetite.

After the repast I called the Missus aside.

"Somethin' tells me we're not goin' to live through three days o' this," I says. "What about takin' the train from Fort Pierce and beatin' it for Jacksonville, and then home?"

"But that'd get us to Chicago too quick," says she. "We told people how long we was goin' to be gone and if we got back ahead o' time they'd think they was somethin' queer."

"They's too much queer on this boat," I says. "But you're goin' to have your own way from now on."

We landed in Fort Pierce about six. It was only two or three blocks to the hotel, but when they laid out that part o' town they overlooked some o' the modern conveniences, includin' sidewalks. We staggered through the sand with our grips and sure had worked up a hunger by the time we reached Ye Inn.

"Got reservations for us here?" I ast the clerk.

"Yes," he says, and led us to 'em in person. The room he showed us didn't have no bath, or even a chair that you could set on w'ile you pulled off your socks.

"Where's the bath?" I ast him.

"This way," he says, and I followed him down the hall, outdoors and up an alley.

Finally we come to a bathroom complete in all details, except that it didn't have no door. I went back to the room, got the Missus and went down to supper. Well, sir, I wish you could of been present at that supper. The choice o' meats was calves' liver and onions or calves' liver and onions. And I bet if them calves had of been still livin' yet they could of gave us some personal reminiscences about Garfield.

The Missus give the banquet one look and then laughed for the first time in several days.

"The guy that named this burg got the capitals mixed," I says. "It should of been Port Fierce."

And she laughed still heartier. Takin' advantage, I says:

"How about the train from here to Jacksonville?"

"You win!" says she. "We can't get home too soon to suit me."

VII

The mornin' we landed in Chicago it was about eight above and a wind was comin' offen the Lake a mile a minute. But it didn't feaze us.

"Lord!" says the Missus. "Ain't it grand to be home!"

"You said somethin'," says I. "But wouldn't it of been grander if we hadn't never left?"

"I don't know about that," she says. "I think we both of us learned a lesson."

"Yes," I says; "and the tuition wasn't only a matter o' close to seven hundred bucks!"

"Oh," says she, "we'll get that back easy!"

"How?" I ast her. "Do you expect some tips on the market from Mrs. Potter and the rest o' your new friends?"

"No," she says. "We'll win it. We'll win it in the rummy game with the Hatches."

JOHN DOS PASSOS

1896–1970

Ernest Hemingway and John Dos Passos

I N 1924, JOHN Dos Passos was on the move. He was in Baltimore, Washington, D.C., Savannah, New Orleans, and finally Florida. In New Orleans, he came close to completing most of his book, *Manhattan Transfer*. He moved across the Florida Panhandle, then down the peninsula along the west coast and across Florida to Palm Beach, then becoming a winter getaway for millionaires and the powerful.

He found Florida to be "fabulous and movie-like," and marveled at the building boom, which made Florida the fastest growing state in the nation in the 1920s. He was fascinated by the people who thought Florida was the get-rich capital of the nation. "One arrives on foot, works a year, buys an orange grove from his wages, then in five years travels in a limousine, in ten years is the founder of a city, is a millionaire or a senator—it's the American Eden," he said with tongue in cheek.

His next stop was something of a surprise. Today, Key West is a lush resort and a destination for millions, but in 1924, it was a rundown relic, its economy failing and its best days seemingly behind it. Although the island became home to a string of famous writers, it claimed little fame in 1924.

Dos Passos chose Key West, explaining that he had "islomania," an obsession with islands. The impact of Dos Passos on Key West cannot be overstated. He was the first significant author to visit the island, but more importantly he was well liked in the New York and Paris literary communities. He became a public relations advocate for the island, writing to friends about the island's wonders. He told Ernest Hemingway to go to Key West: "It's the best place for Ole Hem to dry out his bones."

Manhattan Transfer was published in 1925, pushing him into the first rank of American writers with a style that introduced stream-of-consciousness writing. He returned to Key West in 1928 with plans to meet Hemingway, who was returning to Europe. It was a life-changing visit, for he met Katharine Smith in Key West. Smith—known as Katy—stopped off in Key West to visit friends while returning from Mexico. It was not love at first sight. Dos Passos was busy finishing his book, *The 42nd Parallel*. Then he traveled to the Soviet Union. The following year they reconnected in Key West and five months later they married. He was thirty-three, and although she claimed to be thirty-four, she was about to turn thirty-eight.

For Dos Passos, Key West was an escape. He wrote to Edmund Wilson: "[I was] licking my wounds, fishing, eating wild herons and turtle steak, drinking Spanish wine and Cuban rum and generally remaking the inner man." He called it "a swell little jumping off place—the one spot in America desperately unprosperous."

His 1934 trip to Key West was a bit of a disappointment because Hemingway was not there, but Dos Passos was able to relax and improve his health. The health of Key West itself was not as robust; the city was broke, and its operations taken over by the federal government.

Key West in the late 1930s was more isolated than it had been since the 1800s. The railroad linking Miami and Key West had been completed in 1912, Henry Flagler's miracle construction project that no one believed could be a reality. It opened the island up to large numbers of tourists. In 1935, a massive hurricane heavily damaged the structure and the bankrupt Florida East Coast Railway lacked the money to rebuild it. Eventually, the state took over the railway to Key West and turned it into a highway. While the railroad was out, getting to Key West was difficult. Dos Passos wrote to a friend, "The railroad had folded and now you arrived by car ferry from a point below Homestead on the mainland. There were three separate ferry rides and sandy roads through the scrubby keys between." Despite the difficulty, Dos Passos called it a "most delightful trip, with long cues of pelicans scrambling up off the water and manofwar birds in the sky and bobbygulls on the buoys and mullet jumping in the milky shallows."

Dos Passos had originally lured Ernest Hemingway to Key West, inviting him repeatedly while they were in Europe. The two fished together frequently, although Dos Passos' wife, Katy, complained about Hemingway's irresponsibility.

Like Robert Frost, Dos Passos had a run-in with poet Wallace Stevens. Stevens, who seemed to relish Key West primarily as a place to get away from his conservative life as a Connecticut insurance executive, came to the island to drink. On one such drunk, he barged into Hemingway's house and began berating the writer as a cad. Stevens left the Hemingway home and staggered to the Dos Passos home. Interrupting a dinner party, Stevens said, "So you're Dos Passos, and here I find you, playing cheap things on the phonograph and surrounded by women in pajamas. I thought you were a cripple [it is not quite clear what he meant by that, perhaps another term for radical] and a man of culture! Women in pajamas!" Dos Passos said Stevens was the only person he considered throwing out of his home. Dos Passos thought Stevens was envious of the lives that Hemingway and Dos Passos lived; he could not live the life of an artist and hated them for it.

In 1936 Dos Passos returned with the page proofs for his book, *The Big Money*, making corrections and last-minute changes.

Beginning with the Spanish Civil War, Dos Passos visited Key West less frequently. He had considered himself a supporter of Soviet aspirations, but the war in Spain led him to rethink his views. "I have come to think, especially since my trip to Spain, that civil liberties must be protected at every stage.... The trouble with an all powerful secret police in the hands of fanatics, or of anybody, is that once it gets started there's no stopping it.... I am afraid that's what's happening in Russia."

The Spanish war caused a split with his best Key West friend, Hemingway, who supported the Russian-backed Spanish forces. Then World War II came, and Dos Passos became a war correspondent. In 1947, his beloved Katy died in an automobile crash; Dos Passos was driving and lost an eye in the wreck. His visits to Key West came to an end, but his legacy in establishing Key West as a writer's colony is secure.

Under the Tropic
by John Dos Passos

Some of the best times in those years were with Hem and Pauline in Key West. The time that stands out was in late April and early May of 1929.

It is hot in April in Key West when the trade wind drops. We trolled back and forth between the wharves and an old white steamboat that had gone on a reef in a hurricane. She had lost her stack and the engines had been taken out. Waldo painted a picture of her that still hangs in the upstairs hall at Spence's Point. When Charles took his boat up into a bight away from the town, an unbelievable sweetness of blossoming limes came out along with the mosquitoes from among the mangroves.

Hem had brought along a couple of bottles of champagne which perched on the ice that kept the mullet fresh in the bait bucket. The rule was that you couldn't have a drink until somebody caught a fish. The sun set in a wash of gaudy pinks and ochres. We kept fishing on into the moonlight. I'm not sure whether we caught any tarpon that night, but we certainly had one hooked because I remember the arc of dark silver against the moon's sheen on the water when the fish jumped.

The tarpon seemed only to bite when the tide was low and the water warm in the channels. When they stopped striking and we had finished the champagne Charles said with a yawn that he had to go to work at the store at seven o'clock next morning and headed us in to the dock.

If we hadn't pulled in a tarpon I was probably just as glad because catching tarpon always seemed a waste to me. I hated to see the great silver monsters lying in the dust on the wharf. They aren't fit to eat. About the only use is for mounting. Some people make knicknacks out of the dried scales. Sheer vanity catching tarpon.

We went to the Asturian's for a bite before going to bed. French-fried yellowtail and bonito with tomato sauce were his specialities. It was a delight to be able to chatter amiably on all sorts of topics without tripping over that damn Party line. No taboos. Everybody said the first thing that came into his head. After the ideological bickerings of the New York theater Key West seemed like the Garden of Eden.

Hem was the greatest fellow in the world to go around with when everything went right. That spring was a marvelous season for tarpon. Every evening Charles would take us out tarpon fishing and we would fish and drink and talk and talk and talk far into the moonlit night. Days, after Hem and I had knocked off our stint—we were both very early risers—we would go out to the reef with Bra.

Bra was a Conch. That's what they called white people from Spanish Wells in the Bahamas. His real name was Sanders. Hem, who had gotten to be a Conch right along with him, talked Captain Sanders into taking us out. Nobody had heard of a party boat. Fifteen dollars was considered a fair price for the day.

Fishingboats were still smacks whether they had sails or not. They carried a livebox built into the boat amidships to keep the fish alive. Key West had an iceplant, but at the fishmarket down at the wharf they would scoop up your yellowtails with a net out of a big vat when you bought them. Another great tank was full of green turtles.

Shipping sea turtles was an important industry.

There was endless fascination in the variety of creatures you pulled up off the reef. Never much of a sports fisherman, I liked going along, just to be out on the varicolored water. I always announced that I fished for the pot. Although as competitive as a race horse, Hem wasn't yet so much the professional sportsman as to spoil the fun. Such was my enthusiasm for the great pale moonstruck snappers known locally as mutton fish that Katy got to calling me Muttonfish. It stuck for a while as a nickname.

For several winters after that Katy and I made a point of spending as much time as we could at Key West. It wasn't quite under the tropic but it was mighty close to it. No doctor's prescription was ever pleasanter to take.

The railroad had folded and now you arrived by car-ferry from a point below Homestead on the mainland. There were three separate ferryrides and sandy roads through the scrubby keys between. It took half a day and was a most delightful trip, with long cues of pelicans scrambling up off the water and manofwar birds in the sky and boobygulls on the buoys, and mullet jumping in the milky shallows.

Hem and I kept planning a trip to Bimini, but it always had to be put off for some reason or other. The first time we started out we had hardly reached the purple water of the Gulf Stream when old Hem shot himself in the leg—in the fleshy part, fortunately—with his own rifle trying to shoot a shark that was making for a sailfish somebody had alongside and was trying to gaff. We had to turn back to take him to the sawbones at the hospital. Katy was so mad she would hardly speak to him.

Hem's leg had hardly healed when a package arrived for him from

Oak Park. It was from his mother. It contained a chocolate cake, a roll of Mrs. Hemingway's paintings of the Garden of the Gods which she suggested he might get hung at the Salon when he next went to Paris, and the gun with which his father shot himself. Katy, who had known her of old, had explained to me that Mrs. Hemingway was a very odd lady indeed. Hem was the only man I ever knew who really hated his mother.

It was on the first of Hem's *Pilar*s that we finally made it to the Bahamas. The big money fishing camp at Cat Cay had gone broke in the collapse of the first Florida boom and was still closed down. There were a few yachtsmen and sports fishermen about but the tiny island of Bimini proper was very much out of the world. There was a wharf and some native shacks under the coconut palms and a store that had some kind of a barroom attached, where we drank rum in the evenings, and a magnificent broad beach on the Gulf Stream side. There was an official residency and a couple of sunbeaten bungalows screened against the sandflies up on the dunes. Katy and I occupied one of them for a week to give Hem more room on the *Pilar.*

We had gotten to calling Hem the Old Master because nobody could stop him from laying down the law, or sometimes the Mahatma on account of his having appeared in a rowboat with a towel wrapped around his head to keep off the sun. He had more crotchety moments than in the old days, but he was a barrel of monkeys when he wanted to be. Life still seemed enormously comical to all of us. Nobody ever got so mad that some fresh crack didn't bring him around. We drank a good deal but only cheerfully. We carried things off with great fits of laughing.

If I'm not mistaken this trip to Bimini was the first time the Old

Master really went out after tuna. He'd been reading Zane Grey's book about catching great tuna on the seven seas (and a surprisingly well-written book it is) and wanted to go Zane Grey one better.

We had caught a few smallish yellowfins along with some rainbow-colored dolphins on the way over across the Gulf Stream from the upper end of Hawk Channel. It was in the spring of the year and the wiseacres all claimed that the tuna were running.

Katy and I were delighted with the island. We never tired of walking on the beach and watching the highslung landcrabs shuttle like harness racers among the fallen coconuts. We did a lot of bathing in the comfortable surf on the great beach. Hem was scornful of our shell collection.

We got hold of an agreeable storytelling Negro with a small sailboat who took us sailing over the marly waters of the Great Bahama Bank and fishing for bonefish in the shallows between the coral heads. The Mahatma used to kid us about our taste for going out in rowboats together, said people did that before they were married, not after.

The Bimini Negroes were great fun. They made up songs about every incident of the day. Every little job like hauling a boat ashore was a choral event. It was the first time any of us had heard

My Mama don't want no peas no rice no coconut oil
All she wants is handy brandy and champagne.

They immediately made up songs about old Hem. I wish I remembered the words. All my recollections of that week are laced with the lilt of those Bimini songs.

Anyway while Katy and I were unashamedly sightseeing and sailing and rowing and dabbling in folklore—all occupations frowned on by serious fishermen—the Old Master was cruising the deep. He'd brought tuna rigs along and was trolling with that implacable impatient persistence of his.

We were ashore when the Old Master first tangled with his great tuna. It had been hooked early in the morning by a man named Cook who was caretaker at Cat Cay. It must have been an enormous fish because as soon as it sounded it ran out all the line. Cook's hands were cut to shreds when he turned it over to Ernest, who came alongside with the *Pilar* in the early afternoon. Hem went on playing it from Cook's boat and sent the *Pilar* in to fetch us so that we should see the sport. I've forgotten who was at the wheel but we cruised alongside while the battle continued.

Among the assembled yachtsmen there was a gentleman who had a large white yacht named the *Moana*. William B. Leeds, of a family famous in the international set, had invited the Old Master aboard for drinks a couple of days before. The Old Master had come away charmed by Bill Leeds' hospitality but even more charmed by the fact that Leeds owned a Thompson submachine gun. Just at that moment a submachine gun was what the Old Master wanted more than anything in the world.

From a boy he had been fond of firearms but now he was particularly interested in a submachine gun as a way of fighting the sharks. Bimini was infested with sharks that season. They even bothered us bathing on the beach, but particularly they had an exasperating way of cutting off a hooked fish just as you were about to get him into the boat. The Old Master tried potting them with his rifle but unless you shoot him right through his tiny brain a rifle bullet doesn't make much impression on a shark. The night before he fought the tuna he'd been trying all sorts of expedients over the rum collinses to get Leeds to part with his submachine gun. He kept suggesting that they match for it or that they cut a hand of poker for it or shoot at a target for it. I believe he even offered to buy it. But Leeds was holding on to his submachine gun which he told me later had been given to him by the inventor's son who was a good friend of his.

It was late afternoon by the time Katy and I got out to the scene of the battle. By dusk the tuna began to weaken. The Old Master was reeling in on him. Everybody was on the ropes but the tuna was still hooked. We were very much excited to be in for the kill. There was a ring of spectator boats around, including Leeds with his machine gun on the launch from the *Moana*.

It was getting dark. The wind had dropped but a nasty looking squall was making up on the horizon. In the last gloaming the Old Master inched the fish alongside. Nobody had seen him yet. One man was ready with the gaff. The rest of us, hunched on top of the cabin of the *Pilar,* peered into the water with our flashlights.

We all saw him at once, dark, silvery and immense. Eight hundred pounds, nine hundred pounds, a thousand pounds, people guessed in hornswoggled whispers. All I knew was that he was a very big fish. He was moving sluggishly. He seemed licked. The man with the gaff made a lunge and missed. The silver flash was gone. The reel whined as the fish sounded.

The Old Master's expletives were sibilant and low.

The fish took half the reel; then the Old Master began hauling in on him again. He didn't feel right. Somebody suggested he might be dead. Bill Leeds had been keeping the sharks at bay with his machine gun, but now he laid off for fear a ricochet might hit someone. The

Old Master reeled and reeled.

The stormcloud ate up a third of the starry sky. Lightning flickered on its fringes. Most of the small boats had put back to shore.

Leeds from his launch was inviting us to take cover on his yacht but the Old Master was doggedly reeling in.

At last in a great wash of silver and spume the tuna came to the surface ten or fifteen yards astern of the boat. The sharks hadn't touched him. We could see his whole great smooth length. The Old Master was reeling in fast. Then suddenly they came. In the light of our flashlights we could see the sharks streaking in across the dark water. Like torpedoes. Like speedboats. One struck. Another. Another. The water was murky with blood. By the time we hauled the tuna in over the stern there was nothing left but his head and his backbone and his tail.

Getting Katy and me aboard the *Moana* was a real victory for Old Hem. He'd been trying to cotton up to Leeds on account of that machine gun, and maybe too because he thought Leeds was so stinking rich. Katy had taken a scunner to poor Leeds and declared she'd rather die than go aboard his yacht. There was an oily and rather pimpish old Spaniard in the party whom we called Don Propina. We'd both taken a scunner to him. Anyway Ernest won. The squall blew up so hard there was nothing for it but to take refuge on the yacht. We climbed up the gangplank in the first horizontal sheets of rain and sat wet and shivering under the ventilation ducts in the saloon. To serve us right for being so snooty we both caught colds in the head.

Leeds hospitably put us up for the night. We turned in early, so we never knew exactly how it happened; but when we shoved off from the yacht in the lovely early morning sunlight the Old Master had the submachine gun affectionately cradled in the crotch of his arm.

It must have been a loan because Bill Leeds wrote me later that he didn't make Hem a present of the machine gun until a couple of years after when the Old Master was leaving for the civil war in Spain. Leeds agreed that what we saw was a preview of *The Old Man and the Sea,* though the tales the Canary Islander told Hem in Havana certainly played their part.

Nobody ever had much luck trying to trace a fish story to its source.

It was probably the following spring that Hem and Waldo and I rented Bra's boat to go out to the Dry Tortugas. These are the westernmost islets of the string of coral islands that make up the Florida Keys. We'd made the long choppy trip across the banks hoping to catch up with one of the schools of big king mackerel that move east and north out of the Gulf of Mexico in the spring. We hadn't caught many big fish.

Waldo set up his easel at one of the embrasures of the vast stone fort and painted. I had my cot and notebook in another shady nook. The sun was hot and the tradewind cool. The place was enormous and entirely empty. We kept expecting to meet poor old Dr. Mudd coming out of one of the tunnels. No sound but the querulous shrieking of the terns. The water was incredibly clear, delicious for swimming. We saw no shark or barracuda, only a variety of reef fish: yellowtails, angelfish, searobbins, all sorts of tiny jewellike creatures we didn't know the names of swarming under the coralheads. A couple of days went by; it was one of the times I understood the meaning of the word halcyon.

Ernest had brought along Arnold Gingrich, who was just starting *Esquire*. The man was in a trance. It was a world he'd never dreamed of. He was mosquitobitten, half seasick, scorched with sunburn, astonished, half scared, half pleased. It was as much fun to see Ernest play an editor as to see him play a marlin.

Gingrich never took his fascinated eyes off Old Hem. Hem would reel in gently letting his prey have plenty of line. The editor was hooked. Sure he would print anything Hemingway cared to let him have at a thousand dollars a whack. (In those days it never occurred to us anyone got paid more than that. We lived outside of the world of agents and big time New York Lunches.) Ernest was practicing up on skills he'd later apply to high literary finance. He got Gingrich so tame he even sold him a few pieces of mine for good measure.

Bra meanwhile was spending his time dredging up conches. Tourists had appeared in Key West. Bra had discovered to his amazement that tourists would buy the great rosy scalloped shells. He had the whole bow of the boat piled up with them. The night before we started back to Key West he made us one of the best conch chowders I ever ate. That with fried yellowtail seasoned with a brine and lime concoction he called Old Sour, made a royal feast. We washed it down with a little too much Bacardi rum.

We were tied up to a pier across from the fort. While we were eating and drinking, a couple of Cuban smacks that had been fishing in deep water for red snapper came alongside. They were a ragged sunbaked friendly crew. We handed around tin cups of Bacardi. Hem's Spanish became remarkably fluent. From out of his beard Waldo produced that mixture of French, Italian, and bastard Castilian that had carried him for years through the Mediterranean countries. Bra, who disdained foreign tongues, made himself friendly with shrugs and grunts. Gingrich sat speechless and goggleeyed while we climbed around each other's boats jabbering like a band of monkeys.

There were feats of strength, tales of huge blue marlin hooked and lost, of crocodiles sighted in the Gulf and rattlesnakes twenty feet long seen swimming out to sea. Night fell absolutely windless. There was no moon. Our friends pushed their boats off, anchored a few hundred feet out and turned in. We moved out from the pier to catch what breeze there was. The stars looked big as Christmastree ornaments, clustered overhead and reflected in the sea. The three small craft seemed suspended in the midst of an enormous starstudded indigo sphere.

It was hot in the cabin. Weighed down with heat and Bacardi we lay sweating in the narrow bunks. Sleep came in a glare of heat.

We were wakened by a knocking on the deck. It was the elderly grizzled man who was skipper of one of the smacks. "Amigos, par despedirnos." Redeyed, with heads like lumps of lead, we scrambled on deck.

He pointed. Against the first violet streak in the east we could see a man on the bow of the smack shaking some liquid in a large glass carboy. They were sailing for Havana with the first breeze. They wanted to honor us with a farewell drink before they left.

Everybody climbed up on the narrow planking of the pier. Of course there was no ice. It was a warm eggnog made with a kind of cheap aguardiente that smelt like wood alcohol. Obediently we brought out our tin cups. We were hung over. We felt squeamish. It made us retch. We couldn't insult our amigos. We expected to die but they were our amigos and we drank it.

It was then that Ernest brought out his rifle and started to shoot. By this time it was silvery gloaming. You could feel the sun burning under the horizon. He shot a baked-bean can floating halfway to the shore. We threw out more cans for him. He shot bits of paper the Cubans spread out on wooden chips from their skiff. He shot several terns. He shot through a pole at the end of the pier. Anything we'd point at he would hit. He shot sitting. He shot standing. He shot lying on his belly. He shot backward, with the rifle held between his legs.

So far as we could see he never missed. Finally he ran out of ammunition. We drank down the last of the fishermen's punch. The amigos shook hands. The amigos waved. They weighed anchor and hoisted the grimy sails on their smacks and steered closehauled into the east as the first breath of the trade lightened the heavy air.

We headed back to Key West. There was an oily swell over the banks on the way back. What wind there was settled into the stern. Bra's conches had begun to rot and stank abominably. The punch set badly. Our faces were green. Our lips were cold. Nobody actually threw up, but we were a pallid and silent crew until we reached the lee of the first low patches of mangroves that lay in the approaches of Key West.

WALLACE STEVENS

1879–1955

WALLACE STEVENS FINALLY won the Pulitzer Prize for poetry the year he died, a third of a century after he began writing poems. But which Stevens won the Pulitzer Prize? Was it the straight-laced Hartford attorney who became a vice president of one of the nation's largest companies, or was it the feuding, fighting, hard-drinking man who escaped to Key West each year?

Stevens was born in 1879 in Pennsylvania, the son of a wealthy lawyer. He attended Harvard University, then received his law degree from New York University.

He fell in love with Elsie Moll Kachel, a woman his family considered beneath their social position, and married her despite his family's objections. He and his father never spoke again.

In 1916 he joined the Hartford Accident and Indemnity Company, a century-old firm that grew dramatically after weathering disasters such as the Chicago Fire and the San Francisco Earthquake as other firms failed.

By day, he studied numbers, rising steadily until he became a vice president in 1934. At night, he retreated to a dark corner of his large home and wrote poetry.

He sampled the literary scene in Paris and New York, finding both to be lacking. In 1922, he made his first trip to Key West as part of a business trip. Stevens was one of the first writers to arrive in Key West before it became a leading literary colony. He usually stayed at the Casa Marina, a luxurious retreat built by Henry Flagler. He was also a regular at the Long Key Fishing Camp, an exclusive resort where he fished with friends.

One attraction of Key West was that he could use business as an excuse for trips, allowing the Hartford to underwrite most of his expenses. Over the next eighteen years, he spent several weeks a year in Key West and came down for occasional shorter business trips. He wrote to his wife, "This is one of the choicest places I've ever been to. The place is a paradise."

He wrote of Key West, "I was christened a charter member of the Long Key Fishing Club of Atlanta. The christening occupied about three days, and required just two cases of Scotch. When I traveled home, I was not able to tell whether I was travelling on a sound or a smell. As I remember it, it was very much like a cloud full of Cuban senoritas, coconut palms, and waiters carrying ice water." To a friend, he wrote, "This place is paradise—midsummer weather, the sky brilliantly clear and intensely blue, the sea blue and green beyond what you have ever seen."

His wife was a passionate homemaker—some said she was obsessed with housekeeping—and remained behind in Hartford. That was fine with Stevens, who went fishing and drinking with friends.

The small island began to attract more writers, including two who became Stevens' enemies, Ernest Hemingway and Robert Frost.

Stevens met Frost at the Casa Marina, and initially the two became friends. Stevens had been coming to Key West for a dozen years before Frost made his first trip in 1935. Frost was already a well-known poet, with two Pulitzer Prizes to his credit. Stevens had published only a single volume of poetry with far less notice.

Although Stevens welcomed Frost with a basket of fruit, that night things went terribly wrong. Stevens was drunk and made comments Frost did not like. Later, in a speech at the University of Miami, Frost talked about Stevens' drinking.

In 1954, a year before Stevens died, he was asked to speak at Frost's eightieth birthday celebration but turned it down with a put-down of the nation's best known poet: "I do not know his work well enough to be either impressed or unimpressed."

He also feuded with Hemingway. In 1936, the two were in Key West at the same time. "This year he came again pleasant like the cholera," Hemingway wrote.

In Hemingway's version, his sister Ura came home crying because of critical comments Stevens had made about Hemingway's writing. Hemingway found Stevens and told it this way: "So who should show up but poor old Papa and Mr. Stevens swung that same fabled punch but fertunately [sic] missed and I knocked all of him down several times and gave him a good beating." Stevens was able to land one solid punch—which may or may not have sent Hemingway to the ground—but Stevens broke his hand in two places.

Hemingway said later that Stevens tried to make up, but the feud continued. Hemingway wrote, "I don't know anybody needed to be hit worse than Mr. S."

Novelist John Dos Passos also saw Stevens drunk when the poet showed up uninvited at a party in the Dos Passos home, and Stevens managed to offend Marjorie Kinnan Rawlings, the author of *The Yearling*. He visited her at Cross Creek and called her a "very remarkable woman in her own right as distinct from her literary right."

Stevens wrote extensively about Florida, beginning with his first book of poetry, *Harmonium*.

By 1934, Key West was suffering through the Great Depression. The town's government had gone bankrupt and the federal government stepped in and took over. By then Stevens had become a Hartford vice president, but the company had frozen his salary as a result of the economic slowdown, and although the impact was minor for him, Stevens did not have to look far to see the impact of the Depression. Stevens was disturbed by what he saw: the homeless men, the poverty, and the hopelessness.

Stevens opened his 1936 book *Ideas of Order* with the poem "Farewell to Florida," which tells of leaving his paradise in Key West. (The first stanza appears here.)

> Go on high ship, since now, upon the shore,
> The snake has left its skin upon the floor.
> Key West sank downward under massive clouds
> And silvers and greens spread over the sea. The moon
> Is at the mast-head and the past is dead.
> Her mind will never speak to me again.
> I am free. High above the mast the moon
> Rides clear of her mind and the waves make a refrain
> Of this: that the snake has shed its skin upon
> The floor. Go on through the darkness. The waves fly back.

Stevens' visits stopped at the beginning of the American entry into World War II. The government seized his beloved Casa Marina Hotel for military use and Key West was no longer the secluded getaway he had discovered in 1922. It had become a popular resort, which displeased Stevens. To a friend he wrote, "Key West is no longer quite the delightful affectation it once was. Who wants to share green cocoanut ice cream with these strange monsters who snooze in the porches of his once forlorn hotel." Where he had once been the only writer of any renown, he now shared the island with dozens of authors. "Key West, unfortunately, is becoming rather literary and artistic."

Although known as a poet, Stevens did write an article for the Sunday magazine of the *Atlanta Journal* about the early cattle kings of Florida.

Cattle Kings of Florida
by Wallace Stevens

Saddle bags filled with gold left lying on the front porch or even in the stable!

Coffee cans or kitchen pots filled to the brim with the yellow Spanish coins and left unguarded on kitchen shelves of isolated ranch homes!

Such tales told by the few surviving pioneer cattle kings of Florida contrast strangely with present day customs. A single gold coin is more or less of a curiosity today while anyone in Atlanta, or Florida either, with a sizable bag of gold would watch it with a shot gun until they could procure an armored car to move it to the deposit vaults of some bank.

And yet the Florida tales are true, as any old time cow hunter who trailed the herds down to Punta Rassa in the '70s and '80s will testify. The little port a few miles from Fort Myers, on the Gulf of Mexico, is only a cable station with a few fishing racks now, but in the early days it saw thousands of Florida's free range cattle rafted out to Spanish ships bound for Havana and in turn saw thousands of Spain's golden coins turned over to the cattle barons who lived on scattered and unfenced ranches in the interior.

Fort Myers itself wasn't much of a town then and didn't offer many facilities for recreation. Some of the early cattlemen, the Tolles and the Hendrys and a few others, made their homes there, but most of them poured the gold into their saddle bags and after a few drinks around mounted their shaggy and tired looking ponies and rode northward toward Polk or DeSoto Counties.

Although their mounts had several times the speed and spirit their appearances indicated, it usually took several days to cover the trail back home. Camp was made by the cattlemen wherever nightfall found them and the tired riders would dump their saddle bags wherever it was handiest. If a friend dropped in after camp was made and wanted to borrow money, or if the cattle owner owed him money, the visitor was frequently told to find the saddle bags and count out what he needed or what was due him.

Honesty wasn't questioned in money matters on the range. From all reports, the cattle kings would and did steal cows from each other. But stealing money was taboo among the home folks and tourists and other visiting gentry were still practically unknown in Florida below Jacksonville and St. Augustine.

One of the famous cattle kings of this period was Jacob Summerlin, a cowboy philanthropist of the early days whose generosity made him rather a patron saint of the south Florida range, and who left eternal monuments to his credit in Bartow and Orlando.

There are many still living who knew Summerlin personally and he has several descendants still residing in Polk County. Innumerable stories are told of his saddle pockets filled with gold and how any tale of distress or want, particularly on the part of widow or orphan, always found him digging out a handful of coins for the unfortunate one.

Despite his wealth he was said to have always dressed only in the cotton trousers and shirt, leather boots and five-gallon hat of the range. Thus, without any outward manifestation of having any money it was said to be a favorite trick of his to ride into some settler's yard where he was not known and beg a meal for himself and his horse. If the family was hospitable, as practically all pioneer families were, he would keep up his disguise until leaving; then he would give each child a Spanish ten-dollar gold piece; and if he had learned during his visit that the family lacked any particular necessity which money could buy, that would be forthcoming, too.

Summerlin was said to have been an orphan boy and to have had practically no schooling. That he deeply missed his lack of an opportunity for a higher education was shown when he purchased a large tract of land near the heart of Bartow, county seat of Polk County, and deeded it to trustees to sell in city lots and "form a free school for the poor white children." Schools up to that time in south Florida had been largely operated under the fee system, with few but the children of the well-to-do able to attend. Summerlin's donation financed the erection of the first brick school building in the southern portion of the state and initiated the free school system through the entire region, for, although his first intention was only a school for the poor children who could not attend the fee schools, his idea was enlarged upon by the trustees and a public school opened. The main public school in Bartow today is still known as Summerlin Institute, although, of course, it is now supported entirely by tax money.

Summerlin also donated ten-acre tracts of land within the town to each of the then established churches of Bartow and gave the town of Orlando the land surrounding many of the beautiful little lakes, forming the basis of Orlando's present park system around its lake shores—one of its chief claims to fame.

Another instance illustrating conditions when the Cuban cattle trade was booming was related to the writer some years ago by the late T. L. Wilson, of Bartow, who, before his death, became one of the most prominent attorneys and bankers of south Florida and was well known in Atlanta through his activities as a member of the war finance board appointed by President Woodrow Wilson.

Colonel Wilson was the son of a farmer and small cattleman who came from Georgia just after the War Between the States. "Tom" grew up as a pioneer Cracker boy, without much book learning but with a pretty thorough knowledge of the out-of-doors. He started out to become a cattle king on his own account and had acquired a herd of a couple of hundred head by the time he was eighteen.

But one stormy night while he was riding herd down in the cypress flats and palmetto prairies near the present site of Immokalee, in Collier County, one thing went wrong after another. The cattle stampeded at every lightning flash. His horse slipped and fell with him half a dozen times while he was working in the dark. Wet and muddy and cold he stuck it out until daylight and then turned the job over to the cow hand he had riding with him with the brief remark that he was through with bovine playmates forever, or words to that effect.

He rode into Fort Myers, reaching the home of an uncle there after the family had gone to bed. He woke his relative up and after a short explanation of the situation, offered him his herd at the market price, saying he was going to take the money and study law.

The uncle didn't think much of his nephew's decision. In a land where most of the crime concerned shooting matches, and the shootees unable to go to court after it was over as a usual thing, he didn't see much promise in becoming a lawyer. But he agreed to buy the cattle if the boy insisted on selling.

"You'll see my saddle bags on the porch as you go out," he said. "I just sold a bunch at Punta Rassa this morning and am pretty tired, so I won't get up. You count out your money and go ahead, if you're bound you won't spend the night."

Mr. Wilson counted out the nearly two thousand dollars that his cattle came to and left for home. And he stated that there was probably a thousand dollars more still in the bags left on the porch for the night.

The youth never regretted his change of profession from a financial viewpoint at least. He went direct from the range to Washington and Lee University at Lexington, and was said to have been one of the two men ever to complete the law course there in one year, and that without even a complete grammar school education. He was admitted to the bar before he was twenty-one by a special act of the Florida legislature, and from that time on his success justified his choice of a career.

The old order of cattle raising began to change generally after the Spanish-American War. Cuba settled down under its new regime and began to raise more of its own beef. Florida's own steady growth furnished a constantly increasing home market, but at the same time the new towns and farms and groves springing up all over the former vast open range cut into the pasturage and made it more difficult and costly to handle the big herds.

Many of the cattle kings held on. Most of the big ones had built up very sizable fortunes when the yellow coins from Spain were rolling in so freely. Some of them went into other activities as the changes became more marked. Others who felt that they could not be satisfied with any other life began to alter their methods. Many voluntarily fenced their vast pastures long before the townsfolk and grove owners began to advocate a fence law in the more settled regions.

The old careless days of half a century ago with their easy money will probably never return, but the manner in which the Florida cattle industry is adapting itself to the new conditions indicates that it will be a big business there for a long time to come.

ELIZABETH BISHOP

1911–1979

ELIZABETH BISHOP HAD a comfortable but chaotic childhood, shuttled from relative to relative after the death of her parents. She graduated from Vassar College, then traveled extensively, using funds from a family trust and from her lover, Louise Crane, the heiress to the Crane Stationery fortune.

She came to the island in the late 1930s to fish and fell in love with it, drawn to the colors and lights of Key West, which gave her a setting and an inspiration for both her poems and her watercolors. In 1938, she and Crane purchased a home at 624 White Street. Bishop spent long stretches there for the next decade, at first with Crane, and later with Marjorie Stevens. She became friends with Pauline Hemingway, the ex-wife of Ernest Hemingway, as well as with Tennessee Williams and other writers.

She described her home in a letter to a friend. "It is very well made, with slightly arched beams so that it looks either like a ship's cabin or a freight car." While she was in Key West, her first volume of poems, *North and South,* was published and went on to win the Pulitzer Prize.

Behind her seemingly idyllic life there were demons. She battled alcoholism all of her adult life, probably causing the breakup with Crane, and certainly ending the relationship with Stevens. After the breakup with Stevens, Key West lost its charm and she sold the house with the provision that future owners make no structural changes.

Without the house as her anchor, she became a nomad, traveling the world as her funds slowly ran out, until she settled in Brazil, where she lived with Lota de Macedo Soares for sixteen years. When Soares died in 1967, Bishop returned to the United States and began drinking more heavily. She died in 1979, Key West a distant memory.

Florida

by Elizabeth Bishop

The state with the prettiest name,
the state that floats in brackish water,
held together by mangrove roots
that bear while living oysters in clusters,
and when dead strew white swamps with skeletons,
dotted as if bombarded, with green hummocks
like ancient cannon-balls sprouting grass.
The state full of long S-shaped birds, blue and white,
and unseen hysterical birds who rush up the scale
every time in a tantrum.
Tanagers embarrassed by their flashiness,
and pelicans whose delight it is to clown;
who coast for fun on the strong tidal currents
in and out among the mangrove islands
and stand on the sand-bars drying their damp gold wings
on sun-lit evenings.
Enormous turtles, helpless and mild,
die and leave their barnacled shells on the beaches,
and their large white skulls with round eye-sockets
twice the size of a man's.
The palm trees clatter in the stiff breeze
like the bills of the pelicans. The tropical rain comes down
to freshen the tide-looped strings of fading shells:
Job's Tear, the Chinese Alphabet, the scarce Junonia,
parti-colored pectins and Ladies' Ears,
arranged as on a gray rag of rotted calico,
the buried Indian Princess's skirt;
with these the monotonous, endless, sagging coast-line
is delicately ornamented.

Thirty or more buzzards are drifting down, down, down,
over something they have spotted in the swamp,
in circles like stirred-up flakes of sediment
sinking through water.
Smoke from woods-fires filters fine blue solvents.
On stumps and dead trees the charring is like black velvet.
The mosquitoes
go hunting to the tune of their ferocious obbligatos.
After dark, the fireflies map the heavens in the marsh
until the moon rises.
Cold white, not bright, the moonlight is coarse-meshed,
and the careless, corrupt state is all black specks
too far apart, and ugly whites; the poorest
post-card of itself.
After dark, the pools seem to have slipped away.
The alligator, who has five distinct calls:
friendliness, love, mating, war, and a warning—
whimpers and speaks in the throat
of the Indian Princess.

ERNEST HEMINGWAY

1899–1961

John Dos Passos had been telling Ernest Hemingway about the wonders of Key West for years, urging him to visit and see for himself. Finally, in 1928, Hemingway relented, agreeing to a stopover on a trip from Havana. The real reason for the visit was to pick up a new Model A Ford Roadster, a gift from his wife Pauline's wealthy Uncle Gus. When Hemingway arrived, there was no car waiting, just the owners of the Trev-Mor Ford Agency, who told him the car had not arrived. The dealership owners, Benjamin Trevor and George Morris, offered a solution: Hemingway could stay in an apartment above their dealership.

It took two weeks for the car to arrive and during that time, Hemingway fell in love with the island. In his room at the Trev-Mor Hotel, he finished *A Farewell to Arms*. The two-week wait turned into a nearly three decades' relationship with Key West, which helped him achieve his greatest fame. The same wealthy uncle who purchased the car bought them a home at 907 Whitehead Street as a wedding present. Uncle Gus was a prime force in creating what would become Warner-Lambert, the giant pharmaceutical and personal products company.

The home was built in 1851, and for more than a century it was the largest on the island. Asa Tift, a wealthy ship builder and captain, used his slaves to build the house before a series of tragedies befell his family. Within three years, his wife and two of his three children were dead of yellow fever. He remained in the house until 1889, passing it on to his surviving daughter. The Tift descendants had financial troubles, and the house went to the Hemingways for $8,000 in back taxes.

The house was sixteen feet above sea level, the second-highest point on the island, and was the first to have indoor plumbing and an upstairs bathroom with running water—supplied by a cistern fed from rain from the roof. It also had the first swimming pool in Key West, which Pauline Hemingway built for $20,000 while her husband was covering the Spanish Civil War. When he returned, he was less than pleased.

The house was across the street from the lighthouse, and friends joked that the beam from the lighthouse made it easy for him to find his way home after a long night of drinking, usually at Sloppy Joe's.

His days were predictable. He wrote in the morning before it became too hot, working in a room on the second floor of the pool house. Then after a few hours of writing, he would put his work aside to go fishing, or hang around with his friends, usually at a bar. Shortly after he moved to Key West, *A Farewell to Arms* was published in early 1929 to wide critical acclaim. He followed that with *Death in the Afternoon, The Green Hills of Africa*, and *The Snows of Kilimanjaro*. He wrote *To Have and Have Not*, his only novel set in the United States, and supposedly featuring the characters he had met in Key West, in the room overlooking the pool. The last book he wrote in Key West was *For Whom the Bell Tolls*.

As his fame grew, so did the unwanted and unannounced visitors. He was upset when city officials distributed his address to tourists, and in a letter to the editor of *Esquire* magazine, said, "To discourage visitors while he is at work, your correspondent has hired an aged Negro who appears to be the victim of an odd disease resembling leprosy who meets visitors at the gate and says, 'I'se Mr. Hemingway and I'se crazy about you.'" He also hired someone who looked like him to hang around his house—hundreds of people left Key West thinking they had met the famous writer and obtained an autograph. Finally he hired a friend to build a high brick wall around the house to guard his privacy.

To pursue his hobby of boxing, he erected a ring in his backyard to stage boxing matches, and he hired residents to box. He also refereed fights at the Blue Heaven, a bar that featured regular bouts.

In 1934 he purchased a boat, the *Pilar,* and took frequent fishing trips, often with Dos Passos. On one trip, they were trolling for dolphins and found a school of them not far from Key West. Hemingway was hauling in dolphins when two large sharks attacked the dolphins. Hemingway grabbed a rifle, shot the shark and was pulling it into the boat so that Dos Passos could take a picture. Hemingway picked up a Colt .22 revolver and was about to finish off the shark when the shark suddenly jerked, snapping the gaff pole which struck the pistol. The gun fired and the bullet struck a piece of brass on the boat, shattered, and a piece of the lead entered Hemingway's leg. They returned to Key West, where Hemingway recovered quickly enough to take another fishing trip a week later.

Hemingway shared his love of Key West with other writers. In a 1936 letter to the Russian writer Ivan Kashkin—who translated Hemingway into Russian—Hemingway wrote, "I wish you could come down here, the weather is wonderful now, like the finest sort of spring day and it is wonderful out in the Gulf stream."

Around Christmas 1936, he met journalist Martha Gelhorn at Sloppy Joe's bar, the start of an affair that led to marriage in 1940, and divorce five years later. Pauline Hemingway got the house in Key West.

One legend that has circulated is that Hemingway kept six-toed cats at the house. Like many legends, this appears to be false. His widow Mary called the story of the cats, "an outright lie," and called selling the cats as descendants of Hemingway's cats as a "Rank exploitation of Ernest's name." His son, Patrick, said that while his father had peacocks, there were no cats. Still, tourists come from throughout the world to see the cats.

Although Hemingway owned the home from 1931 until his death thirty years later, he did not live in it after his divorce in the 1940s. Pauline Hemingway lived in the home with her two sons until her death in 1951. After his divorce from Pauline, Hemingway lived primarily in Cuba and Idaho, but would stop at the Key West home while traveling between the two. He had long struggled with depression—his father committed suicide—and was increasingly troubled by illness. In 1961 he shot himself to death in his Idaho home. The Key West home sold in 1964 for $80,000 and eventually became a museum.

***

O N September 2, 1935, a hurricane struck the Florida Keys, one of the most powerful hurricanes ever to strike the United States. The winds were steady at 160 miles per hour with gusts up to 200 miles per hour. Weather forecasting in the United States ignored warnings from Cuban forecasters about the severity of the approaching storm, and it happened over the Labor Day weekend, when most government workers and potential rescue officials were off.

Hundreds of World War I veterans, often hapless men who had wandered aimlessly for more than fifteen years trying to find their place, were working on the railroad linking Miami and the Keys as part of a federal relief program. Emergency warnings were inadequate, and even when the warnings finally came, the government failed to send them help in time. The storm killed between 400 and 600 people, including 265 of the veterans. Hemingway, who had seen death in nearly every form, left Key West for the worker's camp as soon as the storm passed to offer his help. Writing in *The Masses*, he placed the blame for the deaths squarely on President Roosevelt. Hemingway did not like Roosevelt, but his article was particularly vicious, making it clear that he thought the veterans were murdered and that the Roosevelt administration was responsible.

Who Murdered the Vets?
A First-Hand Report on the Florida Hurricane
by Ernest Hemingway

I have led my ragamuffins where they are peppered; there's not three of my hundred and fifty left alive, and they are for the town's end, to beg during life. —Shakespeare

Yes, and now we drown those three.

Whom did they annoy and to whom was their possible presence a political danger?

Who sent them down to the Florida Keys and left them there in hurricane months?

Who is responsible for their deaths?

The writer of this article lives a long way from Washington and would not know the answers to those questions. But he does know that wealthy people, yachtsmen, fishermen such as President Hoover and President Roosevelt, do not come to the Florida Keys in hurricane months. Hurricane months are August, September and October, and in those months you see no yachts along the Keys. You do not see them because yacht owners know there would be great danger, unescapable danger, to their property if a storm should come. For the same reason, you cannot interest any very wealthy people in fishing off the coast of Cuba in the summer when the biggest fish are there. There is a known danger to property. But veterans, especially the bonus-marching variety of veterans, are not property. They are only human beings, unsuccessful human beings, and all they have to lose is their lives. They are doing coolie labor for a top wage of $45 a month and they have been put down on the Florida Keys where they can't make trouble. It is hurricane months, sure, but if anything comes up, you can always evacuate them, can't you?

This is the way a storm comes. On Saturday evening at Key West, having finished working, you go out to the porch to have a drink and read the evening paper. The first thing you see in the paper is a storm warning. You know that work is off until it is past, and you are angry and upset because you were going well.

The location of the tropical disturbance is given as east of Long Island in the Bahamas, and the direction it is traveling is approximately toward Key West. You get out the September storm chart which gives the tracks and dates of forty storms of hurricane intensity during that month since 1900. And by taking the rate of movement of the storm as given in the Weather Bureau Advisory you calculate that it cannot reach us before Monday noon at the earliest. Sunday you spend making the boat as safe as you can. When they refuse to haul her out on the ways because there are too many boats ahead, you buy $52 worth of new heavy hawser and shift her to what seems the safest part of the submarine base and tie her up there. Monday you nail up the shutters on the house and get everything movable inside. There are northeast storm warnings flying, and at five o'clock the wind is blowing heavily and steadily from the northeast. They have hoisted the big red flags with a black square in the middle, one over the other that means a hurricane. The wind is rising hourly, and the barometer is falling. All the people of the town are nailing up their houses.

You go down to the boat and wrap the lines with canvas where they will chafe when the surge starts, and believe that she has a good chance to ride it out if it comes from any direction but the northwest where the opening of the sub-basin is; provided no other boat smashes into you and sinks you. There is a booze boat seized by the Coast Guard tied next to you and you notice her stern lines are only tied to ringbolts in the stern, and you start bellyaching about that.

"For Christ sake, you know those lousy ringbolts will pull right out of her stern and then she'll come down on us."

"If she does, you can cut her loose or sink her."

"Sure, and maybe we can't get to her too. What's the use of letting a piece of junk like that sink a good boat?"

From the last advisory you figure we will not get it until midnight, and at ten o'clock you leave the Weather Bureau and go home to see if you can get two hours' sleep before it starts, leaving the car in front of the house because you do not trust the rickety garage, putting the barometer and a flashlight by the bed for when the electric lights go. At midnight the wind is howling, the glass is 29.55 and dropping while you watch it, and rain is coming in sheets. You dress, find the car drowned out, make your way to the boat with a flashlight with branches falling and wires going down. The flashlight shorts in the rain, and the wind is now coming in heavy gusts from the northwest. The captured boat has pulled her ringbolts out, and by quick handling by Jose Rodriguez, a Spanish sailor, was swung clear before she hit us. She is now pounding against the dock.

The wind is bad and you have to crouch over to make headway against it. You figure if we get the hurricane from there you will lose the boat and you never will have enough money to get another. You feel like hell. But a little after two o'clock it backs into the west and by the law of circular storms you know the storm has passed over the Keys above us. Now the boat is well sheltered by the sea wall and the breakwater and at five o'clock, the glass having been steady for an hour, you get back to the house. As you make your way in without a light you find a tree is down across the walk and a strange empty look in the front yard shows the big old sappodillo tree is down too. You turn in.

That's what happens when one misses you. And that is about the minimum of time you have to prepare for a hurricane; two full days. Sometimes you have longer.

But what happened on the Keys?

On Tuesday, as the storm made its way up the Gulf of Mexico, it was so wild not a boat could leave Key West and there was no communication with the Keys beyond the ferry, nor with the mainland. No one knew what the storm had done, where it had passed. No train came in and there was no news by plane. Nobody knew the horror that was on the Keys. It was not until the next day that a boat got through to Matecumbe Key from Key West.

Now, as this is written five days after the storm, nobody knows how many are dead. The Red Cross, which has steadily played down the number, announcing first 46 then 150, finally saying the dead would not pass 300, today lists the dead and missing as 446, but the total of veterans dead and missing alone numbers 442 and there have been 70 bodies of civilians recovered. The total of dead may well pass a thousand as many bodies were swept out to sea and never will be found.

It is not necessary to go into the deaths of the civilians and their families since they were on the Keys of their own free will; they made their living there, had property and knew the hazards involved. But the veterans had been sent there; they had no opportunity to leave, nor any protection against hurricanes; and they never had a chance for their lives.

During the war, troops and sometimes individual soldiers who incurred the displeasure of their superior officers, were sometimes sent into positions of extreme danger and kept there repeatedly until they were no longer problems. I do not believe anyone, knowingly, would send U.S. war veterans into any such positions in time of peace. But the Florida Keys, in hurricane months, in the matter of casualties recorded during the building of the Florida East Coast Railway to Key West, when nearly a thousand men were killed by hurricanes, can be classed as such a position. And ignorance has never been accepted as an excuse for murder or for manslaughter.

Who sent nearly a thousand war veterans, many of them husky, hard-working and simply out of luck, but many of them close to the border of pathological cases, to live in frame shacks on the Florida Keys in hurricane months?

Why were the men not evacuated on Sunday, or at latest, Monday morning, when it was known there was a possibility of a hurricane striking the Keys *and evacuation was their only possible protection?*

Who advised against sending the train from Miami to evacuate the veterans until four-thirty o'clock on Monday, so that it was blown off the tracks before it ever reached the lower camps?

These are questions that someone will have to answer, and answer satisfactorily, unless the clearing of Anacostia Flats is going to seem an act of kindness compared to the clearing of Upper and Lower Matecumbe.

When we reached Lower Matecumbe there were bodies floating in the ferry slip. The brush was all brown as though autumn had come to these islands where there is no autumn but only a more dangerous summer, but that was because the leaves had all been blown away. There was two feet of sand over the highest part of the island where the sea had carried it and all the heavy bridge-building machines were on their sides. The island looked like the abandoned bed of a river where the sea had swept it. The railroad embankment was gone and the men who had cowered behind it and finally, when the water came, clung to the rails, were all gone with it. You could find them face down and face up in the mangroves. The biggest bunch of the dead were in the tangled, always green but now brown mangroves behind the tank cars and the water towers. They hung on there, in shelter, until the wind and the rising water carried them away. They didn't all let go at once but only when they could hold on no longer. Then further on you found them high in the trees where the water had swept them. You found them everywhere and in the sun all of them were beginning to be too big for their blue jeans and jackets that they could never fill when they were on the bum and hungry.

I'd known a lot of them at Josie Grunt's place and around the town when they would come in for pay day, and some of them were punch drunk and some of them were smart; some had been on the bum since the Argonne almost and some had lost their jobs the year before last Christmas; some had wives and some couldn't remember; some were good guys, and others put their pay checks in the Postal Savings and then came over to cadge in on the drinks when better men were drunk; some liked to fight and others liked to walk around the town; and they were all what you get after a war. But who sent them there to die?

They're better off, I can hear whoever sent them say, explaining to himself. What good were they? You can't account for accidents or acts of God. They were well-fed, well-housed, well-treated and, let us suppose, now they are well dead.

But I would like to make whoever sent them there carry just one out through the mangroves, or turn one over that lay in the sun along the fill, or tie five together so they won't float out, or smell that smell you thought you'd never smell again, with luck when rich bastards make a war. The lack of luck goes on until all who take part in it are gone.

So now you hold your nose, and you, you that put in the literary columns that you were staying in Miami to see a hurricane because you needed it in your next novel and now you were afraid you would not see one, you can go on reading the paper, and you'll get all you need for your next novel; but I would like to lead you by the seat of your well-worn-by-writing-to-the-literary-columns pants up to that bunch of mangroves where there is a woman, bloated big as a balloon and upside down and there's another face down in the brush next to her and explain to you they are two damned nice girls who ran a sandwich place and filling station and that where they are is their hard luck. And you could make a note of it for your next novel and how is your next novel coming, brother writer, comrade shit?

But just then one of eight survivors from that camp of 187 not counting 12 who went to Miami to play ball (how's that for casualties, you guys who remember percentages?) comes along and he says, "That's my old lady. Fat, ain't she?" But that guy is nuts, now, so we can dispense with him, and we have to go back and get in a boat before we can check up on Camp Five.

Camp Five was where eight survived out of 187, but we only find 67 of those plus two more along the fill makes 69. But all the rest are in the mangroves. It doesn't take a bird dog to locate them. On the other hand, there are no buzzards. Absolutely no buzzards. How's that? Would you believe it? The wind killed all the buzzards and all the big winged birds like pelicans too. You can find them in the grass that's washed along the fill. Hey, there's another one. He's got low shoes, put him down, man, looks about sixty, low shoes, copper-riveted overalls, blue percale shirt without collar, storm jacket, by Jesus that's the thing to wear, nothing in his pockets. Turn him over. Face tumefied beyond recognition. Hell, he don't look like a veteran. He's too old. He's got grey hair. You'll have grey hair yourself this time next week. And across his back there was a great big blister as wide as his back and all ready to burst where his storm jacket had slipped down. Turn him over again. Sure he's a veteran. I know him. What's he got low shoes on for then? Maybe he made some money shooting craps and bought them. You don't know that guy. You can't tell him now. I know him, he hasn't got any thumb. That's how I know him. The land crabs ate his thumb. You think you know everybody. Well you waited a long time to get sick brother. Sixty-seven of them and you get sick at the sixty-eighth. And so you walk the fill, where there is any fill and it's calm and clear and blue and almost the way it is when the millionaires come down in the winter except for the sand-flies, the mosquitoes and the smell of the dead that always smell the same in all countries that you go to—and now they smell like that in your own country. Or is it just that dead soldiers smell the same no matter what their nationality or who sends them to die?

Who sent them down there?

I hope he reads this-and how does he feel?

He will die too, himself, perhaps even without a hurricane warning, but maybe it will be an easy death, that's the best you get, *so* that you do not have to hang onto something until you can't hang on, until your fingers won't hold on, and it is dark. And the wind makes a noise like a locomotive passing, with a shriek on top of that, because the wind has a scream exactly as it has in books, and then the fill goes and the high wall of water rolls you over and over and then, whatever it is, you get it and we find you now of no importance, stinking in the mangroves.

You're dead now, brother, but who left you there in the hurricane months on the Keys where a thousand men died before you when they were building the road that's now washed out?

Who left you there? And what's the punishment for manslaughter now?

TENNESSEE WILLIAMS
1911–1983

TENNESSEE WILLIAMS FIRST came to Florida after his graduation from the University of Iowa—his third college—in 1939. He worked briefly as a telegraph operator, one of a series of short attempts at employment. A few years later, he was thirty years old when he came to Key West seeking a refuge after his play *Band of Angels* opened to disastrous reviews in Boston—he hoped the South might offer that refuge. He wanted to rewrite *Band of Angels*—and swim. "Key West was the southernmost point in America. I figured I'd be able to swim there," he said.

He first lived in a cabin behind what had once been a grand mansion, a cabin that had been home to slaves eighty years earlier. He wrote to a friend, "I am occupying the old servant's quarters in back of this 90-year-old house. It has been converted into an attractive living space with a shower. The rent is $7 a week."

He said his apartment was "at the center of the action for the pub-crawlers and the night people, Navy officers, singers, entertainers, artists, and writers, and some members of the town's social set."

In 1942, with the war under way, Williams took a job with the U.S. Corps of Engineers in Jacksonville, decoding messages. He later wrote, "[with] the awful shortage of manpower in those war years, even I impressed the personnel manager as an employable person." He and another man—whom Williams claimed had been prematurely discharged from an asylum—worked the overnight shift. He spent most of his time writing his plays, paying scant attention to the messages that needed to be decoded. One night he overlooked an important message and was fired. "Our boss thought it best to let me go and retain the services of the certified loony."

By the time he returned to Key West after the war, he was famous. *The Glass Menagerie* was a hit on Broadway and he had won a New York Drama Critics' Circle Award for Best Play.

In many ways, Williams replaced Hemingway as the leading writer on the island, but the two could not have been more different. The crowd Williams hung with was far different from the Hemingway crowd. Williams moved to a cottage, often entertaining such writers as Carson Mc-

Cullers, Christopher Isherwood, and Gore Vidal at the piano bar at the Tradewinds. He later moved to a hotel where he completed *Summer and Smoke*.

By 1949 Williams had made enough money from writing *The Glass Menagerie* and *A Streetcar Named Desire* to buy an old Bahamian home at 1431 Duncan Street. While Hemingway's home was one of the finest on the island, the Williams home was modest, located in a poorer part of town. It was there he wrote *Night of the Iguana.*

Williams told an interviewer, "This is the most fantastic place that I have been yet in America. It is even more colorful than Frisco, New Orleans or Santa Fe. There are comparatively few tourists and the town is the real stuff. It still belongs to the natives who are known as 'conks.' "

The movie version of his Broadway play, *The Rose Tattoo*, was filmed on the island in 1956, becoming a hit and winning three Academy Awards including Best Picture. When he died, the local Key West theater on Duval Street presented repeated showings of the movie in his honor. The movie was filmed in Key West at Williams' urging, rather than in Mississippi, where the play takes place.

Generally, Key West was forgiving, even welcoming of Williams' homosexuality, although the occasional minister came through preaching fire and brimstone and urging redemption. His presence attracted other gays and the Williams cottage became a stopover for many of them. In 1979 a minister, upset at what he saw as growing rowdiness on the island, took out an advertisement in the *Key West Citizen:* "If I were the chief of police, I would get me a hundred good men, give them each a baseball bat and have them walk down Duval Street and dare one of these freaks to stick his head over the sidewalk. That is the way it was done in Key West in the days I remember and love." He told an interviewer, "We'll either have a revival of our society or the homosexuals will take it over in five years."

The ad appeared amidst growing tension over the gay presence in Key West—with Williams its best-known representative. It touched off a series of events: His gardener was found dead in a pool of blood, bullet wounds in his head and neck. Days later, the Williams home was burglarized, and it turned out that his discarded writing notes were stolen—undoubtedly by someone who thought they may be worth something.

Finally, one night Williams and his biographer Dotson Rader were leaving a gay disco club called the Monster off Duval Street when they were attacked by four or five young men. Williams was knocked down and Rader punched. Williams refused to run and said, "There are punks here," and he predicted accurately the violence would subside.

Although his only home was in Key West, he traveled extensively and he spent most of his life in hotel rooms. He died in a New York hotel room in 1983, a strange tragedy in which he inhaled an eyedropper bottle cap, and choked to death. Before his death, Williams had planned his funeral, asking that one of his favorite poems, the Wallace Stevens poem, "The Idea of Order in Key West," be read. He wanted to be buried at sea, near where poet Hart Crane had jumped overboard and committed suicide, but his brother had him buried in St. Louis.

Although Williams is best remembered for his plays, he also wrote essays, stories, and poems, beginning in college. His poems were published in a book titled *Androgyne, Mon Amour.* "The Diving Bell" was written by Williams in Key West and inspired by the divers whom he saw sailing out each morning and returning in the evening.

The Diving Bell

by Tennessee Williams

I want to go under the sea in a diving-bell
and return to the surface with ominous wonders to tell.
I want to be able to say:
"The base is unstable, it's probably unable
to weather much weather,
being all hung together by a couple of blond hairs caught
in a fine-toothed comb."
I want to be able to say through a P.A. system,
Authority giving a sonorous tone to the vowels,
"I'm speaking from Neptune's bowels.
The sea's floor is nacreous, filmy
with milk in the wind, the light of an overcast morning."
I want to give warning:
"The pediment of our land is a lady's comb,
the basement is moored to the dome
by a pair of blond hairs caught in a delicate
tortoise-shell comb."
I think it's safer to roam
than to stay in a mortgaged home
And so—
I want to go under the sea in a bubble of glass
containing a sofa upholstered in green corduroy
and a girl for practical purposes and a boy
well-versed in the classics.

I want to be first to go down there where action is slow
but thought is surprisingly quick.
It's only a dare-devil's trick,
the length of a burning wick
between tu-whit and tu-who!
Oh, it's pretty and blue
but not at all to be trusted. No matter how deep you go
there's not very much below
the deceptive shimmer and glow
which is all for show
of sunken galleons encrusted with barnacles and doubloons,
an undersea tango palace with instant come and go moons . . .

JOHN F. KENNEDY

1917–1963

THE TWO LITERARY works that John F. Kennedy is best known for are *Pro-files in Courage* and his 1961 Inaugural Address in which he told the American people, "Ask not what your country can do for you; ask what you can do for your country." While we know that both were written while Kennedy was at his family home in Palm Beach, we do not know—and will never know—just what role Kennedy played in writing them.

The Kennedy family always assumed that Joseph P. Kennedy Jr., the eldest Kennedy son, was destined for a political career that might take him to the White House. When Joe Kennedy died during World War II, attention turned to the second son, John. Before his election to Congress in 1946, John Kennedy often talked of a career as a writer or in journalism. Even after his election, he told a friend that he was still considering a career as a writer.

Profiles in Courage might never have been written if it had not been for Kennedy's serious health problems. Throughout his life, Kennedy fought a series of illnesses. Hospitalized more than three dozen times during his life, he received the last rites three times as death seemed imminent.

Problems with his back began in the late 1930s and lasted until his death. He was hospitalized in 1940 in Boston with pain in his lower back, then admitted to three hospitals in 1944 for back treatment, including his first back surgery. Despite the surgery, his problems persisted.

Joseph Kennedy had purchased the Palm Beach beach-front mansion in 1933 as a playground for his children. For John Kennedy, the home became a place to recover from his operations.

Kennedy represented Massachusetts three terms in the House of Representatives, and in 1952 he won a Senate seat. Two years later, he came up with an idea he thought would make a compelling series of magazine articles. He assembled a list of senators who had taken courageous stands, risking their political careers to do what they believed was right. It might have remained just an idea if not for Kennedy's worsening back problems. In late 1954 he went to Palm Beach to recover from back surgery, and now his idea about courageous senators came back, but instead of magazine articles, he decided to write a book.

The book, *Profiles in Courage,* was published in early 1956 to positive reviews and tremendous sales. It spent nearly two years on the best seller list, and has remained in print since, with millions of copies sold. In 1957 the book won the Pulitzer Prize for biography. There was controversy over the prize—it had not been a finalist, but somehow emerged as a winner, many believe because of the lobbying of respected *New York Times* columnist Arthur Krock, a close friend of Joseph P. Kennedy.

The book did more than make Kennedy even wealthier. In the Senate he had been known as a lightweight. Majority Leader Lyndon Johnson would sometimes dismiss him as "that boy" or "Johnny." But the book publication and the Pulitzer had given him national prestige, and winning journalism's highest award had created a bond with the thousands of reporters who saw the award as the holy grail.

But almost from the date of publication, questions were raised over who really wrote the book. There was speculation that the real author was Ted Sorenson, a Kennedy speechwriter and close confidant. On December 14, 1957, columnist Drew Pearson was interviewed by Mike Wallace on ABC. Pearson didn't pull any punches when he said, "John F. Kennedy is the only man in history that I know who won a Pulitzer Prize for a book that was ghostwritten for him." Wallace replied, "You know for a fact, Drew, that the book *Profiles in Courage* was written for Senator Kennedy?" Pearson said yes and Wallace said, "And Kennedy accepted a Pulitzer Prize for it? And he never acknowledged the fact?" Pearson said, "No, he has not. You know there's a little wisecrack around the Senate about Jack. . . . 'Jack, I wish you had a little less profile and more courage.' "

When he ran for president in 1960, Washington insiders learned that the Kennedy family could play hardball, but executives at ABC got their lesson in late 1957. The Kennedy family hired leading Washington attorney Clark Clifford, who threatened to sue; both Bobby Kennedy and his father protested directly; and the network was shown copies of John Kennedy's notes for the book.

ABC network, the weakest of the networks, backed down without a fight, and a week later, an ABC executive read a statement on national television apologizing. Still the rumors would not die and the controversy continued. An analysis by historian Herbert Parmet shows that Kennedy was more of a director than an author. Kennedy clearly gets credit for coming up with the idea and drafted long memos about what he wanted, and he came up with the framework. His secretary, Gloria Sitrin, said that because of his back problems, Kennedy could not sit for long periods and dictated many pages to her. But Sorenson apparently did much of the writing, although many others were involved. Jacqueline Kennedy asked one of her history professors, Jules Davids of Georgetown University, to help and he contributed to the book. And finally, Senate researchers were called in to gather and check facts. Parmet believes Kennedy wrote the first and last chapters and was heavily involved in the other parts of the book.

For nearly half a century, Sorenson claimed that Kennedy had written the book and rejected attempts to give him the credit. But in 2008, Sorensen published his memoirs and finally painted a far different picture of what had happened than he had in his previous claims. Sorensen agreed with Parmet that Kennedy had "worked particularly hard and long on the first and last chapters, setting the tone and philosophy of the book." However, Sorenson said he did the first draft of most of the book. Sorenson also claimed that Kennedy had paid him generously over a period of years—which suggests that Kennedy wanted to guarantee Sorenson's silence.

The two were to work together again on Kennedy's inaugural address beginning after the November 1960 election. Here again, it was a collaborative process, involving Kennedy and Sorenson and more than a dozen others. Kennedy spent much of the time between his election and his inauguration at the Palm Beach home.

On November 24, 1960, President-elect Kennedy and his wife had dinner with friends in Washington, then Kennedy flew to Palm Beach, while his wife remained behind in Washington to await the birth of their second child. As Kennedy's private plane approached Palm Beach, he received word that his wife had been taken to the hospital to give birth—several weeks early.

When he landed, he commandeered the larger and faster press plane for the return flight to Washington. His son, John F. Kennedy Jr., was born before the takeoff. When he returned to Palm Beach, he finished selecting his cabinet by the middle of December.

As Christmas approached, he turned to his inaugural address. Most inaugural addresses are quickly forgotten. Abraham Lincoln's second address is the best known, with his call for "With malice toward none, with charity for all." Franklin Roosevelt's first address ("The only thing we have to fear is fear itself,") is also memorable.

On December 23, 1960, Kennedy advisor John Kenneth Galbraith visited Palm Beach and brought with him an inaugural address he had written. A telegram went out to ten men asking for their thoughts on the inaugural address. As with *Profiles in Courage,* Sorenson was writing in Washington while Kennedy dictated memos and called with suggestions.

On January 15, just a week before the inauguration ceremonies, Sorenson flew to Palm Beach bringing drafts of an inaugural address written by at least five other men.

The following day the two men met to work on the speech. The initial meeting lasted just seventy-five minutes. Kennedy headed for other meetings and Sorenson headed for his typewriter. They met the following morning to work on the speech again, although Kennedy was distracted by other demands. Those who were there recall Kennedy talking on the patio while Sorenson typed nearby.

They flew back to Washington, working on the speech during the flight, and by the time they landed, the inaugural address was complete, including the line, "Ask not what your country can do for you; ask what you can do for your country."

1961 Inaugural Address
by John F. Kennedy

Vice President Johnson, Mr. Speaker, Mr. Chief Justice, President Eisenhower, Vice President Nixon, President Truman, reverend clergy, fellow citizens, we observe today not a victory of party, but a celebration of freedom—symbolizing an end, as well as a beginning—signifying renewal, as well as change. For I have sworn before you and Almighty God the same solemn oath our forebears prescribed nearly a century and three quarters ago.

The world is very different now. For man holds in his mortal hands the power to abolish all forms of human poverty and all forms of human life. And yet the same revolutionary beliefs for which our forebears fought are still at issue around the globe—the belief that the rights of man come not from the generosity of the state, but from the hand of God.

We dare not forget today that we are the heirs of that first revolution. Let the word go forth from this time and place, to friend and foe alike, that the torch has been passed to a new generation of Americans—born in this century, tempered by war, disciplined by a hard and bitter peace, proud of our ancient heritage—and unwilling to witness or permit the slow undoing of those human rights to which this Nation has always been committed, and to which we are committed today at home and around the world.

Let every nation know, whether it wishes us well or ill, that we shall pay any price, bear any burden, meet any hardship, support any friend, oppose any foe, in order to assure the survival and the success of liberty.

This much we pledge—and more.

To those old allies whose cultural and spiritual origins we share, we pledge the loyalty of faithful friends. United, there is little we cannot do in a host of cooperative ventures. Divided, there is little we can do—for we dare not meet a powerful challenge at odds and split asunder.

To those new States whom we welcome to the ranks of the free, we pledge our word that one form of colonial control shall not have passed away merely to be replaced by a far more iron tyranny. We shall not always expect to find them supporting our view. But we shall always hope to find them strongly supporting their own freedom—and to remember that, in the past, those who foolishly sought power by riding the back of the tiger ended up inside.

To those peoples in the huts and villages across the globe struggling to break the bonds of mass misery, we pledge our best efforts to help them help themselves, for whatever period is required—not because the Communists may be doing it, not because we seek their votes, but because it is right. If a free society cannot help the many who are poor, it cannot save the few who are rich.

To our sister republics south of our border, we offer a special pledge—to convert our good words into good deeds—in a new alliance for progress—to assist free men and free governments in casting off the chains of poverty. But this peaceful revolution of hope cannot become the prey of hostile powers. Let all our neighbors know that we shall join with them to oppose aggression or subversion anywhere in the Americas. And let every other power know that this Hemisphere intends to remain the master of its own house.

To that world assembly of sovereign states, the United Nations, our last best hope in an age where the instruments of war have far outpaced the instruments of peace, we renew our pledge of support—to prevent it from becoming merely a forum for invective—to strengthen its shield of the new and the weak—and to enlarge the area in which its writ may run.

Finally, to those nations who would make themselves our adversary, we offer not a pledge but a request: that both sides begin anew the quest for peace, before the dark powers of destruction unleashed by science engulf all humanity in planned or accidental self-destruction.

We dare not tempt them with weakness. For only when our arms are sufficient beyond doubt can we be certain beyond doubt that they will never be employed.

But neither can two great and powerful groups of nations take comfort from our present course—both sides overburdened by the cost of modern weapons, both rightly alarmed by the steady spread of the deadly atom, yet both racing to alter that uncertain balance of terror that stays the hand of mankind's final war.

So let us begin anew—remembering on both sides that civility is not a sign of weakness, and sincerity is always subject to proof. Let us never negotiate out of fear. But let us never fear to negotiate.

Let both sides explore what problems unite us instead of belaboring those problems which divide us.

Let both sides, for the first time, formulate serious and precise proposals for the inspection and control of arms—and bring the absolute power to destroy other nations under the absolute control of all nations.

Let both sides seek to invoke the wonders of science instead of its terrors. Together let us explore the stars, conquer the deserts, eradicate disease, tap the ocean depths, and encourage the arts and commerce.

Let both sides unite to heed in all corners of the earth the command of Isaiah—to "undo the heavy burdens . . . and to let the oppressed go free."

And if a beachhead of cooperation may push back the jungle of suspicion, let both sides join in creating a new endeavor, not a new balance of power, but a new world of law, where the strong are just and the weak secure and the peace preserved.

All this will not be finished in the first 100 days. Nor will it be finished in the first 1,000 days, nor in the life of this Administration, nor even perhaps in our lifetime on this planet. But let us begin.

In your hands, my fellow citizens, more than in mine, will rest the final success or failure of our course. Since this country was founded, each generation of Americans has been summoned to give testimony to its national loyalty. The graves of young Americans who answered the call to service surround the globe.

Now the trumpet summons us again—not as a call to bear arms, though arms we need; not as a call to battle, though embattled we are—but a call to bear the burden of a long twilight struggle, year in and year out, "rejoicing in hope, patient in tribulation"—a struggle against the common enemies of man: tyranny, poverty, disease, and war itself.

Can we forge against these enemies a grand and global alliance, North and South, East and West, that can assure a more fruitful life for all mankind? Will you join in that historic effort?

In the long history of the world, only a few generations have been granted the role of defending freedom in its hour of maximum danger. I do not shrink from this responsibility—I welcome it. I do not believe that any of us would exchange places with any other people or any other generation. The energy, the faith, the devotion which we bring to this endeavor will light our country and all who serve it—and the glow from that fire can truly light the world.

And so, my fellow Americans: ask not what your country can do for you—ask what you can do for your country.

My fellow citizens of the world: ask not what America will do for you, but what together we can do for the freedom of man.

Finally, whether you are citizens of America or citizens of the world, ask of us the same high standards of strength and sacrifice which we ask of you. With a good conscience our only sure reward, with history the final judge of our deeds, let us go forth to lead the land we love, asking His blessing and His help, but knowing that here on earth God's work must truly be our own.

PATRICK D. SMITH

1927–

T HAS BEEN an improbable journey for Patrick Smith, whose rise to literary fame was slow, but who has had several brushes with history and
emerged as Florida's unofficial novelist laureate. His book *A Land Remembered* has become a classic, required reading in schools, and even the
name of a restaurant in a luxury hotel that seeks to recapture Florida's
past.

He was born in Mississippi and began writing for a weekly newspaper
when he was in ninth grade. After high school, he served in the Merchant
Marine and then went to the University of Mississippi. After graduation, he
drifted through a variety of jobs.

He wrote a book about a boy growing up in Mississippi but had no
idea how to get it published. He went to the local small-town library,
pulled down a book and checked the name of the publisher. The book
was published by Little, Brown. He mailed the manuscript with a note:
"Dear Editor: Please publish this book." Little, Brown, one of the nation's
most prestigious publishers, said, "Yes." He went to Boston to work on
the final editing of his manuscript and found himself sharing an office with
another new author, J. D. Salinger. The two could not have been more different, Smith, the courtly, proper Southerner, and Salinger, the author of
Catcher in the Rye, who was in the process of fighting Little, Brown over
the number of times he could use a certain expletive in his book. At one
point, Salinger asked Smith for advice. Smith replied, "If I had that word in
my book even one time my mother would kill me."

In 1962 he took a job as the public relations director at the University of Mississippi, a job that usually involved sending out press releases to
state newspapers about events at the school. But 1962 was anything but
usual at Ole Miss. James Meredith was set to become the first African-
American student at the school, creating turmoil and the threat of violence. Smith was selected to escort Meredith to class. He had help, federal
marshals and Justice Department officials, but rioting broke out and two
people died.

His assignment led him to write the novel *The Beginning,* which drew
on the Meredith experience. The book came out as Smith was taking a

new job in Florida, handling public relations for Brevard Community College. His new home state gave him a wealth of ideas for books. He set off to write about the Seminole Indians living in the Everglades. Smith spent weekends in the Everglades doing research but had trouble getting the Indians to open up to him. An encounter with James Billie, who would become chairman of the tribe, gave him the access he needed. In 1973, *Forever Island* was published, the story of a young Seminole resisting development on his land. *Reader's Digest* selected *Forever Island* for its hugely popular condensed books.

His next book took him undercover, to write a book about conditions for migrant workers. He got a job picking vegetables south of Miami with migrant workers. He worried that if his disguise was discovered, he would be beaten—or worse. The result was *Angel City*, which drew international attention. The miserable working conditions were exposed by Smith, and the Florida Legislature passed legislation to regulate working conditions for migrant workers. His book was turned into a 1980 television movie.

His next undertaking was his greatest work, and one that continues to define him as a writer. He began working on *A Land Remembered* by reading every book on Florida history he could find. Then he hit the road, spending two years interviewing Floridians whose roots in Florida went back to the early 1800s.

The result was a book that traced a family—the MacIveys—over two centuries. He sent the manuscript to a new publishing house, Pineapple Press, in Sarasota. Pineapple was only two years old and saw the potential in Smith's manuscript. A favorable review in *The New York Times* gave the book a national following, and since 1984 it has sold hundreds of thousands of copies.

Smith and his wife still live in the same modest Cocoa home they bought when they first moved to Florida in 1967. He has received a long list of honors, both from Florida and his native Mississippi.

Fried Mullet and Grits

by Patrick D. Smith

It was mid-afternoon when Alvin Binder pulled the black Buick Regal off the two-lane asphalt highway and came to a stop on the right shoulder. Across the road, adjacent to a sandy lane leading off into the woods, there was a faded red sign:

TURKEY CREEK FISH CAMP BOATS - BAIT - CABINS
2 MILES

On an impulse he pulled across the highway and started down the narrow lane. Huge oak trees formed an overhead canopy, and beneath them were thick clumps of palmetto surrounded by a carpet of ferns.

He drove slowly, glancing both right and left, wondering if this were the right thing to do. If he kept going he could make Fort Lauderdale by nightfall.

The lane made a right turn and then came into a clearing bordered on the south by a slow flowing stream, and then a long stretch of sawgrass. On the left there was an unpainted building with a porch on its front. Off to the right side there was a row of six small cabins, also unpainted and highly weathered.

Alvin Binder parked the car and went inside the main building. Behind a counter there were shelves filled with canned goods, and a cooler to the left contained beer, soda and milk. Just then a short rotund man came from a room at the rear of the store. He was about the same age as Alvin, sixty-five, and his face was burned leather brown. He said, "Howdy. Something I can do for you?"

For a moment Alvin didn't know if the man could do something for him or not. He finally said, "Well, I don't know. I was on my way to Fort Lauderdale and saw your sign. I usually go down the turnpike, but this time I decided to take some backroads instead. I've never done this before."

The man extended his hand and said, "I'm Sim Lowry. You want something cold to drink? A beer or a soda?"

"Coke will do fine."

Sim popped open a can and handed it to Alvin. He then said, "Where you coming from?"

"Marion, Ohio. My wife and I have been spending two weeks each year in a time-share condo in Fort Lauderdale. She died six months ago, and I'm on my way there to make arrangements to sell my share of the condo. Wouldn't be the same there without Mary."

Sim could see the sadness in the stranger's eyes. He said, "You're welcome to spend the night here if you're a mind to. All the cabins are empty. The water's so low now nobody comes out here to fish. We need a real good soaking rain. Can let you have a cabin for ten bucks. There's no TV or air conditioning, but it does have a ceiling fan. And you can eat with me and the missus tonight and in the morning. No charge. Tonight we're having cooter stew, swamp cabbage and corn pone. In the morning it'll be fried mullet and grits, with some biscuits too."

"Sounds like a good deal to me," Alvin said, still a bit uncertain about what he was doing. "Which cabin do I take?"

"The first one," Sim responded. "It's not locked. Just go on over and settle in, then come back and we'll visit for a spell. That is, if you want to."

"Thanks," Alvin said. "I'll do that. I'll be back here shortly."

When he emerged from the cabin Alvin gazed southward. In the distance to the right there was a line of giant bald cypress trees, some towering a hundred feet, marking the beginning of a swamp. Limbs were dotted with egrets and white ibis. Blue herons waded slowly along the shallows of the creek, pecking at something beneath the black water. To the east, sawgrass stretched away to the horizon.

Sim was sitting in a rocker on the front porch of the store, so Alvin crossed over and took a chair beside him.

"Nice and quiet out here," Alvin said.

"That's the way we like it," Sim responded. "I got no hankering for city life."

"How long have you been here?" Alvin asked curiously.

"Owned this fish camp for forty years. Before that, me and my daddy was in the cattle business up north of here. I got tired of sitting in a saddle all day, so I came down here and built this camp. We don't have any frills out here, but it suits us fine. We make do O.K. What do you do up in Ohio?"

"I owned an appliance store, but I sold it five years ago and retired. That's when we bought the time-share condo. I guess I should have bought a camper instead, and taken Mary to a lot of different places we've never seen. Like this. But it's too late for that now."

A plump woman suddenly burst through the screen door. She was wearing a blue cotton dress and white canvas shoes. She said to Alvin, "I'm Ruthie. You men come on in inside now. Swamp cabbage is best when it's piping hot. It's time to eat."

Sim and Alvin got up and followed her inside.

After supper, Sim and Alvin were back on the porch when a dusty pickup truck pulled in and parked. A man of about forty lumbered out of the truck and joined them. He was as slim as a fence rail and dressed in faded overalls without shirt or shoes. He said, "Evening, Sim. Thought I'd stop by for a beer."

"As usual," Sim said. "I'll get it for you."

Sim went into the store, returned and handed the can to the new arrival. He said, "This is Alvin Binder from Ohio. He's staying the night with us. And this varmint here who looks like a scarecrow is Junior Rawson. He lives not far from here, out in the swamp."

"Pleased to meet you," Alvin said.

"Likewise."

Junior took a deep draw on the beer and then said, "If this place is givin you the willies, it's a pity ole Biff Sutter ain't around right now. You'd get some free entertainment. Biff is always playing jokes on somebody. He was at a flea market one time and this guy had a gorilla suit for sale. It was pretty wore out, but was O.K. Biff bought it for twenty dollars.

"They's always been a rumor out here about a swamp ape. Some folks calls it a skunk ape, cause it's supposed to smell like a skunk. Some folks even swear they've seen it. Well, ole Biff got to putting on that monkey suit and running around in the woods when tourists came by in a fishing boat. He'd jump up and down and shout, 'Woogla woogla wah wah.' Scared the living daylights out-en them tourists, and their eyeballs popped right out of the sockets.

"One thing he didn't figure on was Uncle Benro. He's about eighty years old, half blind, and can't hear too good either. Everywhere he goes he carries a double-barrel twelve-gauge shotgun loaded with number eight birdshot, and he's liable to shoot at anything that moves. We see him coming we just hide behind a tree till he's passed by.

"One day Biff was on the bank of a canal, jumping up and down and shouting 'woogla woogla wah wah.' He didn't see Uncle Benro coming up behind him. Uncle Benro throwed up that blunderbus and unloaded both barrels right in the direction of Biff's behind. Black fur flew everywhere. That 'woogla woogla wah wah' changed to 'yipe yipe yipe,' and the last them tourists seen of Biff he was cutting through the swamp eighty miles per hour. Shortly after that, Biff traded what was left of the gorilla suit for the mangiest dog I ever seen. That dog wasn't worth a cuss for nothing, but Biff said he was going to train him to climb trees and bark like a squirrel. That would get the attention of them tourists for sure. Biggest squirrel they ever seen sitting on the limb of a tree."

Sim didn't even crack a smile, but Alvin erupted in laughter. Alvin finally said, "Seems you have some characters out here."

"That ain't nothing," Junior said. "You stay around for a while I'll tell you some tales that'll make your ears stand up like a rabbit's."

Junior then got up, stretched, and said, "I got to go now and gig some frogs if I can scare the gators away from them. With this low water, the gators and frogs are kinda crowded together. It was good to meet you, Mister Binder. You come back and visit with us sometime."

"I just might do that," Alvin said. He watched the old pickup truck disappear around the bend of the road, then he said to Sim, "Guess I'll turn in now. It's been a long day."

"I'll roust you out for breakfast," Sim said. "You'll like fried mullet and grits. Real cracker food."

Alvin sat on the bed for a moment, then he got up and walked down to the dock. The moon was high now, casting a soft silver glow through the trees and across the sawgrass. At first he could not understand what it was that so enthralled him, and then he realized it was the absence of human sights and sounds: no street lights, no rumbling automobiles, no shrill laughter drifting upward from a crowded beach, no sirens shrieking in the night. And no television blaring in a thick-carpeted room. All he and Mary ever did in the condo at night was watch TV. They could have as well been in a New York City hotel room as a Florida condo. This thought had not occurred to him before.

The moonlight was bright enough for him to see a small stream meandering snake-like through the sawgrass, and he wondered where it led to. In the distance there was the dim outline of a shell mound—one probably built by Indians centuries ago. In his imagination he joined them, snatching roasted oysters from a roaring fire. And then he felt a sudden release, as if nature flushed all the sorrow and sadness from his mind. He wished he had brought Mary to this place, for he was sure she would have enjoyed it.

He lingered for an hour more, drinking deeply of the magic that seemed to envelop all the world; then he went back into the cabin and closed the door. He slept soundly for the first time in six months.

Breakfast was all that Sim promised. He enjoyed three helpings of fried mullet fillets and grits, four buttermilk biscuits, and six cups of strong black coffee made in an old-fashioned stove-top percolator. He felt a warm glow as he walked back to the cabin and packed to leave.

Once again he gazed out at the great expanse of natural, untouched land, wishing he had time to explore it. Next time he would.

Sim came off the porch and down to the car. He shook Alvin's hand warmly and said, "It was good to have you here, Alvin. It's a pity you don't have more time to spend with us."

"Do you reserve these cabins?" Alvin asked.

"Well, sort of," Sim said. "Some regular customers come at the same time each year, and we hold a cabin open for them. "

"I want one for the first two weeks in October each year. Can you do that?"

"I'll mark it in my book."

Alvin got into the Buick reluctantly, then he waved his hand and pointed the car back toward the asphalt highway.

ISAAC BASHEVIS SINGER

1902–1991

I N 1948, ISAAC Bashevis Singer and his wife boarded a train in New York in the middle of winter for a trip to Miami, their first. He recalled later, "I could hardly believe my eyes—the water, the buildings, the indescribable glow, and the palm trees. The palm trees especially made an impression on me."

The couple checked in at the Hotel Pierre, one of the dozens of Art Deco hotels built in the 1930s. The Pierre was best known for its low prices and Singer paid eight dollars a day for a room. "We were young and we had little money and that seemed a bit much, but we got a room that had a balcony. I stood on that balcony and stared at a palm tree for hours and I was happy."

The journey to Miami had begun more than a decade earlier when Singer emigrated from Poland amid the growing Nazi threat from neighboring Germany. A year earlier he had published his first novel, *Satan in Goray.* In New York, he went to work for the Yiddish-language newspaper, *The Forward,* and began to build his reputation as a great writer. In all, he published eighteen novels, fourteen children's books, and hundreds of newspaper articles. Although he wrote only in Yiddish, his work appeared in *Esquire* and *Playboy.*

Arriving in Miami, he said, "I had a feeling I had come to paradise."

After the Pierre, he moved to another classic Art Deco hotel, the Crown, where he wrote his first major novel and the first to be published in English, *The Family Moskatt.* The book traces a Jewish family in Poland from 1911 to 1930, a subject Singer knew very well. He also began producing stories set in Miami Beach, including "Alone," "Old Love," "The Hotel," and "A Party in Miami Beach."

He returned to New York, but visited Florida often and finally moved permanently to the Miami suburb of Surfside in 1973.

One of his grandchildren came to visit in 1982 and said her grandfather took her to the block-long "Isaac Bashevis Singer Boulevard." He insisted she take photos of him next to the sign. She recalled years later that when her grandfather said "Let's go for a walk," he meant walking up and down the corridor outside his apartment forty times.

In 1978 he won the Nobel Prize, further increasing his world renown and pushing up sales of his works. For most of his life, he had struggled with money, but now he was making over half a million dollars a year. The University of Miami named him a distinguished professor with an attractive salary. He was so successful that for the first time in his life he had to get an unlisted telephone number.

But he was lonely and depressed by his advancing years. At a University of Miami function, someone lightheartedly asked, "How does it feel to be seventy-seven years young?" Singer, who had been in a good mood, turned angry and said, "Don't ask such questions! No one is years young. A man is years old. And it is not a joke. It is nothing to joke about. It is a terrible thing to be old, not a joke."

His personal life had always been something of a mess. He had left behind a common-law wife in Poland, remarried, but was involved with other women. In Miami, he broke with his longtime mistress, Dobe, and his faithful secretary, Dvora. His relationship with his wife, Alma, was strained. Sometimes he would embarrass her in public; other times he would praise her, as he did in an interview with *People* magazine in 1982. "My wife is a saint. For the 42 years of our marriage she had to put up with a lot of nonsense, including supporting my writing as a buyer for department stores in the days when one article for the Jewish daily, *Forward,* earned $25. Alma is like my Rock of Ages."

By the late 1980s, his health was beginning to fail. He suffered from Alzheimer's disease and often could not recognize longtime friends. But it was a strange strain of Alzheimer's. He could go all day without recognizing family members, then say, "I certainly am the greatest Yiddish writer living."

He moved to the Douglas Gardens Rest Home, where he could be cared for around the clock. He died there in 1991.

His story "Alone" is set in Miami and deals with a lonely man who lives in a hotel that closes suddenly. He moves to a seedier hotel run by a deformed Cuban girl. The story contains most of the elements that made up Miami in the 1970s, including Jewish and Cuban residents who were often looking for cheap rooms in rundown hotels that had become relics from the 1920s and 1930s. For most readers, it was a different view of Miami Beach, a dark look at a sunny city.

Alone

by Isaac Bashevis Singer

Many times in the past I have wished the impossible to happen—and then it happened. But though my wish came true, it was in such a topsy-turvy way that it appeared the Hidden Powers were trying to show me I didn't understand my own needs. That's what occurred that summer in Miami Beach. I had been living in a large hotel full of South American tourists who had come to Miami to cool off, as well as with people like myself who suffered from hay fever. I was fed up with the whole business—splashing about in the ocean with those noisy guests; hearing Spanish all day long; eating heavy meals twice each day. If I read a Yiddish newspaper or book, the others looked at me with astonishment. So it happened that taking a walk one day, I said out loud: "I wish I were alone in a hotel." An imp must have overheard me, for immediately he began to set a trap.

When I came down to breakfast the next morning, I found the hotel lobby in confusion. Guests stood about in small groups, their voices louder than usual. Valises were piled all over. Bellboys were running about pushing carts loaded with clothing. I asked someone what was the matter. "Didn't you hear the announcement over the public-address system? They've closed the hotel." "Why?" I asked. "They're bankrupt." The man moved away, annoyed at my ignorance. Here was a riddle: the hotel was closing! Yet so far as I knew, it did a good business. And how could you suddenly close a hotel with hundreds of guests? But in America I had decided it was better not to ask too many questions.

The air conditioning had already been shut off and the air in the lobby was musty. A long line of guests stood at the cashier's desk to pay their bills. Everywhere there was turmoil. People crushed out cigarettes on the marble floor. Children tore leaves and flowers off the potted tropical plants. Some South Americans, who only yesterday had pretended to be full-blooded Latins, were now talking loudly in Yiddish. I myself had very little to pack, only one valise. Taking it, I went in search of another hotel. Outside, the burning sun reminded me of the Talmudic story of how, on the plains of Mamre, God had removed the sun from its case so that no strangers would bother Abraham. I felt a little giddy. The days of my bachelorhood came back when, carefree, I used to pack all my belongings in one valise, leave, and within five minutes find myself another room. Passing a small hotel, which looked somewhat run-down, I read the sign: "Off Season Rates from $2 a Day." What could be cheaper? I went inside. There was no air conditioning. A hunchbacked girl with black piercing eyes stood behind the desk. I asked her if I could have a room.

"The whole hotel," she answered.

"No one is here?"

"Nobody." The girl laughed, displaying a broken row of teeth with large gaps between. She spoke with a Spanish accent.

She had come from Cuba, she told me. I took a room. The hunchback led me into a narrow elevator, which took us up to the third floor. There we walked down a long, dark corridor meagerly lit by a single bulb. She opened a door and let me into my room, like a prisoner into his cell. The window, covered by mosquito netting, looked out over the Atlantic. On the walls the paint was peeling, and the rug on the floor was threadbare and colorless. The bathroom smelled of mildew, the closet of moth repellent. The bed linen, though clean, was damp. I unpacked my things and went downstairs. Everything was mine alone: the swimming pool, the beach, the ocean. In the patio stood a group of dilapidated canvas chairs. All around the sun beat down. The sea was yellow, the waves low and lazy, barely moving, as if they too were fatigued by the stifling heat. Only occasionally, out of duty, they tossed up a few specks of foam. A single sea gull stood on the water trying to decide whether or not to catch a fish. Here before me, drenched in sunlight, was a summer melancholy—odd, since melancholy usually suggests autumn. Mankind, it seemed, had perished in some catastrophe, and I was left, like Noah—but in an empty ark, without sons, without a wife, without any animals. I could have swum naked, nevertheless I put on my bathing suit. The water was so warm, the ocean might have been a bathtub. Loose bunches of seaweed floated about. Shyness had held me back in the first hotel—here it was solitude. Who can play games in an empty world? I could swim a little, but who would rescue me if something went wrong? The Hidden Powers had provided me with an empty hotel—but they could just as easily provide me with an undertow, a deep hole, a shark, or a sea serpent. Those who toy with the unknown must be doubly careful.

After a while I came out of the water and lay down on one of the limp canvas beach chairs. My body was pale, my skull bare, and though my eyes were protected by tinted glasses, the sun's rays glared through. The light-blue sky was cloudless. The air smelled of salt, fish, and mangoes. There was no division, I felt, between the organic and the inorganic. Everything around me, each grain of sand, each pebble, was breathing, growing, lusting. Through the heavenly channels, which, says the Cabala, control the flow of Divine Mercy, came truths impossible to grasp in a northern climate. I had lost all ambition; I felt lazy; my few wants were petty and material—a glass of lemonade or orange juice. In my fancy a hot-eyed woman moved into the hotel for a few nights. I hadn't meant I wanted a hotel completely to myself. The imp had either misunderstood or was pretending to. Like all forms of life, I, too, wanted to be fruitful, wanted to multiply—or at least to go through the motions. I was prepared to forget any moral or aesthetic demands. I was ready to cover my guilt with a sheet and to give way wholly, like a blind man, to the sense of touch. At the same time the eternal question tapped in my brain: Who is behind the world of appearance? Is it Substance with its Infinite Attributes? Is it the Monad of all Monads? Is it the Absolute, Blind Will, the Unconscious? Some kind of superior being has to be hidden in back of all these illusions.

On the sea, oily-yellow near the shore, glassy-green farther out, a sail walked over the water like a shrouded corpse. Bent forward, it looked as if it were trying to call something up from the depths. Overhead flew a small airplane trailing a sign: MARGOLIES' RESTAURANT—KOSHER, 7 COURSES, $1.75. So the Creation had not yet returned to primeval chaos. They still served soup with kasha and kneidlach, knishes and stuffed derma at Margolies' restaurant.

In that case perhaps tomorrow I would receive a letter. I had been promised my mail would be forwarded. It was my only link, in Miami, with the outside world. I'm always amazed that someone has written me, taken the trouble to stamp and mail the envelope. I look for cryptic meanings, even on the blank side of the paper.

II

When you are alone, how long the day can be! I read a book and two newspapers, drank a cup of coffee in a cafeteria, worked a crossword puzzle. I stopped at a store that auctioned Oriental rugs, went into another where Wall Street stocks were sold. True, I was on Collins Avenue in Miami Beach, but I felt like a ghost, cut off from everything. I went into the library and asked a question—the librarian grew frightened. I was like a man who had died, whose space had already been filled. I passed many hotels, each with its special decorations and attractions. The palm trees were topped by half-wilted fans of leaves, and their coconuts hung like heavy testicles. Everything seemed motionless, even the shiny new automobiles gliding over the asphalt. Every object continued its existence with that effortless force which is, perhaps, the essence of all being.

I bought a magazine, but was unable to read past the first few lines. Getting on a bus, I let myself be taken aimlessly over causeways, islands with ponds, streets lined with villas. The inhabitants, building on a wasteland, had planted trees and flowering plants from all parts of the world; they had filled up shallow inlets along the shore; they had created architectural wonders and had worked out elaborate schemes for pleasure. A planned hedonism. But the boredom of the desert remained. No loud music could dispel it, no garishness wipe it out. We passed a cactus plant whose blades and dusty needles had brought forth a red flower. We rode near a lake surrounded by groups of flamingos airing their wings, and the water mirrored their long beaks and pink feathers. An assembly of birds. Wild ducks flew about, quacking—the swampland refused to give way.

I looked out the open window of the bus. All that I saw was new, yet it appeared old and weary: grandmothers with dyed hair and rouged cheeks, girls in bikinis barely covering their shame, tanned young men guzzling Coca-Cola on water skis.

An old man lay sprawled on the deck of a yacht, warming his rheumatic legs, his white-haired chest open to the sun. He smiled wanly. Nearby, the mistress to whom he had willed his fortune picked at her toes with red fingernails, as certain of her charms as that the sun would rise tomorrow. A dog stood at the stern, gazing haughtily at the yacht's wake, yawning.

It took a long time to reach the end of the line. Once there, I got on another bus. We rode past a pier where freshly caught fish were being weighed. Their bizarre colors, gory skin wounds, glassy eyes, mouths full of congealed blood, sharp pointed teeth—all were evidence of a wickedness as deep as the abyss. Men gutted the fishes with an unholy joy. The bus passed a snake farm, a monkey colony. I saw houses eaten up by termites and a pond of brackish water in which the descendants of the primeval snake crawled and slithered. Parrots screeched with strident voices. At times, strange smells blew in through the bus window, stenches so dense they made my head throb.

Thank God the summer day is shorter in the South than in the

North. Evening fell suddenly, without any dusk. Over the lagoons and highways, so thick no light could penetrate, hovered a jungle darkness. Automobiles, headlamps on, slid forward. The moon emerged extraordinarily large and red; it hung in the sky like a geographer's globe bearing a map not of this world. The night had an aura of miracle and cosmic change. A hope I had never forsaken awoke in me: Was I destined to witness an upheaval in the solar system? Perhaps the moon was about to fall down. Perhaps the earth, tearing itself out of its orbit around the sun, would wander into new constellations.

The bus meandered through unknown regions until it returned to Lincoln Road and the fancy stores, half-empty in summer but still stocked with whatever a rich tourist might desire—an ermine wrap, a chinchilla collar, a twelve-carat diamond, an original Picasso drawing. The dandified salesmen, sure in their knowledge that beyond nirvana pulses karma, conversed among themselves in their air-conditioned interiors. I wasn't hungry; nevertheless, I went into a restaurant where a waitress with a newly bleached permanent served me a full meal, quietly and without fuss. I gave her a half-dollar. When I left, my stomach ached and my head was heavy. The late-evening air, baked by the sun, choked me as I came out. On a nearby building a neon sign flashed the temperature—it was ninety-six, and the humidity almost as much! I didn't need a weatherman. Already, lightning flared in the glowing sky, although I didn't hear thunder. A huge cloud was descending from above, thick as a mountain, full of fire and of water. Single drops of rain hit my bald head. The palm trees looked petrified, expecting the onslaught. I hurried back toward my empty hotel, wanting to get there before the rain; besides, I hoped some mail had come for me. But I had covered barely half the distance when the storm broke. One gush and I was drenched as if by a huge wave. A fiery rod lit up the sky and, the same moment, I heard the thunder crack—a sign the lightning was near me. I wanted to run inside somewhere, but chairs blown from nearby porches somersaulted in front of me, blocking my way. Signs were falling down. The top of a palm tree, torn off by the wind, careened past my feet. I saw a second palm tree sheathed in sackcloth, bent to the wind, ready to kneel. In my confusion I kept on running. Sinking into puddles so deep I almost drowned, I rushed forward with the lightness of boyhood. The danger had made me daring, and I screamed and sang, shouting to the storm in its own key. By this time all traffic had stopped, even the automobiles had been abandoned. But I ran on, determined to escape such madness or else go under. I had to get that special-delivery letter, which no one had written and I never received.

I still don't know how I recognized my hotel. I entered the lobby and stood motionless for a few moments, dripping water on the rug. In the mirror across the room, my half-dissolved image reflected itself like a figure in a cubist painting. I managed to get to the elevator and ride up to the third floor. The door of my room stood ajar: inside, mosquitoes, moths, fireflies, and gnats fluttered and buzzed about, sheltering from the storm. The wind had torn down the mosquito net and scattered the papers I had left on the table. The rugs were soaked. I walked over to the window and looked at the ocean. The waves rose like mountains in the middle of seas—monstrous billows ready once and for all to overflow the shores and float the land away. The waters roared with spite and sprayed white foam into the darkness of the night. The waves were barking at the Creator like packs of hounds. With all the strength I had left, I pulled the window down and lowered the blind. I squatted to put my wet books and manuscripts in order. I was hot. Sweat poured from my body, mingling with rivulets of rain water. I peeled off my clothes and they lay near my feet like shells. I felt like a creature who has just emerged from a cocoon.

III

The storm had still not reached its climax. The howling wind knocked and banged as if with mighty hammers. The hotel seemed like a ship floating on the ocean. Something came off and crashed down—the roof, a balcony, part of the foundation. Iron bars broke. Metal groaned. Windows tore loose from their casements. The window-panes rattled. The heavy blind on my window billowed up as easily as a curtain. The room was lit with the glare of a great conflagration. Then came a clap of thunder so strong I laughed in fear. A white figure materialized from the darkness. My heart plummeted, my brain trembled in its socket. I always knew that sooner or later one of that brood would show himself to me bodily, full of horrors that are never told because no one who has seen them has survived to tell the story. I lay there silently, ready for the end.

Then I heard a voice: "Excuse please, señor, I am much afraid. You are asleep?" It was the Cuban hunchback.

"No, come in," I answered her.

"I shake. I think I die with fear," the woman said. "A hurricane like this never come before. You are the only one in this hotel. Please excuse that I disturb you."

"You aren't disturbing me. I would put on the light but I'm not dressed."

"No, no. It is not necessary. . . . I am afraid to be alone. Please let me stay here until the storm is over."

"Certainly. You can lie down if you want. I'll sit on the chair."

"No, I will sit on the chair. Where is the chair, señor? I do not see it."

I got up, found the woman in the darkness, and led her to the armchair. She dragged herself after me, trembling. I wanted to go to the closet and get some clothing. But I stumbled into the bed and fell on top of it. I covered myself quickly with the sheet so that the stranger would not see me naked when the lightning flashed. Soon after, there was another bolt and I saw her sitting in the chair, a deformed creature in an overlarge nightgown, with a hunched back, disheveled hair, long hairy arms, and crooked legs, like a tubercular monkey. Her eyes were wide with an animal's fear.

"Don't be afraid," I said. "The storm will soon be over."

"Yes, yes."

I rested my head on the pillow and lay still with the eerie feeling that the mocking imp was fulfilling my last wish. I had wanted a hotel to myself—and I had it. I had dreamed of a woman coming, like Ruth to Boaz, to my room—a woman had come. Each time the lightning flashed, my eyes met hers. She stared at me intently, as silent as a witch casting a spell. I feared the woman more than I did the hurricane. I had visited Havana once and, there, found the forces of darkness still in possession of their ancient powers. Not even the dead were left in peace—their bones were dug up. At night I had heard the screams of cannibals and the cries of maidens whose blood was sprinkled on the altars of idolaters. She came from there. I wanted to pronounce an incantation against the evil eye and pray to the spirits who have the final word not to let this hag overpower me. Something in me cried out Shaddai, destroy Satan. Meanwhile, the thunder crashed, the seas roared and broke with watery laughter. The walls of my room turned scarlet. In the hellish glare the Cuban witch crouched low like an animal ready to seize its prey—mouth open, showing rotted teeth; matted hair, black on her arms and legs; and feet covered with carbuncles and bunions. Her nightgown had slipped down, and her wrinkled breasts sagged weightlessly. Only the snout and tail were missing.

I must have slept. In my dream I entered a town of steep, narrow streets and barred shutters, under the murky light of an eclipse, in the silence of a Black Sabbath. Catholic funeral processions followed one after the other endlessly, with crosses and coffins, halberds and burning torches. Not one but many corpses were being carried to the graveyard—a complete tribe annihilated. Incense burned. Moaning voices cried a song of utter grief. Swiftly, the coffins changed and took on the form of phylacteries, black and shiny, with knots and thongs. They divided into many compartments—coffins for twins, quadruplets, quintuplets.

I opened my eyes. Somebody was sitting on my bed—the Cuban woman. She began to talk thickly in her broken English.

"Do not fear. I won't hurt you. I am a human being, not a beast. My back is broken. But I was not born this way. I fell off a table when I was a child. My mother was too poor to take me to the doctor. My father, he no good, always drunk. He go with bad women, and my mother, she work in a tobacco factory. She cough out her lungs. Why do you shake? A hunchback is not contagious. You will not catch it from me. I have a soul like anyone else—men desire me. Even my boss. He trust me and leave me here in the hotel alone. You are a Jew, eh? He is also a Jew . . . from Turkey. He can speak—how do you say it?—Arabic. He marry a German señora, but she is a Nazi. Her first husband was a Nazi. She curse the boss and try to poison him. He sue her but the judge is on her side. I think she bribe him—or give him something else. The boss, he has to pay her—how do you call it?—alimony."

"Why did he marry her in the first place?" I asked, just to say something.

"Well, he love her. He is very much a man, red blood, you know. You have been in love?"

"Yes."

"Where is the señora? Did you marry her?"

"No. They shot her."

"Who?"

"Those same Nazis."

"Uh-huh . . . and you were left alone?"

"No, I have a wife."

"Where is your wife?"

"In New York."

"And you are true to her, eh?"

"Yes, I'm faithful."

"Always?"

"Always."

"One time to have fun is all right."

"No, my dear, I want to live out my life honestly."

"Who cares what you do? No one see."

"God sees."

"Well, if you speak of God, I go. But you are a liar. If I not a cripple, you no speak of God. He punish such lies, you pig!"

She spat on me, then got off the bed, and slammed the door behind her. I wiped myself off immediately, but her spittle burned me as if it were hot. I felt my forehead puffing up in the darkness, and my skin itched with a drawing sensation, as if leeches were sucking my blood. I went into the bathroom to wash myself. I wet a towel for a compress and wrapped it around my forehead. I had forgotten about the hurricane. It had stopped without my noticing. I went to sleep, and when I woke up again it was almost noon. My nose was stopped up, my throat was tight, my knees ached. My lower lip was swollen and had broken out in a large cold sore. My clothes were still on the floor, soaking in a huge puddle. The insects that had come in for refuge the night before were clamped to the wall, dead. I opened the window. The air blowing in was cool, though still humid. The sky was an autumn gray and the sea leaden, barely rocking under its own heaviness. I managed to dress and go downstairs. Behind the desk stood the hunchback, pale, thin, with her hair drawn back, and a glint in her black eyes. She wore an old-fashioned blouse edged with yellowed lace. She glanced at me mockingly. "You have to move out," she said. "The boss call and tell me to lock up the hotel."

"Isn't there a letter for me?"

"No letter."

"Please give me my bill."

"No bill."

The Cuban woman looked at me crookedly—a witch who had failed in her witchcraft, a silent partner of the demons surrounding me and of their cunning tricks.

HUNTER THOMPSON

1937–2005

HUNTER THOMPSON JOINED the Air Force with grand plans of becoming a pilot, but after basic training in Texas and Illinois, his application to become an aviator was rejected. In 1956 he transferred to Eglin Air Force Base in the Florida Panhandle, not far from the Alabama border. It was a great assignment—some of his friends went to the Arctic Circle—and Thompson counted his blessings.

Still, Thompson was Thompson, and even a plum posting did not make him happy. He threw a liquor bottle at a camp guard and earned a reprimand. Bored, Thompson discovered that the base offered night classes at Florida State University and he signed up for a literature course. The director of the program started talking with Thompson about writing and Thompson ended up as the sports editor of the camp newspaper, *The Command Courier*.

He was unqualified for the job, and his work was something of a disaster. There was quite a bit of lying involved—Thompson made up experience he did not have. His spelling was terrible, he often made up words, and he wrote English as if it were a foreign language. But he did get to cover the Eglin Eagles, the base football team. Ordinarily, covering a base football team would not have been a significant achievement, but this team included Bart Starr, Zeke Bratkowski, and Max McGee. The three National Football League greats had been called up to active duty and were sidetracked to the Eglin Eagles. It meant Thompson got to travel the country covering the team—including a victory over Rutgers.

Despite his journalistic limitations, he got a side job as a sports columnist for the Fort Walton Beach newspaper—using a pen name to avoid problems with the Air Force. Still problems with the Air Force were constant. Thompson simply could not bow to authority, clashing frequently with officers. The Air Force wanted Thompson gone, but Thompson did not want a dishonorable discharge. A compromise was reached; the Air Force got rid of a problem and Thompson got his honorable discharge.

Thompson left Florida, returning home to Louisville, but he had found his career—writing. He headed north, taking a job as a sports editor for a tiny Pennsylvania newspaper, then to New York City, where he took classes at Columbia University and worked briefly as a copyboy for *Time* magazine. He was fired by *Time*, predictably for insubordination, then fired by the *Middletown Daily Record*, and ended up in Puerto Rico. He got married and went through several more jobs before ending up in San Francisco just as the city was becoming the center for the hippie culture. His career took off, with articles in leading magazines and his adventures with the Hells Angels.

He returned to Florida in the late 1960s, going to Key West, as far away from Eglin Air Force Base as possible and still remaining in the state. He had a home in Colorado that was always his prime refuge, but as it was for so many writers, Key West became his getaway. Thompson made friends easily in Key West, getting to know Jimmy Buffett and Thomas Mc-Guane. The painter Russell Chatham became a close friend, and the two went fishing together. Thompson found a house on the beach, only a few blocks from Hemingway's former home.

He divorced in 1980 and was usually joined in Key West by Laila Nabulsi, a producer for the hit television show *Saturday Night Live*. The two walked the streets unrecognized, which did not please the attention-craving Thompson. Hunter purchased a bullhorn and used it as a toy, usually to tell people to get off the beach in front of his house. He also called attention to himself by driving his Buick convertible through the streets of Key West, yelling for pedestrians to get out of the way.

Thompson, desperate for money to pay for his divorce and always close to broke, turned to screenwriting in Key West as a way to wealth. He picked up tips on screenwriting from McGuane, who wrote and directed *Ninety-Two in the Shade*, which was set in Key West. Paul Schrader, who wrote *Taxi Driver*, was in Key West to write his *Raging Bull* screenplay and Thompson asked him for tips on writing movies.

Thompson picked drug smuggling in Key West for his subject and on the advice of Schrader, set about writing a "treatment," the outline used to sell a movie to Hollywood studios. Paramount Pictures bought the treatment, called *Cigarette Key*, giving Thompson some money up front. Hunter wrote his script in Buffett's apartment, but after seeing the script the studio killed the project.

He wrote a few magazine pieces while in Key West, one on the Mariel boatlift of 1980 and another on treasure hunter Mel Fisher, but his writing trailed off. Thompson's work had become known as "gonzo journalism," an uncertain term used to describe a writing form where the writer plays a role in the story and objectivity is discarded. The writer draws on his personal experiences and injects himself into the narrative. One of those stories was "The Gonzo Salvage Company," the story of treasure hunting in the Keys.

In 1986, he came back to Key West, intent on carrying out a half-baked idea that only Thompson could embrace. He was going to make a pilot for a television show—perhaps a morning television program—starring himself. He considered a number of titles including "The Gonzo Tour" and "Breakfast with Hunter," the latter being the suggestion of Jack Nicholson.

The crew stayed in Thompson's favorite motel, the Sugar Loaf Lodge on Sugar Loaf Key. Hunter loved the fame and money a television show could bring. Television was hard work, calling for early rising and many re-takes. For Thompson, daybreak came at noon, and even once awakened, he took time to truly rouse himself.

At the end of a week, there was less than two hours of film featuring Thompson. Like so many other things in Thompson's life, this one dissolved.

On February 20, 2005, Thompson was at his home in Colorado when he put a 455-caliber automatic in his mouth and pulled the trigger.

The Gonzo Salvage Company

by Hunter Thompson

The TV is out tonight. The set went black about halfway through "Miami Vice," just as Don Johnson dropped a KGB thug with a single 200-yard shot from his high-tech belly gun.

The storm got serious after that, and the mood in The Keys turned mean. Junk cars crashed in the mango swamps and fishheads whipped on each other with sharkhooks in all-night bars and roadhouses along Highway A1A. These people will tolerate almost anything except being cut off in the middle of "Miami Vice."

On nights like these it is better not to answer the telephone. It can only mean trouble: Some friend has been crushed on the highway by a falling power pole, or it might be the Coast Guard calling to say that your boat was stolen by dope fiends who just called on the radio to say they are sinking somewhere off Sand Key and they've given you as their local credit reference, to pay for the rescue operation.

In my case it was a just-reported shipwreck involving total strangers. An 88-foot tramp motor-sailor called *The Tampa Bay Queen* had gone on the reef in Hawk Channel, and all hands had abandoned ship.

There were only three of them, as it turned out. They had all washed ashore on a ice chest, raving incoherently about green sharks and coral heads and their ship breaking up like a matchbox while they screamed for help on a dead radio.

"Why not?" I thought. We are, after all, in Business—and besides, I had never covered a shipwreck, not even a small one . . . and there was also talk about "losing the cargo" and the cruel imperatives of "salvage rights."

None of this talk seemed worth going out in a storm to investigate at the time, but that is not how The Business works. I went out, and not long after midnight I found myself huddled with these people in a local motel where they'd been given shelter for the night . . . and by dawn I was so deep in the story that I'd hired a 36-foot Cigarette boat to take me and the captain out to his doomed wreck, at first light, so he could recover whatever was left of it.

"We'll have to move quick," he said, "before the cannibals get there. They'll strip her naked by noon."

The sun came up hot and bright that morning. The storm was over and the chop in the channel was down to 3 feet, which means nothing to a fast Cigarette boat. We were running 40 mph by the time we got out of the bay, and about 40 minutes later we were tying up to the wreck of *The Tampa Bay Queen.* It was lying on the bottom, tilted over at a 45-degree angle, and the sea had already broken it open.

There was no hope of saving anything except the new nylon sails and the V-8 engine and six nickel-plated brass winches, which the distraught captain said were worth $5,000 each—and maybe the 80-foot teakwood mast, which would fetch about $100 a foot in Key West, and looked like a thing of beauty.

We climbed up the steep rotted deck and the captain set about slashing down the sails with a butcher knife and ordering the first mate to take a hatchet to the winches. "Never mind a screwdriver," he shouted. "Just rip 'em out by the stumps."

The first mate was in no mood to take orders. He had not been paid in three weeks, he said, and he was wearing fancy black leather pilot's boots with elevator heels and slick leather soles, which caused him to constantly lose his footing and go sliding down the deck. We would hear him scream as he went off, and then there would be a splash. I spent most of my time pulling him back up the deck, and finally we lashed him to the mast with a steel safety cable, which allowed him to tend to his work.

By this time I had worked up a serious sweat, and the mystique of this filthy shipwreck had long since worn off. The captain was clearly a swine and the first mate was a middle-aged bellboy from New Jersey and the ship was probably stolen . . . But here I was out on the high sea with these people, doing manual labor in the morning and bleeding from every knuckle. It was time, I felt, for a beer.

I was moving crabwise along the deck, homing in on the cooler we'd left in the Cigarette boat, when I saw the scavengers coming in. They had been circling the wreck for a while, two half-naked thugs in a small skiff, and the captain had recognized them instantly.

"God help us now," he muttered. "Here they come. These are the ones I was worried about." He looked nervously out at the two burly brutes in the cannibal boat, and he said he could see in their eyes that they were getting ready to board us and claim the whole wreck for themselves.

"It won't be much longer," he said. "These bastards are worse than pirates. We may have to fight for it."

I shrugged and moved off toward the beer cooler, at the other end of the wreck. The captain was obviously crazy, and I had lost my feel for The Story. All I wanted was a cold can of beer.

By the time I got to the Cigarette boat, however, the thugs had made their move and were tying up alongside us, grinning like wolves as they crouched between me and the cooler. I stared down at them and swore never again to answer my phone after midnight.

"Was this your boat?" one of them asked. "We heard you whimpering all night on the radio. It was a shame."

The next few minutes were tense, and by the end of that time I had two new partners and my own marine salvage business. The terms of the deal were not complex, and the spirit was deeply humane.

The captain refused to cooperate at first, screeching hoarsely from the other end of the wreck that he had silent partners in Tampa who would soon come back and kill all of us. . . .

But you hear a lot of talk like that in The Keys, so we ignored him and drank all the beer and hammered out a three-way agreement that would give the captain until sundown to take anything he wanted, and after that the wreck would be ours.

It was the Law of the Sea, they said. Civilization ends at the waterline. Beyond that, we all enter the food chain, and not always right at the top.

The captain seemed to understand, and so did I. He would be lucky to get back to shore with anything at all, and I had come close to getting my throat slit.

It was almost dark when we dropped him off on the dock, where he quickly sold out to a Cuban for $5,000 in cash. Mother ocean had prevailed once again, and I was now in the marine salvage business.

RUSSELL BANKS

1940–

RUSSELL BANKS WAS 18 when he first came to Florida—a young man with a mission. He hoped to join up with Fidel Castro, then fighting in the jungles of Cuba, months away from taking Havana, driving dictator Fulgencio Batista from power, and becoming the nation's prime minister. Banks dropped out of Colgate University to join Castro, but never got closer to Cuba than south Florida. "I was a New England kid, coming out of that world. All of a sudden I could smell the Gulf Stream. There were palm trees, and people who didn't look like me, sound like me. Half a century later, I still get off the airplane and feel the same rush, that same hit," he once said.

He worked a bit, moving furniture at a St. Petersburg hotel, decorating windows in a Lakeland department store, and getting married—the first of four times—before entering the University of North Carolina. He went on to achieve world-wide fame, not as a revolutionary, but as an author. He has always kept his bond with Florida, including using Florida as a backdrop for many of his writings. His wrote the classic *Continental Drift* in 1985, which combines two plots: In one, a New Englander heads for Florida to make his mark (similar to Banks), and the second tells of a Haitian who also comes to Florida seeking opportunity.

Two of his books, *Affliction* and *The Sweet Hereafter*, became movies. I lis success enabled him to buy a condo overlooking Biscayne Bay, a far cry from his revolutionary days. He also has a New England home, close to the Canadian border—saying he likes the two extremes.

His condominium overlooks the Julia Tuttle Causeway, which connects Miami Beach to the mainland. In 2007 he read articles in *The Miami Herald* about sex offenders who live under the causeway because state law says they cannot live within 2,500 feet of children—an almost impossible task in a crowded city.

In his books Banks is drawn to those who live on the edge, and his novel about the sex offenders, *Lost Memory of Skin*, fits the pattern well. Only Banks would write sympathetically about the problems faced by a group of outcasts. The book focuses on a twenty-two-year-old boy who was declared a sex offender, even though he was a virgin. He had used the

Internet to make a date with a person he thought was a fourteen-year-old girl, who turned out to be a police officer. As Banks found out in three years of research, the term "sex offender" is a huge umbrella covering everything from true sexual predators prone to violence, to men caught urinating behind a building.

Banks became so associated with Florida that when the *Conde Nast Traveler* magazine was assembling its *Book of Unforgettable Journeys*, Banks wrote the essay about Florida. The result was "Primal Dreams," a beautiful story about the Everglades National Park and the ongoing battle to save it.

Primal Dreams

by Russell Banks

When you come into Miami International Airport from Newark, as I recently did, and drive south and west for two hours on Florida's Turnpike, you have to travel through the end of the twentieth century in North America. Condos and malls and housing developments, like orange-capped mushrooms, spring up from horizon to horizon.

Fast-food outlets, trailer parks, used-car lots with banners crackling in the breeze, and in Homestead the lingering wreckage of Hurricane Andrew—stripped live oak trees, decapitated palms, boarded-up buildings, temporary housing—give way to tomato and sugarcane fields, where migrant workers from Jamaica and Mexico toil under the subtropical sun. It's the inescapable present.

But then, suddenly, you drive through the entrance to Everglades

National Park, and it's as if you've passed through a gate into another time altogether, a distant, lost time aeons before the arrival of the first Europeans, before even the rumored arrival of the Arawak in dugouts fleeing the Caribbean archipelago and the invading Caribs.

Out on the Anhinga Trail, barely beyond earshot of the cars and RVs lumbering toward the lodge and marina in Flamingo at the southern end of the park, the only sounds you hear are the wind riffling through the saw grass, the plash of fish feeding on insects and on one another, and the great long-necked anhingas diving or emerging from the mahogany waters of a sluggish, seaward-moving slough.

You hear a hundred frogs cheeping and croaking and the sweet wet whistle of a red-winged blackbird. A primeval six-foot-long alligator passes silently through the deep slough to the opposite side, coasts to a stop in the shallows, and lurks, a corrugated log with eyes. An anhinga rises from the water and flies, like a pterodactyl, to a cluster of nearby mangrove roots and cumbrously spreads and turns its enormous wings, glistening black kites silhouetted against the noontime sun.

A rough carpet of water lilies—clenched, fist-sized buds about to bloom—floats on the surface of the slough, while just below, long-nosed gars luff in threes and fours and bass and bluegills collect in schools, abundant and wary of the next upper link in the food chain, but strangely secure, like carp in a Japanese pool, as if here they have no unnatural enemies. And they don't. A large soft-shell turtle hauls herself out of the water and patiently begins to lay her dozens of eggs in the gray limestone soil, depositing them like wet vanilla-colored seeds. Farther down the embankment lies the wreckage of an old nest broken open by birds, the leathery shells smashed and drying in the sun. A dark blue racer snake slides into the brush. Mosquitoes gather in slow, buzzing swirls. The sun is high, and it's hot, ninety degrees, with a slight breeze blowing from the east. It's mid-May, yes—but what century?

In our time, much of travel that is freely elected by the traveler is time-travel. We go to Paris, tour Venice, visit Athens and the Holy Land, mainly to glimpse the past and walk about the cobbled streets with a guidebook and a furled umbrella—emulating as best we can Henry James in Rome, Flaubert in Cairo. Or we fly to Tokyo, Beijing, Brasilia, perhaps, for a safe, cautious peek into the future. Sometimes, for both the past and the future at once, we make our way to cities such as Lagos, Mexico City, Lima. It's time-travel, but it's strictly to the past and future of humanity that we've gone.

For some of us, that's not enough. We want to travel even farther in time, to view and imagine anew the planet earth without billions of human beings on it. For this we get up an expedition and float down the Amazon on a raft, or we go off to Africa and clone ourselves a Teddy Roosevelt safari, this time shooting off to the Arctic or to un-inhabited deserts or to mountaintops—alone, more or less, and view the planet as it was before we started killing it.

But who can afford that? Who has the time? With only a week or two available and a modest amount of cash in hand, most of us are obliged to look for places closer to home. For me, when in search of this type of time-travel, one of the most satisfying places to go is the Florida Everglades. The reasons are many and complex. First off, and of no small importance, the Everglades is easy to get to, especially for a traveler living in the eastern United States. The park is a smooth seventy-mile drive from downtown Miami. And it is vast in size; you can get lost there. It is the second-largest national park in the Lower 48—2,200 square miles, an area approximately the size of Delaware. And despite its proximity to one of the most densely populated regions of America, it is, for its size, one of the least-visited parks in the system, especially from April to November, so you can be alone there, or nearly so.

But more to the point, every time I climb into my time machine (usually an air-conditioned rental car picked up at the Miami International Airport) and travel into the Everglades, I journey to a place that has a shivering personal resonance for me. I almost always go by myself. It's less distracting that way, and I don't want to be distracted, because, once there, my imagination is instantly touched at its center and all the world seems significant and personalized, as in a powerful dream. It's my dreamtime, and I don't want anyone, even someone I love and trust, to wake me.

Most people, if they're lucky, have a place or two where this happens, but for me it occurs in the Everglades. Who knows why? Childhood visions of pre-Columbian Florida and the Caribbean, maybe, induced by hagiographic stories of Columbus, DeSoto, and that master of time-travelers, Ponce de Leon, in which I helplessly identified with the wide-eyed European explorers. Followed years later by adolescent pilgrimages to the Keys in naive search of Ernest Hemingway's source of inspiration—as vain an enterprise as Ponce's, of course, but who knew that then?

And then, over the years, repeated visits to the Glades, by accidental or casual circumstances, building up a patina of personal associations, until now I always enter the park with an expectance based on nostalgia for a lost self-nostalgia for the New England boy reading about the Arawak and Columbus, for the youth trying to become a novelist, for the reckless young man footloose in South Florida.

And it's an expectancy that is almost always met. I park my time machine and walk out onto the Anhinga or the Gumbo Limbo trail, step by step moving along on the catwalk of my own personal time line. I keep going back, and with increasing clarity, I see more of the place and more of my past selves. And more of the past of the planet as well.

Beyond any other national park, perhaps, the Everglades bears repeated visits, justifying a traveler's return trips, but maybe requiring them too. Without intending it, over the years I've acquired from these visits a gradual accumulation of information—about my layered self, I suppose, and, more important, about the place—which has helped me learn to look at the Everglades and see it for what it is instead of for what it isn't.

The first few times I didn't get it. There are no high mountains, no rushing cataracts, no grand panoramic vistas. There's no rain forest, no powerful continent-draining rivers, no rocky seashore. No, the Glades is quiet and low and slow, a shallow, almost invisible river of grass, an intricate, extremely fragile subtropical ecosystem that seems shy and difficult of access to the human eye, which is, of course, one of the reasons humans have come so close to destroying it—and may yet succeed.

To see the Everglades for what it is and not what it isn't, however, you have to develop a kind of bifocal vision, as if you were floating down the Mississippi on a raft with Huck Finn. You have to learn to switch your gaze constantly from the concrete to the abstract, from the nearby riverbank to the distant sky. You need an almost Thoreauvian eye for detail and the interrelatedness of nature's minutiae, for it is a 1.5-million-acre Walden Pond we're talking about here, the largest wetland in the United States. From November through May there are between fifty thousand and a hundred thousand wading birds in the Everglades.

More than one hundred species of butterflies have been identified in the park. Fifty species of reptiles, including twenty-six species of snakes and sixteen of turtles. Eighteen species of amphibians. Three hundred forty-seven species of birds. Forty species of mammals. More than one thousand species of plants. There are fifty-two varieties of the live oaks along the short Gumbo Limbo Trail, where, as you stroll, you can catch the skunklike smell of white stopper buds opening, used in ancient times by the Arawak and the first white settlers as a specific against dysentery.

The Gumbo Limbo Trail winds through great twisted old live oak trees with epiphytes and bromeliads clinging to the trunks and upper branches and dead-looking brown resurrection ferns at the roots that burst greenly into life after a rain. The trail is circular and begins and ends at the hundred-foot-tall royal palms of Paradise Key. The key is a hammock, a gentle, almost imperceptible rise in the blond, watery plain, more like a solidified limestone sea swell than an actual key or island. The majestic palms, which these days tower photogenically in front of Miami hotels and cluster around the old Bebe Rebozo compound of Key Biscayne and a thousand other estates, appeared first on the continent here in the Everglades, their seed carried by wind and water from the Caribbean thousands of years ago to catch and eventually prosper on this very hammock.

A short way off the trail, I notice a small, still pool of water covered with bright green slime—duckweed—which, seen up close, turns into a glistening skin, as clean and beautiful and serene as snakeskin over the dark, turbulent, fecund water below. I lean down and look closer and imagine I can see into the thrashing molecular soup of life itself.

But the swarming details of the Everglades can overwhelm you. It's almost too much to absorb and organize. In this finely delineated and particularized landscape, to gain perspective you have to step away from time to time and abstract it. Thus, along with Thoreau's eye, you need to develop an almost Melvillean appreciation for the vast circular canopy of blue that stretches unbroken from horizon to horizon and the broad watery swale under your feet. It's as if you are at sea and are standing upon a shimmering grassy plain that floats like the Sargasso between the firmament above and the firmament below.

The light is spectacular and shifts constantly, as clouds build and dissipate and build again. But the intensity of the light and its movement are dizzying. And to steady yourself, you shift your gaze almost involuntarily back to what's close at hand, clinging to it as if to the rail of a ship. In so abstract a landscape, to ground yourself you have to look again at the details.

And so it goes—back and forth, the long view and the short, the abstract and the concrete—for here you are situated in an infinitely complex world whose parts, and the tissue of connections between them, can be seen only if the viewer keeps shifting his focal point. By comparison, the city of man, from nearby Miami to distant Calcutta, seems stilled, frozen, caught in a snapshot in relatively recent time, and serving either as all foreground or all background, with no movement between them. The central figure, the subject, is always us; humanity is the figure and the ground; we are content as well as context. In the Everglades, the central figure is the ancient planet itself and its immense plenitude.

Sometimes, instead of visiting the southern end of the Everglades, I drive out from Miami along Route 41, the old Tamiami Trail, cross through the Miccosukee Indian Reservation, pass the airboat rentals (banned inside the park but ready to rent all around it) and the solitary fishermen sitting by the canals built by the Army Corps of Engineers, to reach the north side of the park and spend the day at Shark Valley.

It's less a valley than a broad, shallow slough twelve miles wide, a one-to-three-foot-deep scimitar-shaped depression in the limestone bedrock that carries the overflow from Lake Okeechobee in a tectonically slow drift south and west at barely one hundred feet per day, sliding the fresh, nutrient-rich waters across the saw grass plain to the mangrove estuaries of the Gulf of Mexico. Out here, South Florida seems freshly emerged from the ocean, still dripping and draining back into the Gulf, as if the Ice Age had ended only yesterday. Its highest point is barely eight feet above sea level, but from it you can see for miles.

At the Shark Valley Visitors Center there's an open rubber-tired tram that carts tourists into the Glades a ways, with a Park Service guide on a loudspeaker who'll describe what you're seeing. But there's also a bike-rental shop and a fifteen-mile bike path to an observation tower and numerous trails where you can walk in silence. In a half hour, I'm under the hot May sun a few miles out on the bicycle path, pedaling a wobbly old one-speed bike I rented next to the visitors center. I'm finally far enough into the Glades that I can no longer hear the visitors or their cars and RVs or the guide on the tram, so I pull off the path and stop.

Purple pickerelweed is flowering everywhere, and bladderwort, like yellow stars, blooms against the dark water of the slough. Deer-flies cruise by and then swerve hungrily back toward me, a new warm-blooded mammal, and hairless, too. All I can hear now is the sound of the links of the food chain clanking. Herons and egrets stand knee-deep in water, waiting motionless, like the fishermen I saw earlier on the Tamiami Trail alongside the canal, and now and then I hear the splash of a gar or a bass busting into the air for a low-flying dragonfly. For a long time, without making a ripple, a six-foot alligator on the far side of the slough stalks a spindly white egret, drawing closer and closer, undetected, until suddenly there is a great, furious roil and splash of water, then feathers floating, and silence as the gator slides away.

Later, out at the observation tower, I pause halfway up and look down, and in the copse below, a rust-colored fawn with pale spots across its belly lies curled and hidden by its mother. Intent only on protecting her offspring from the huge gator snoozing in the slough fifty feet away, she obviously has not considered aerial reconnaissance, especially by a human. Down below, the fawn is as still as a statue in the cool shade of the copse, and lovely, but I feel oddly invasive for watching and quickly resume climbing to the top of the tower. There I gaze out across the watery, veldlike plain of saw grass, where in the west I can make out a bank of cumulus clouds piling up over the Gulf near Everglades City, promising rain. For a moment I consider hurry-ing back to the car, but then decide no, let the rain come down. And within the hour it does, and as I walk my rented bike the eight miles back to the visitors center, I find myself feeling finally invisible, lost in time and space, afloat inside a dream of a lost and coherent world.

Crossing Shark Valley by foot in the warm torrential rain, it's almost inconceivable somehow that my points of departure—Newark, New Jersey, and Miami, Florida—are in the same time zone as the Everglades. Not just longitudinally, as on a map, but literally, as on a calendar or a wristwatch.

Here and in Newark and Miami, today's headlines and stock quotes are the same, the historical facts still hold, and thus all three places bear, at least abstractly, the same relation to the onrushing millennium, to its ethnic cleansings, genocidal massacres, famines, global floods of refugees, children gunning each other down with automatic weapons, wanton destruction of the planet—everything that drives a modern man or woman nearly mad with grief and despair, so that finally all one wants is to get out of this time zone. "Anywhere, so long as it's out of this world," said Baudelaire. And here I am, out of that world. Astonishing!

Later in the day, after the rain has passed east toward Miami and the Atlantic, I drive out on Route 41 to Everglades City in the northwest corner of the Everglades, where there is another visitors center and a marina located at the entrance to the Ten Thousand Islands, a huge chain of mangrove islands that stretches about forty miles from Marco Island in the north to Pavilion Key. It was Ponce de Leon who guessed there were ten thousand islands, but the modern count, via satellite, is 14,022. The number keeps changing, because most of the "islands," even those several miles across, are built on clustered red mangroves and are constantly being broken apart and restructured by hurricanes.

It's close to five o'clock, though midafternoon bright at this time of year. The sky is washed clean of clouds, and the still surface of the cordovan-colored waters of Chokoloskee Bay is glazed with a taut silvery skin. In these calm tidal waters there is an abundance of snook, tarpon, redfish, blue crabs, and bottlenose dolphins, feeding, breeding, and being preyed upon by each other, by the thousands of cormorants, ospreys, cranes, pelicans, egrets, and ibis that flock year-round on the mangrove islets and rookeries, and by the sport and commercial fishermen from the tiny villages of Everglades City and Chokoloskee as well.

They're not preyed upon in such numbers as to endanger them yet—except, of course, for the elusive mysterious manatee, that fifty-million-year-old watery relative to the elephant, a seagoing cow with flippers. The manatees are protected, but their death rate may exceed their birth rate. These gentle two-thousand-pound animals are being decimated and cruelly wounded by the propellers of the fishing and pleasure boats that roar up and down the waterways here. Nine out of ten of the remaining eighteen hundred manatees bear ugly prop scars on their smooth backs. But there are about 700,000 registered power-boats in Florida, and, thanks to persistent lobbying in Tallahassee by the owners, there are no speed limits in these peaceful, secluded waters.

The boats race along the thousands of interlaced channels and crisscross the myriad of unnamed bays at thirty to fifty miles an hour, chopping through anything too slow or confused by the noise to get out of the way. Generally the manatees keep to the channels among the islands, feeding on sea grass in waters so darkened by the tannin from the roots and dead leaves of the red mangrove that the animal cannot see the bottom of the boat approaching; nor can it hear the roar of the motor until the boat is nearly on top of it, and thus cannot flee in time to elude death or maiming.

There's enough daylight left to tempt me to rent a canoe at the visitors center, and I push out into the Chokoloskee Bay and paddle slowly along one of the scores of channels that cut into and around Sandfly Island in the general direction of the Turner River Canoe Trail, the start of the Wilderness Waterway that winds for ninety-nine miles through the most extensive mangrove forest in America, all the way to Flamingo and Florida Bay in the south. All I want today, however, is a few hours of solitude on the water, a closer look than was available onshore at the cormorants and frigate birds and the tricolor Louisiana heron I glimpsed heading low over the bay toward Sandfly Island.

Halfway out, barely a quarter mile from shore, a pod of bottle-nose dolphins, maybe four or five, swimming a short way off my bow, notice the canoe and slice through the water to investigate, their dorsal fins racing toward me like black knife blades. After circling the intruder several times, they move off again, apparently satisfied or bored, but the last in the pod—an adolescent probably—makes a show-off's grinning leap. It practically stands on the water and plops over, splashing me and rocking the canoe, and then cruises back to join the others.

I move out into the bay another half mile and notice that atop many of the channel markers, ospreys have built their nests, turning the poles into tall, branchless trees. They are incredibly stable birds, mating for life (fifteen to twenty years), and they use the same nest year after year. Off to my right a ways, one of the smaller islands has been converted into a rookery by a huge flock of fork-tailed frigate birds. There seems to be a great flurry of activity, so I paddle over. Fifty or more parent frigate birds are huddling protectively over their fuzzy gray hatchlings, while another fifty make a great racket and fight off dozens of predatory, sharp-beaked cormorants screeching and hungrily diving for the offspring. I draw near in my canoe and watch the fight for a long while, an invisible witness to a savage siege and great acts of parental courage and sacrifice.

To see what's there, most national parks get you up high on a mountain or make you gape into a canyon or a gorge, playing with scale and fostering delusions of human grandeur without your even having to leave your car. "This car climbed Pikes Peak, Whiteface Mountain, Mount Washington," and so on. In the Everglades, though, you're kept on the same plane as the natural world. You can't see the Everglades at all, really, unless you get close up and keep it at eye level, which humbles you a bit. ("This car drove through the Everglades" is not much of a claim.) This sort of viewing is interactive, and your travel backward in time to the continent's beginnings is all the more convincing for it.

It's especially true for us Americans—we whose present is too much with us, whose future looks worse, and whose past is increasingly paved over or deliberately erased—that, for our emotional and intellectual well-being, for our moral health as well, time-travel has become more essential than ever. Maybe it's this need that explains the growing popularity and proliferation of historical theme parks, the desire to build a Disney World near a Civil War battlefield, for instance, or the whole Jurassic Park concept, which surely, as much as the animated dinosaurs, accounts for the extraordinary popularity of the movie.

It's the idea of safe passage to the distant past that appeals. (One wonders, is that what's behind the success of *The Flintstones?*) This idea may also account for the rapidly increasing popularity of our national parks. The total number of visitors is up ten percent overall in the last decade, and it's much greater in some parks (seventy percent in Yosemite, for instance), bringing, especially in those located within easy striking distance of urban areas, traffic jams, environmental damage, graffiti, crime—all the woes of life in the here and now that we're trying to escape.

The Everglades, which in an odd way is more demanding of its visitors' imaginations than most other parks, has not yet suffered as they have. The greatest danger to the Glades comes from outside the park, from the agriculture industry and real estate developers who for generations have been blocking and draining off its freshwater sources in central and southeastern Florida for human use and polluting the rest with chemical fertilizers and runoff. In recent years, the National Park Service, the state of Florida, and the U.S. Army Corps of Engineers have begun cooperating to restore the old flow of water from Okeechobee as much as possible and to control with great rigor the amount of pollution allowed to enter the system.

In May of this year [1994], Florida governor Lawton Chiles signed the Everglades Forever Act, a complicated, expensive compromise between the environmentalists and the agricultural interests, brokered with the assistance of Interior Secretary Bruce Babbitt.

The bill requires the state to construct forty thousand acres of filtration marshes around Lake Okeechobee at a cost of $700 million, with the farmers paying a third of the costs and the rest coming from Florida taxpayers. No one is happy with the deal, which suggests that it's as good a deal as anyone is going to get right now. This act sets a temporary clean-water goal of fifty parts of phosphorus per billion parts of water while delaying a final goal for up to ten more years, which means that the pollution from chemical fertilizers, though diminished, will nonetheless continue. It's a start, but saving the Everglades is an ongoing, extremely costly fight, and for some species it may be too late. A Florida panther, for instance, whose numbers have dwindled to less than thirty, was recently found dead inside the park, and its body contained mercury at a level that would kill a human being.

The sky in the west fades to pale rose. Ragged silver-blue strips of cloud along the horizon glow red at the edges, as if about to burst into flame. I turn my canoe back toward the marina and am paddling fairly energetically now, for I don't want to get caught out here after dark among ten thousand islands and ten million mosquitoes. You could easily get lost in this maze of channels and not be found for days and be extremely ill by then. I'm reluctant to leave this primeval world, however. Once again, the peaceful, impersonal beauty of the Everglades has soothed and nourished my mind and heart and has restored some of the broken connections to my layered selves and memories. It's time, however, to return to the city of man.

Then suddenly, a few yards ahead of my canoe, I see a swelling disturbance in the water. It smooths and rises, and the water parts and spills, as first one, then two large, sleek-backed, pale gray manatees surface and exhale gusts of mist into the air. They slowly roll and dive, but a second later they reappear, and this time there is a calf the size of a dolphin nestled safely between them. I can hear the three animals inhaling huge quantities of air, and then they dive again and are gone. The water seethes and settles and is still. A low-flying pelican cruises down the channel ahead of me and disappears in the dusk.

For a long time I sit there in my canoe, thrilled by the memory of the sight, feeling unexpectedly, undeservedly blessed. Jurassic Park, indeed. This is the real thing! For a few wondrous seconds, a creature from the Paleocene has let me enter its world and has come close enough almost to touch. It's as if the old planet earth itself contained a virtue, a profound generosity of spirit, that has allowed it to reach forward in time all the way to the end of the twentieth century in North America, and has brought me into its embrace.

CARL HIAASEN

1953–

H IS GRANDFATHER—ALSO NAMED Carl—came from Norway, one of millions of immigrants who flocked to the United States, settling in the Dakotas, a prime gathering place for Scandinavians. The government offered free land, 160 acres to anyone who would work the land for five years.

It was another land rush that brought the grandfather to Florida, the chance to make a fortune in the Florida land boom of the 1920s. The prices kept going up, and the possibilities seemed unlimited. He settled in south Florida, the heart of the land boom, and opened a law office, representing the land buyers and sellers who were changing the face of Florida.

Carl's son, Odel, joined him in the law firm, and in 1953, Odel's son, Carl, was born in Plantation. Although he was named for his grandfather, the two came to have far different views about land development in Florida.

The Plantation of his childhood featured open spaces and plenty of trees and brush. As Hiaasen grew up, he could see the open spaces as trees gave way to the developers.

He began writing in high school, producing a satirical newspaper called "More Trash," and found he could make people laugh. He was seventeen when he married his high school girlfriend. Then he went to Emory University for two years and graduated from the University of Florida. With his degree in journalism, he started working at a small newspaper in Cocoa, Florida. Two years later, he moved to the state's largest newspaper, *The Miami Herald*, and three years later, he joined the newspaper's investigative team.

A friend at the *Herald*, William Montalbano, suggested that the two of them write a book, and it led to three novels. The duo might have continued cranking out books, but his friend went to China as a foreign correspondent, and Hiaasen began to write books on his own.

In 1986, he wrote *Tourist Season*, an instant hit, about a newspaper columnist who rails against development in Florida, then resorts to terrorism to stop the growth.

More best sellers followed including *Double Whammy* and *Skin Tight*.

While he continued to write his column for the *Herald*, he spent less and less time in the *Herald* newsroom and more time at home writing books—three columns a week became one column a week.

His book *Striptease* became an unsuccessful movie. One reviewer wrote that the movie was a "muddled and dumbed-down adaptation of Carl Hiaasen's bitingly funny book." It did produce a great poster featuring a naked but carefully covered Demi Moore.

He and his wife, Connie, divorced in 1996 after a quarter century of marriage, and Hiaasen moved to Islamorada in the Florida Keys. While the Keys have become home to scores of writers, Hiaasen was not a member of the hard-drinking, hard-partying group who called the Keys home. Instead of a night of drinking and carousing, Hiaasen would go to a restaurant and read as he ate dinner. The restaurant manager, Fenia Clizer, noticed him and noted that he was not the typical customer the restaurant attracted. They married and moved to Vero Beach.

Hiaasen is blessed. Like Damon Runyon and Edna Buchanan, he is helped out by the facts of life in Miami to keep his writing fresh. Any time a writer in south Florida gets writer's block, there is certain to be a body to wash up on shore, a politician caught in a cheap motel with someone other than his wife, or a scam so bizarre it provides a writer with inspiration.

Hiaasen has continued to write about the environment. Both in his novels and column he has railed at those who would destroy it. In 1995, he wrote an essay about the condition of environmental decline of Florida Bay for *Sports Illustrated*.

The Last Days of Florida Bay
by Carl Hiaasen

On a gum-gray June afternoon, between thundershowers, my son and I are running a 17-foot skiff through the backcountry of Florida Bay. The wind has lain down, the water is silk. Suddenly, a glorious eruption: bottle-nosed dolphins, an acre of them, in a spree of feeding, play and rambunctious lust. From a hundred yards we can hear the slap of flukes and the hiss of blowholes. We can see the misty geysers, the slash of black dorsals, the occasional detonation as a luckless bait fish gets gobbled.

No matter how often I witness the sight, I'm always dazzled. A stranger to these waters could only assume he was traveling in authentic wilderness, pure and thriving. If only it were so.

It's easy, when surrounded by dolphins, to forget that the bay is fatefully situated downstream from the ulcerous sprawl of Florida's Gold Coast. Four-and-a-half million people live only a morning's drive away.

The river that feeds the backcountry is the Everglades, sometimes parched and sometimes flooded. Water that once ran untainted and bountiful is now intercepted and pumped extravagantly to sugarcane fields, swimming pools, golf courses, city reservoirs—and even the Atlantic. What's left is dispensed toward the bay in a criminally negligent fraction of its natural flow. The water isn't as clean as it once was, and it doesn't always arrive in the right season.

That the bay is sick is hardly a surprise. The wonder is that it has survived so long and the dolphins haven't fled to sea forever.

I fell in love with the Florida Keys by staring at a road map. I was about five years old. My grandfather was a storyteller, and my father was a sportfisherman, and I had listened to their exciting tales long enough. I wanted them to take me.

Outdoor magazines extolled the Keys as jewels or gems or a string of pearls dangling languidly from the continental flank. From the map I memorized the islands transected by U.S. 1. They had lyrical, funky names—Sugarloaf, Saddlebunch, Ramrod, Big Coppitt, Lower Matecumbe. To a boy growing up on the steamy, iron-flat apron of the Everglades, it seemed fantastic that an exotic undersea paradise existed only three hours away—maybe less, the way my dad could drive.

This I already knew: The Keys were surrounded by water—the Atlantic, the Gulf of Mexico, Florida Bay—and the water was blue, by god. All you had to do was look at the map.

Except the map was misleading, as I discovered when we rode down the Overseas Highway, me in the backseat, my father and grandfather up front. The water of the Keys was beyond a map printer's blue; it was a preternatural spray of indigo, emerald, turquoise and violet. And the hues changed with each passing cloud.

Another thing I knew about the Keys: The great Ted Williams lived there! In certain sporting circles he was more revered for his fly-casting than for his batting. Riding through Islamorada, I pressed my face to the window in hopes of glimpsing the legendary slugger. He was bound to be at one of the charter docks or tackle shops, grinning that newsreel grin, posing for snapshots next to a gaping 100-pound tarpon.

It was a much different era, before Jet Skis and time-shares and traffic signals came to the Keys. Now they're trying to four-lane U.S. 1 all the way from Florida City to Key Largo. Ted Williams has moved away, and the water isn't always as blue as it should be. Florida Bay is a thousand square miles of hard-bottom shallows, grassy banks and mangrove islands that stretch from the Upper Keys to the rim of the Gulf of Mexico. On low tide the flats become exposed, pungent and crunchy, revealing the labyrinth of spidery ditches by which the backcountry must be navigated. Casual boaters seldom venture here more than once. Getting beached on the banks is no fun; getting lost can be worse. Despite its smooth and placid face, the backcountry sometimes roils to a murderous fury.

In 1948 a promising young jockey named Albert Snider won the Flamingo Stakes at Hialeah. To celebrate he and some friends took a fishing trip to Florida Bay. They anchored their yacht off a small island named Sandy Key.

Snider and two pals got in a rowboat to go redfishing. They were still within sight of the yacht at dusk when a storm blew up out of nowhere. The next morning the Coast Guard launched an extensive air-and-sea search, which lasted for days. Snider and his companions were never found. The racing world was shocked. Snider's mount in the Flamingo, a horse named Citation, was given to one of Snider's best friends, a rider named Arcaro.

That year Citation won the Triple Crown, and the famous jockey gave part of his winnings to Snider's widow. Eddie Arcaro had considered joining his buddy on that fishing trip to Florida Bay but had gone to Santa Anita instead.

Historically the backcountry has belonged to fishermen, smugglers, poachers, bootleggers, fugitives and the occasional professional adventurer. Its gallant snook and tarpon attracted Zane Grey in the 1920s; its imposing eagles, ospreys and herons caught the artistic eye of John James Audubon in the 1830s.

Early this century, plume hunters in Florida Bay wiped out many thousands of wading birds because rich ladies on Park Avenue fancied white feathers in their hats. When the law cracked down and plumed hats went out of style, the egret and heron populations slowly rebounded—only to be ravaged again as wetlands dried up, victimized by drought and greedy water "management" practices. Today most of the backcountry lies within the boundaries of Everglades National Park, so the birds, manatees and crocodiles enjoy a modest degree of protection. The water itself is under no such stewardship.

The decline of Florida Bay has spanned the terms of several park superintendents, who have displayed widely varying degrees of concern and influence. Blame must also be assigned to the state of Florida. It boasts strict pollution laws for rivers and coastlines, but enforcement is a farce in the Everglades, which is used as both a cistern and a sewer by industry and agriculture. By the time freshwater reaches the bay, scientists can do little but draw samples and hope for the best.

To be sure, some of the bay's natural spectacles still appear unharmed by man: A fire flash of roseate spoonbills high in the black mangroves. Or the sparkle of jittery bonefish tails among mangrove shoots at dawn. Or a steep tannic creek so teeming with snappers that you can't see the bottom for the fish.

Here's the heart of the riddle: How can the backcountry look so robust in some places and so moribund in others? How can it change so fast? One day the water is as clear as gin; the next it's like chowder.

Nobody truly knows why. The maddening riddle is now pursued by biologists, ecologists, hydrologists and a wagonload of other Ph.D.'s. Cheering them on are business leaders, tourism promoters and once indifferent politicians.

Not so long ago only fishermen and a handful of scientists gave a damn. One of the first to spot the trouble was captain Hank Brown, a dean among the guides of the Upper Keys. Impassioned but quiet-spoken, Brown has spent more time in the backcountry—roughly 8,000 days—than all the attending academics combined. "The only thing I have going for me," he says, "is that I look at it every day."

In the late 1980s Brown noticed patches of turtle grass dying in the western and central parts of the bay. Soon entire banks went bald, and the water turned muddy. The effect upon backcountry fishing, a major industry of the Keys, was instantaneous.

Flycasting for tarpon, permit and bonefish depends on relatively clear water. Hard-core anglers won't pay $325 a day to flail blindly in the mud. They want to see their quarry; it's the essence of the sport, an indescribable high. As the backcountry got murky, Brown and other guides began losing clients to the still-crystal flats of the Bahamas, Belize and Mexico.

In the fall of 1990, Florida Bay suffered a staggering fish kill in Garfield Bight and other coves. Administrators of Everglades National Park showed scant interest in the problem until Brown and others began directing the media to the scene. For a place that depends on tourism, the only thing worse than the sight of bloated rotten fish is front-page headlines about bloated rotten fish. The kill was investigated. Lack of oxygen was blamed but not explained.

But by far the most shocking symptom of the bay's collapse was the massive floating clouds of algae that seemed to bloom wherever the sea grasses died. Phytoplankton mixed with wind-stirred sediments to transform healthy water into a bilious, rank-smelling broth. "First came the turbidity," Brown recalls. "Then the grass died. Then the root systems disintegrated, and the banks of the channels literally caved in."

In 29 years on the water he had never seen anything so ominous. Hank and his wife, Joy, videotaped the fish kills and the rotting sea grasses and sent out copies on cassettes. Hank went to government meetings to warn about what was happening in Florida Bay. Other guides, young and old, sounded the alarm, too.

One important tourist who heard about the crisis was George Bush. That the president loved fishing in the backcountry was a cause for great optimism by many Keys locals. If *he* couldn't do something to save the place, they reasoned, nobody could. And they made a point of telling him about it. During one bonefishing expedition, a guide scooped a handful of foul mud off the flat to show the president how the sea grass was dying.

But nothing happened after Bush went back to Washington. Nothing. Meanwhile Florida Bay got sicker.

The problem is fresh, clean water. There's not enough of it moving down the peninsula. Getting more will require prompt, stouthearted action, for which Florida's lawmakers are not famous.

When nature controlled the plumbing, good water ran south in a sheet from Lake Okeechobee through the Everglades, finally emptying from Shark River and Taylor Slough into the brackish estuary called Florida Bay. It was a perfect system, except that it did not anticipate the demands of reckless, unchecked urban growth. As

Fort Lauderdale and Miami boomed in the '40s, the Army Corps of Engineers built 1,400 miles of levees and canals. Pump houses were installed to prevent flooding of farms and newly developed subdivisions (real estate brokers still being somewhat sensitive about their image as tawdry swamp peddlers).

In the ravenous euphoria of a land stampede, no thought was given to the possible adverse effects of gouging deep trenches across Florida's wetlands. For engineers the mission was a simple one: Move the water.

Now the federal government and the state of Florida are spending millions trying to fix the mess. In theory the restoration plan would mimic the ancient pattern of Everglades drainage while reducing pathogenic levels of mercury, nitrogen, phosphorus and pesticides. But in fact there's still no official commitment to replenish the total annual volume of freshwater once sent to Florida Bay. Without that, many scientists say, the backcountry will never recover.

So much water has been purloined for urbanization that the bay today receives about one tenth of its historic flow. In the 1980s successive seasons of brutal drought and exceptionally high temperatures conspired with dumb flood-control practices to hasten the crash. No longer brackish, the bay was becoming a hot, briny lagoon—in some places, twice as salty as seawater.

Most experts think huge algae blooms in the backcountry are related, at least indirectly, to the ultrahigh salinity. They believe too much salt in the water can kill sea grasses, triggering a cycle of decay. Dead grass loads the water with nutrients, which in turn gorge the plankton. As the algal mass spreads, it damages more grasses in its path. "Thus a positive growth loop, similar to a cancer cell's, is born," explains Dr. Joseph Zieman, a University of Virginia scientist who has studied Florida Bay extensively.

A minority view is that the blooms are caused by phosphates and other waste swept into the bay from distant cities and farms. Whatever the cause, the effect is arresting. Although the phytoplankton isn't toxic to sea life, it blocks sunlight essential to the habitat of larval lobsters, shellfish, corals and sponges. The onset of the algae was followed by a drastic slump in the Gulf of Mexico's pink-shrimp harvest.

By 1992 the bloom was so prolific that a 450-square-mile area of the bay had been dubbed the Dead Zone. Mark Butler, a biologist at Old Dominion University in Virginia, was conducting a field study of spiny lobsters when a 100-square-mile blanket of algae settled for three months around the Arsnicker Keys. Underwater visibility dropped from 25 feet to six inches.

In a letter to the Florida Keys National Marine Sanctuary, Butler wrote, "When the bloom finally dissipated, we were awed at the devastation. . . . Over 90 percent of the sponges at our study site were either killed or severely damaged."

I was out in the bay on a day when it was happening. With the plankton clogging their membranes, sponges were dying by the hundreds and floating off the bottom. The surface became a bobbing gantlet of brown, decaying clumps of sponge; the water was greenish and grungy. The sight put a knot in my gut.

So widespread and thick was the algae that it could be tracked by satellite photography. Currents eventually carried the inky plumes out of the bay through the bridges of the Keys, toward the Atlantic. There the algae settled on reefs, causing an uproar among dive-shop operators and charter captains. Traitorous winds also puddled the crud around Islamorada, in plain sight of tourists on the Overseas Highway. It was not a pretty postcard.

Once a preoccupation of guides, lobstermen and shrimpers, the worsening conditions in the backcountry suddenly became an establishment crusade. That's because the Keys' economy depends entirely on water as clean, blue and inviting as it appears in the travel brochures.

(To say the aquatic balance of the Keys is fragile isn't a cliché, it's an understatement. Recently scientists flushed a viral tracer into a residential septic tank in Port Largo. Only 11 hours later the virus emerged in a nearby canal; in another 12 hours it turned up offshore.)

As soon as the decline of Florida Bay was identified as a major threat to tourism, the obligatory task forces and blue-ribbon panels were convened. Politicians from Key West to Washington, D.C.—some in dire need of pro-environment credentials—adopted the bay as their ward, their Walden Pond.

Even [George H.W.] Bush finally got on board. In August he hosted a celebrity bone-fish tournament, with proceeds to benefit the Everglades. For those who waited in vain for Bush to do something during his presidency, it's sourly ironic that the gesture comes now, when he's out of office and out of power.

But any newfound support must be welcomed, because time is so precious. Between 60,000 and 100,000 acres of sea grass are dead or damaged in the bay. The die-offs and algae blooms continue to advance across the backcountry in two prongs, one from the gulf and one from the interior.

The worst-hit area remains the so-called Dead Zone, the bay's northwestern quadrant. There, near the once fabled tarpon grounds of Oxfoot Bank, the marine bed is tundra. Redfish, trout and pompano have been displaced by mud-loving bottom feeders such as catfish and mullet. A slight breeze churns the lakes and basins to marl; on each incoming tide the silt-filled water rolls eastward from Sandy Key toward Ninemile Bank and beyond.

From far away it's visible—a march of yellowish muck on the horizon. In July it breached Rabbit Key Basin, clouding one of the backcountry's most pristine lakes. One day you could count the blue-black slabs of tarpon resting along the banks, and the next day you couldn't see your own fingers in the water.

SAVE FLORIDA BAY! plead the bumper stickers.

Theories, models and plans abound. The one thing virtually every expert agrees upon: The bay is doomed without a pure, dependable flow of freshwater. That's only the beginning of recovery, the baseline. Reclaiming that water means rechanneling some canals, filling others and displacing some farmers and homeowners who have moved into the wetlands bordering Everglades National Park. Unfortunately, less controversial options haven't worked.

For instance, the Army Corps of Engineers and the South Florida Water Management District have been trying to transfuse water from the problematic C-111 canal toward Taylor Slough. After two years of experimental pumping, the results are discouraging. "There's no evidence any of that water is making it to the bay," concedes Steve Davis, an ecologist for the water district. Davis and others suspect that what's being pumped toward the backcountry is cresting at the upland marshes and retreating downhill into the same holding canal from which it came. Even in a swamp, gravity rules.

No fewer than 15 government agencies and private conservation groups are working on the mystery of Florida Bay. Support has been strong and bipartisan, but folks in the Keys are nervous about the anti-environment mood in Congress. Meanwhile scientists are lining up for about $5 million worth of grants earmarked for studying the bay.

The camps are sharply divided between those who believe years of further research are needed and those who advocate swift action. Davis says that well-grounded science is important, but the clock is ticking for the backcountry: "We want to move ahead. We don't want to study this thing to death."

So many bureaucracies are involved in the saving of Florida Bay that it's inconceivable that the process would go smoothly, and it hasn't. After a long, heated battle with vegetable growers, the state of Florida this year finally agreed to condemn and purchase the Frog Pond, a tract in southwest Dade County deemed critical to the replenishing of the bay. But no sooner was the deal done than the state offered to lease the disputed land back to the very farmers it had evicted. (Applying the same logic, Gen. Norman Schwarzkopf should have allowed Saddam Hussein to reoccupy Kuwait after the gulf war and pay rent.)

The upgrading of Florida Bay from a problem to an emergency has also spawned predictably petty turf guarding and bickering about who's running the show. In July, for example, scores of scientists met in the Keys to offer strategies for reinvigorating the bay. Conspicuously absent were the staff and biologists of Everglades National Park, wherein the bay is situated. Incredibly, park staffers were forbidden to attend the summit. The brass didn't like the way the meeting had been arranged, so they ordered a boycott.Nothing like team spirit in a time of crisis.

The last 18 months have been blessedly wet. Loads of rain, including a deluge from tropical storm Jerry, drenched the Everglades and continue to nourish Florida Bay. Some shallow banks show a stubble of new sea grass—a promising sign, even if it's only a few meager inches. Salinity in the bay's northeastern reaches has fallen to predrought levels.

Another good sign: The algae blooms aren't as stubborn as in recent summers. Prevailing breezes have kept the discolored waters away from the shorelines of the Upper Keys—a relief for the Chamber of Commerce, because not even the most dogged tourists will snorkel in pea soup.

In some basins and inlets the backcountry looks amazingly healthy. It was a good spring for tarpon, and guides say snook fishing is the best it has been in 20 years. An air of cautious hope has returned to the docks. "The water," says Hank Brown, "is absolutely gorgeous in places. But every time you get your hopes up, a storm comes through, and everything looks like crap again."

All of us who live here would love to think that the worst is over, that Florida Bay is rebounding for good. But most scientists don't think so. The rains are fickle, and by winter the water might be too salty again.

That's why it is imperative that a natural flow be restored as soon as possible, while the political will and funds exist to do it. The engineering isn't as daunting as the politics. Powerful special-interest groups are demanding a say in where the lifeblood of the Everglades goes, how much they get to keep and what they're allowed to dump in the water on its way downstream.

The battle begins up at Lake Okeechobee, where Big Sugar finally (and reluctantly) has agreed to filter phosphates from the runoff of the cane fields. Farther south, the cities siphon heavily from the diked "conservation areas"—cheap, accessible reservoirs that help fuel the breakneck westward growth in Palm Beach, Broward and Dade counties. Even below Miami, on Florida's still rural southern tip, water policy is disproportionately influenced by private interests. In the dry months what would otherwise trickle through the glades to the bay is diverted instead to a small cluster of tomato and avocado farms. Conversely, in the wet season the surplus water is pumped off the fields to protect the crops. The canal network was absurdly designed to flush millions of gallons not into the Everglades (which were made to absorb them) but into Manatee Bay and Barnes Sound, which are saltwater bodies. The effect of such a copious, sudden injection of freshwater is an overdose—lethal on an impressive scale to fish, corals and other marine life.

But it's all for a good cause. Upstream the avocados are plump and safe.

During all my days in the Keys, I met Ted Williams only once. It was several years ago, at a gas station in Islamorada.

He noticed my skiff on the trailer and stalked up to inquire about the bonefishing. Understand that Williams's reputation in the backcountry was as fearsome as it was at the ballpark, so I was a jumble of nerves. But he was as pleasant as anyone could be. We talked about the tides, the wind, where the fish were feeding. Then he got in his station wagon and said goodbye. It wasn't so long afterward that he sold his place and moved away.

I understand why he left, but I wish he hadn't. His unshy temperament would have made him a valuable ally in this battle for Florida Bay: a glaring, impatient presence before county commissions, water boards and legislative committees.

Fortunately the Keys have other fiery defenders. One is Mike Collins, who spends almost as much time haggling in the back rooms of Tallahassee as he does poling the backcountry. Twenty years ago Collins fled Wall Street to become a fishing guide in Florida, the sort of madcap impulse of which urban daydreams and Jimmy Buffett lyrics are made. Changing latitudes, I'm happy to report, did not transform Collins into a laid-back guy. He has been a tenacious and refreshingly blunt-spoken advocate for Florida Bay. So, given the many exasperating obstacles to saving the place, I was mildly surprised to hear Collins say, "I'm pretty optimistic. There's enough will to get it done. And there are some very good people working on it."

We were in his 19-foot skiff, tearing a frothy seam across a glass-calm morning, when he stopped to explore a redfish bank near Buoy Key. The scene was disheartening. Only months earlier the bottom had been lush and green. Now there were silty craters where the turtle grass had died. Leaning hard on the push pole, Collins agreed: It looked bad. But it could bounce back, he said. With a little luck and a little help.

You'll hear this over and over from those who spend their lives in these waters—a firm, almost spiritual confidence in the recuperative powers of nature. "What this does," Collins said of the big rains, "is buy us some time." But he, too, worries that budget cutters might pull the plug on the Everglades, murdering it once and for all. For Collins, who happens to be a Republican, saving Florida Bay isn't an ideological choice, it's a moral one. There is simply no honorable argument against it.

"Look, I've been all over the hemisphere looking for someplace else that compares—the Bahamas, Belize, you name it," he says. "But I always end up back here in the Keys, doing battle with these bird-brained bureaucrats. You've got to fight for it, because there is no place else that comes close."

A few days later I travel to the source: Taylor River, a tributary of the aortal slough through which the Everglades delivers essential freshwater to the eastern bay. At the boat's helm is Frank Mazzotti, a University of Florida scientist who has spent 18 years with endangered crocodiles along the backcountry's most remote coves and beaches. It has been a banner season for the crocs, Mazzotti reports, and a good year for most wildlife, thanks to the rains—which could end tomorrow, or next fall, or five years from now. Another drought is inevitable; the only uncertainties are when it will come and how long will it last.

Mazzotti is no less ardent than Collins, but he's a bit more diplomatic. "It's not that we've killed Florida Bay, though we're damn close," he says. "It's that we've compromised its resilience."

For today, there's water enough to navigate Taylor River, which at its mouth is but a jungly creek—overgrown, slender as a mine shaft, mosquito-choked, strung with ornate, dewy spiderwebs. A whispering current, southbound and strong, puckers around the mangrove roots. Reaching over the gunwale, I touch two fingers to the surface, then to my mouth. No trace of salt.

The water is warm, absolutely fresh. It tastes like hope.

DAVE BARRY
1947–

D AVE BARRY STARTED out with every intention of being a serious journalist, but after a series of strange turns he became the nation's top humor writer.

He grew up in Armonk, New York, the son of a minister, and went to Pleasantville High School, then on to Haverford College near Philadelphia. After working with the Episcopal Church for two years—instead of military service—he finally took his first step in journalism, joining the staff of the *Daily Local News* outside of Philadelphia. He moved to the Philadelphia bureau of the Associated Press in 1975, but hated the job, finding it mind-numbing.

He might have spent his career grinding away at the Associated Press, but then one of those strange turns occurred. A friend offered him a job teaching writing to business executives. The courses offered people a chance to write in English instead of the bureaucratic language that is so common in business communication.

His presentations gave him a chance to try out his humor and he found willing audiences. His wife suggested he stay in journalism with a weekly column in his old newspaper. The column became a hit, and soon editors at other newspapers took notice. There are hundreds of newspaper columnists, many covering the same material of life's foibles. But Barry's humor lacked any pretense—what other columnist would compare wine to bat urine?

In 1981, he gained national attention with a column on childbirth for the *Philadelphia Inquirer.* An editor at *The Miami Herald* saw the column and two years later he joined the paper as a humor columnist. *The Herald,* one of the nation's top newspapers, was part of the Knight-Ridder newspaper chain, and the company's syndicate gave him a national audience.

In the late 1980s, *The New York Times* published a lengthy story about Miami—a popular subject for journalists looking for a story and warm weather. Barry responded with a hilarious send-up of life in New York City. "New York has more commissioners than Des Moines, Iowa, has residents," and cited the mythical "Commissioner for Bicycle Messengers Bearing Down on You at Warp Speed with Mohawk Haircuts and Pupils

Smaller Than Purely Theoretical Particles."

That article, along with several others including a moving piece about his mother, won him the Pulitzer Prize in 1989. His column was appearing in 500 newspapers, his books—with titles such as *The Taming of the Screw*—made regular appearances on the best-seller list, and his life became a television series, *Dave's World,* which ran for four seasons on CBS, starring Harry Anderson as Barry.

He stopped doing his weekly column in 2005—when it appeared in 300 newspapers—but continued writing books, contributing occasionally to the *Herald.* In all, he has produced two dozen books, in addition to eight volumes of his collected columns. With Ridley Pearson, he has produced fourteen novels, and two of his books were turned into films.

He and his wife, Michelle Kaufman, live in South Miami. Kaufman is a sportswriter for the *Herald* and teaches at the University of Miami.

Run for Your Lives!
by Dave Barry

Probably the most striking characteristic of South Floridians, aside from the fact that so many of them apparently received their driver training from Roger Rabbit cartoons, is the way they're always asking each other how they like South Florida. I've lived here for four years, and when I meet people, they inevitably ask, "So, how do you like South Florida?" As if I just got here.

And I'm not alone. Everybody asks everybody this. People who've lived here for decades ask each other this. I'm confident that if Manuel Noriega ever takes the witness stand, the first question he'll be asked is how he likes South Florida.

This is not because of civic pride. It's not like in, for example, Texas, where people will say "How yew like Texas!" but what they clearly mean is "Hey, isn't Texas GREAT compared to whatever armpit of a place you come from?"

No, South Floridians ask with a cringe in their voices. They're insecure. They desperately want you to say that you like South Florida, because this reassures them that they're not total morons for living here. This is a suspicion that nags at South Floridians, especially when something bizarre happens, the kind of thing that seems to happen only down here, such as your second-grader casually mentions that one of her classmates brought a machine gun to Show and Tell; or you're late for work because an alligator attacked the drawbridge operator; or your next-door neighbor stops by to ask if he can borrow a cup of ceremonial sheep testicles; or a former chairperson of the Chamber of Commerce—this actually happened—reports that somebody broke into her bedroom and stole her Uzi. These are the times when, as a Miamian, you ask yourself: "Do I really want to live here? Should I maybe move to Kansas?"

It's natural for us to feel these doubts. Why should we have a good image of ourselves, when nobody else does? Our public relations appear to have been handled by the same firm that represents Charles Manson. For years, the image of South Florida that was broadcast to the world was Miami Vice, which depicted this as a place infested with drugs, violence, corruption, homicidal psychotics and—worst of all—really stupid plots. People take this image seriously. When you travel to other cities, and you tell people you're from Miami, they will frequently stick up their hands. Every few weeks you see a newspaper item about how some organization has announced its annual list of the Ten Nicest Places, or the Ten Healthiest Places, or the Ten Easiest Places To Get A Haircut In While Playing The Trombone Naked During Lent, but whatever the category is, Miami is never in the top group. Miami is always something like No. 2,573, behind Cleveland and various maximum-security prisons.

So, OK, we have an image problem. But one thing you can say about this city: When the going gets tough and the game is on the line, we South Floridians have an amazing ability to suck in our guts, tighten our chin straps, and poke ourselves in the eyeball. Sometimes this is just plain bad luck, as when John Paul II attempted to hold an outdoor Mass here, and a lightning storm nearly turned him into Pope Kabob. But sometimes we have to put real effort into screwing up, as when we hosted the Super Bowl, and national media people, who had come here expecting to be pampered into a stupor, wound up sprinting through Overtown, their clothing singed by the flames from what once were their rental cars.

We also could probably present a friendlier face to our tourist visitors. You get off a plane in Orlando, and you're greeted by a spacious, clean, modern airport with futuristic monorails whisking people about. You get off a plane at the Miami International Airport And Regional Cocaine Distribution Center, and you half expect to be run over by goats. We are talking about a Third or possibly even Fourth World situation here, a seething, babbling mass of confusion that can be very scary if you just got off a plane from, say, Indianapolis. There you are, wearing your brand-new active sportswear, all set for a restful tropical vacation, and suddenly you find yourself in a dirty, ill-lit, confusing airport, trying to thread your way through surging hordes of people shouting and gesturing in numerous languages not including English; massive extended families carrying an astounding variety of baggage, including tires, washing machines, giant radios, tractors, livestock, house parts, etc., and forming huge disorganized clots in front of counters representing dozens of tiny airlines you never heard of with names like Air Yemen, Air Anchovy, Air Apparent, and Air Buster A. Storkwhacker Jr. (proud motto: "If The Engine Don't Start, We Don't Fly!").

Here are some actual MIA airline names: Lacsa, TAN, Lac, Ladeco, Faucett, Saeta, Varig, Viasa. What bothers me about these airlines is, in all the times I've been to the airport, I've never seen any of their airplanes. I'm convinced that some of them don't HAVE any airplanes. The way they work is, they wait until they've sold a bunch of tickets, then go around to garage sales looking for aircraft in their price range. This causes lengthy schedule delays, sometimes resulting in the formation of whole refugee passenger villages in the main airport concourse, with primitive huts and oxen roasting over open fires. This is the scene that you, the Indianapolis tourist, must fight your way through in an effort to reach the Baggage Claim area, only to find it littered with mildewed inactive sportswear outfits containing the remains of former tourists who perished while waiting for their baggage to arrive, apparently from Alpha Centauri.

And if, miraculously, you do get your baggage, and you rent a car, you will find yourself out on Le Jeune Road, or God forbid the Palmetto Expressway, dealing with: South Florida traffic, the nation's last true lawless frontier; a place where you're not even certain that the police are licensed drivers, a place where you are passed on the left, passed on the right, passed by cars driving right on top of your roof, cars that were last inspected during the French and Indian War, cars on which the only maintenance activity ever performed is that occasionally the owner slaps another layer of what appears to be black paint on the windows, cars with actual bullet holes in the doors, that seem to be going out of their way to hit you, which they probably are because, as a rental-car driver, you may well be the only person in all of South Florida who actually has insurance.

You think I'm exaggerating? You think it's not that bad?

You're right! Sometimes it's worse. My favorite Welcome-To-South-Florida story, which is absolutely true, concerns the arrival of the distinguished author Cleveland Amory, who was here to promote one of his books. Picking him up at the airport was a friend of mine, Penny Gardner, who operates a VIP hosting service called Miami Seen. Penny had rented a large car for Amory, and she was just getting into it when a man came sprinting up, grabbed her purse, and leaped into a getaway car, which started racing off, with Penny running after it. So far, of course, there is nothing unusual about this anecdote. It could have happened in front of a distinguished visiting author in any big city. But not what happened next. What happened next was a distinctly South Florida event, namely: A passing motorist, seeing what has happened, stops his car in the middle of the street, leaps out, pulls out a gun and starts shooting at the fleeing car. He fires four or five shots, all of which apparently miss, then, without saying a word to Penny, he hops back into his car and drives off. The Good Samaritan.

Penny, now seriously shaken, rushes over to the rental-car agency, whose employees, in true heartwarming we're-all-in-this-together

South Florida fashion, are loudly informing her, through the glass door, that this incident did NOT occur on their property.

Meanwhile, distinguished author Cleveland Amory is lying down sideways on the car seat, possibly wondering if this is, in fact, the kind of community where people purchase a lot of books. Welcome to South Florida, sir! Anything else we can get for you? Bulletproof vest? Change of underwear?

Of course this does not happen to everybody. Most visitors spend their entire vacations here without once being exposed to gunfire. (Possible tourism slogan: "Visit South Florida! There's Not As Much Gunfire As You Think!") But most of us who live here are definitely aware of crime, if only because of the endless electronic yeeping of burglar alarms, the Official Noise of South Florida. Some of us can't sleep without it; when it's too quiet, we have to throw rocks through our neighbor's windows.

Sometimes it seems as if crime is the only thing we all have in common. We lived next door to a family for six months without ever seeing them, until finally the woman dropped by to tell us their house had been broken into. We had a real nice chat. I bet a lot of South Florida socializing occurs this way. ("Hi! We're the Smiths! We've lived next door for 14 years! Somebody just stole all our major appliances!" "Nice to meet you! We're the Johnsons! Louise here was recently mugged!")

That was the only time we ever talked to that particular neighbor, because of course the family moved, as people are constantly doing down here, to the point where pretty soon you're going to see homes built with permanent motel-style neon signs out front, so you'll be able to simply flip a switch to change your sign from "NOT FOR SALE" to "FOR SALE."

We haven't met our new neighbors yet, and we probably never will. They'll never be burglarized, because they have three irate German shepherds the size of UPS trucks. If we ever tried to go over and introduce ourselves, the coroner's office would need a rake to collect all our body fragments.

Everybody has dogs in our neighborhood, including us. My wife, after reading an article filled with Crimestopper Tips, recently put a typically friendly South-Florida-style welcome sign on our front door that says: "WARNING BAD DOG! !CUIDADO HAY PERRO!" (Our dogs, who are really not bad, just stupid, sometimes sniff the sign curiously, as if thinking, "?Cuidado?")

In our previous neighborhood there was a house occupied by drug dealers. At least that's what we all thought, based on the fact that it was an expensive house occupied by a constantly changing group of highly secretive people with no apparent means of support other than washing their own cars. After a while we thought of it as just another neighborhood landmark: the Liebman's house, the Williams' house, the Drug Dealer's house, etc. Our son would ask us if he could ride his bike, and we, being responsible South Florida parents, would say, "OK, but don't go beyond the Drug Dealer's House!"

Last summer I was having a beer at the bar of a small restaurant on Miami Beach, and a man recognized me from my picture in the newspaper. Here, without embellishment, is how our conversation went:

MAN: You the one who write for the newspaper?

ME: Yes.

MAN: You should write about Colombia! A lot of humor there! You ever been to Colombia?

ME: No.

MAN: Hah! I am from there. Let me be honest. I am a narcotics trafficker.

I swear that's what he said. There were two police officers eating dinner maybe 10 feet away, and he said "I am a narcotics trafficker" in the same open, friendly voice you might use to say "I am a claims adjuster." I half expected him to give me his business card.

At least he was polite. Politeness is something you learn not to automatically expect in South Florida. You learn, for example, that when you go to the movies here, you'll inevitably be sitting near people who are making important cellular-phone calls, or who, to judge from their noise level, are playing Charades.

You learn that, when you're in a store, and you attempt to make a purchase, the salesperson will often react in an irritated manner, as though this is a highly irregular breach of store procedure. "How am I supposed to get anything done," the salesperson is clearly thinking, "if I have to keep waiting on people?"

You learn that wherever you live and wherever you go, you'll be able to enjoy the musical tastes of some thoughtful person nearby with self-inflicted ear damage and a Led Zeppelin Model sound system cranked up to Stadium Mode.

You learn that if you're waiting in line for something, you'll begin to question your own existence because of the number of people who barge in front of you; or, if they're stuck behind you, as in the supermarket, they'll push their shopping carts into your rear end, helpfully nudging you along, over and over, nudge nudge nudge NUDGE NUDGE until your brain fills with rage and you want to whirl around and crush their skulls with your frozen Butterball turkey but you don't dare, for the same reason that you don't dare flip the bird at morons in traffic any more, because you never know when somebody down here might be carrying an Uzi stolen from the former chairperson of the Chamber of Commerce.

Yes, there is definitely some hostility down here. Sometimes you can actually feel it hovering and festering in the air. Maybe Bob Soper should include a Hostility Level in his weather forecast ("Tomorrow will be continued hot with a 60 percent chance of somebody getting fatally shot over what will turn out to be a losing Lotto ticket").

Of course a certain amount of tension is inevitable when you have 274 distinct ethnic communities—with new ones washing ashore every hour—all attempting to co-exist in a relatively small, confined area that is also extremely popular with mosquitoes. Each of these ethnic communities has its own cherished customs and beliefs, with the MOST cherished belief being that everybody ELSE's culture is wrong. Top mathematicians using powerful computers have been unable to find a single issue on which all of South Florida's ethnic communities agree, including the issue of what time it is.

Fortunately, South Florida is blessed with many courageous political leaders who refuse to pander to petty ethnic prejudices; who are willing to speak up for fairness and reason and right, even though this might hurt their re-election chances.

Ha ha! I am of course making a hilarious joke here. South Florida's political leaders hold all kinds of national pandering records. Many of them would need major surgery to have their lips removed from their constituencies' butts. Some of them are attempting to perform the near-impossible feat of pandering to several conflicting constituencies simultaneously; these leaders remind you of those battery-operated toys that rush around randomly, changing direction whenever they hit a wall. BONK they hit the Anglo wall, so they change direction until BONK they hit the Cuban wall, which sends them rushing off into BONK the Haitian wall, which is not to be confused with BONK the native African-American wall, which sends them spinning into BONK the Jewish wall, and so on. This kind of bold leadership has needless to say created a tremendous sense of fellowship, as was demonstrated during the recent visit of Nelson Mandela, when the various ethnic communities displayed a generous spirit of mutual trust and understanding rarely seen outside of Beirut.

So let's sum up what we've got down here. We've got crime. We've got violence. We've got invertebrate political leadership tiptoeing nervously around on an ethnic mine field that explodes at the drop of a mango. We've got rampant rudeness and Gridlock-From-Hell traffic populated by frantic IQ-impaired revenge-crazed Motorists of Doom who don't even obey the laws of physics. Have I left anything out? The humidity? The crowding and overdevelopment and continued aggressive uglification of the landscape? The endless highway deconstruction? The corruption? The water shortage? The cockroaches large enough to be registered with the Bureau of Motor Vehicles? The fact that every minute you live here brings you one minute closer to the inevitable day when the major hurricane they've been warning us about for 20 years now—the Big One, Hurricane Idi Amin—finally arrives, and suddenly Sea Level is the same height as your refrigerator, and you find yourself crouching on your roof, surrounded by water, with every pit bull in the neighborhood swimming furiously your way?

These are just a few of the things that run through my mind

when people ask me how I like South Florida.

And then they look at me, cringing.

And I always say: "I like it a LOT."

And this is the absolute truth. I'm not saying it to be polite. I really like South Florida. Sometimes I love South Florida. But it's not easy to explain why.

Oh, sure, there are the obvious reasons, the official tourism-industry reasons. I like the water. I like the weather (Northerners can have their Change of Seasons; for me, the Change of Seasons always wound up involving jumper cables). I like the sky; we get more great sunsets in a month here than I saw in 20 years in Philadelphia. I like being an hour from the Keys. I like the Miami skyline at night, even though I imagine that as a taxpayer I'm now helping to pay for illuminating the CenTrust Tower. I like hardly ever having to wear a tie to restaurants or even necessarily funerals. I like watching the cruise ships go out, loaded with happy Indianapolis people, and I like it when the ships come back and the passengers have to be unloaded via cranes because they've been eating 17 meals per day and their arms and legs have turned into small useless appendages. I like Bayside and the Grove and Tobacco Road at 1:30 a.m., which is what time it always is inside Tobacco Road, even on Monday afternoon. I like the Book Fair and the Columbus Day Totally Nude Regatta and of course the King Mango Strut, a wondrously demented event that each year proves the important and reassuring scientific law that there is no direct correlation between age and maturity. I even like the Orange Bowl Parade after a certain amount of rum. I like conch fritters. I like being represented by the baddest-ass college football team in the nation. I like being at a Heat game when the crowd is going nuts because we're down by only 15 points going into the fourth quarter and if the team plays really hard there's an outside chance that we can cut it to just 10 by the end of the game. I like South Beach on a Saturday night when the bars are busy and the bands are playing and the Beautiful People are strolling past beautiful yet somehow comical architecture and the world-famous Atlantic Ocean is right there.

I like all these things, and many more. But they're not what makes me sometimes love South Florida. What makes me sometimes love South Florida is this:

It's weird.

And when I say "weird," I do not mean merely "interesting." A LOT of places are interesting. Boston, for example, is a very interesting city with many interesting historic sites and cultural attractions that you can go to and be interested in. But did Boston ever name a street after a man who turned out to be a leading drug dealer? I sincerely doubt it. Here in Dade County, however, where our political leaders spend much of their time naming streets after semi-prominent citizens or close friends or business acquaintances or particularly loyal domestic animals, the Metro Commission named a street the "Leomar Parkway" after prominent developer Leonel Martinez, who later pleaded guilty to running a massive drug operation.

Of course you can just imagine how surprised our local political leaders were when they found out about this.

"I'm surprised because I never expected that to be the case," said Miami Commissioner Victor De Yurre, who was Martinez's real-estate attorney. "The whole thing to me was a shock from day one."

Metro Commissioner Larry Hawkins boldly proposed stripping Martinez's name from the street.

"I think it sends the wrong message, not only to kids in our community, but to drug dealers," he said.

You tell 'em, Larry! It's time we got tough! You drug dealers out there better get one thing straight: If you get caught in THIS town, we're going to strip your name from your street.

So Leomar Parkway is back to being plain old West 132 Avenue, at least until some commissioner decides to honor his proctologist. Meanwhile, U.S. Marshals have seized Martinez's $2.2 million house in Coral Gables' very exclusive Cocoplum area, and they've discovered that the basement contains an entire nightclub featuring a stage, a bar, room for 100 people and men's and women's bathrooms with three stalls each. When I read about this I had to snort in a hearty manner, because when I lived in Coral Gables ("Where Life Itself Is A Zoning Violation"), I once got a ticket for having my living room repainted without a permit. Really. I always had the feeling that if I'd attempted a major project, such as the installation of a sink, Coral Gables would have had me shot. I have met many Coral Gables residents who skulk around performing home repairs in the dead of night for fear of being apprehended by the Building Police. Yet here Mr. Prominent Drug Developer somehow managed to install a nightclub in his basement.

When this was discovered, a Coral Gables official told the *Herald* that having a nightclub in your basement is a "major violation" of the laws, and it "definitely will have to go."

Law and order, that's what we stand for here in South Florida.

In reviewing this incident I'm trying to make two points:

1. Abnormal events occur routinely down here.

2. When you probe beneath the surface of these abnormal events,

you often find even more abnormality, whole unexpected basement nightclubs of abnormality.

There seems to be something in the steamy air here that causes events to spontaneously mutate, like some kind of fast-growing alien jungle vegetation, throbbing and roiling and sending out vines and tendrils in all directions and suddenly erupting into giant mysterious pods that burst open to reveal entirely new and possibly carnivorous life forms that immediately start mutating on their own. Before long some seemingly simple event that you thought you had understood completely has evolved into something completely different and usually far more bizarre. In the relatively short time I've lived here, I've seen this process occur over and over, to the point where I've given it a name: the DeSillers Effect.

This name comes, of course, from the tragicomic case of Maria DeSillers, a Miami woman whose son, Ronnie, fought a brave but losing battle against a liver disease, a battle that received nationwide attention and drew hundreds of thousands of dollars in donations. It was a heart-rending story, and through the news media millions of us followed it to its very sad ending, and we all had a good cry and filed the whole thing away under Sad Memories and prepared to go on with our lives, and then . . .

. . . and then it mutated. It sat and festered in the South Florida heat until a new pod burst open and out popped the state attorney, informing us that Mrs. DeSillers, the grieving mom, had used some of the donation money for a BMW and a car phone and clothes and jewelry and furniture and a big wad of cash for her ex-boyfriend. Admit it: When you read about this in the newspaper, somewhere in the back of your mind there was a voice saying this could have happened only in South Florida.

This is not to say that fascinating events don't occur in other places; it's just that in other places, there's a kind of predictability to these events. For example, New York City has the ongoing Donald Trump saga, which is unquestionably fascinating. But we have all known for a long time that Trump is basically a greedy jerk, and the fascination lies mainly in watching him lumber directly into the various pitfalls that you would expect a greedy jerk to fall into. Likewise Washington, D.C., has Marion Barry, a major source of entertainment, but only because he turned out to be exactly the hypocrite that a lot of people suspected all along. You just know that if he'd been mayor of Miami, something unexpected would have happened during the undercover sting operation—maybe the police would have come bursting out from hiding and they would have started smoking crack, too. Or maybe the videotape would have revealed, upon close examination, that the mayor was actually a woman. But something unexpected would have happened. The DeSillers Effect would have seen to this.

Here are some more flagrant examples of the DeSillers Effect in action:

* The Amazing Flight Of Thomas Root *

Although this incident did not begin in South Florida, the significant fact is that it ended here. You remember: Last July, there were news bulletins about a pilot who had apparently blacked out in his single-engine plane, which was flying on autopilot, with Air Force jets trailing it down the Atlantic Coast as it gradually ran out of fuel. This was your classic Unfolding Drama, and the nation waited breathlessly as the little plane flew farther and farther until OH NO it crashed into

Bahamian waters—but somehow, miraculously, the pilot escaped, and he was dramatically rescued and everybody rejoiced as the lucky pilot was taken to Memorial Hospital in Hollywood, where ZAP powerful DeSillers Effect rays immediately started penetrating every facet of the story, and it was discovered that Root had a gunshot wound in his stomach that had been inflicted by his own gun, but he claimed to have no idea how this happened, and the press permanently attached the title Mystery Pilot in front of his name, and he turned out to be a communications attorney involved in some questionable broadcast-license deals, and he wound up pleading guilty to five federal felony charges and could go to jail, and don't even try to tell me this would have happened if he'd gone down off the coast of San Diego.

* The Stirring Escape Of Nadia Comaneci *

You talk about a classic feel-good story: Here she is, little Nadia, the plucky 'n' perky 'n' petite doll of a gal who stole our hearts in the Olympics, escaping from Communist Tyranny, fleeing to Freedom here in . . . UH OH! Not South Florida, Nadia! Watch out for the DeSil . . . too late. Suddenly Nadia was not nearly as perky or petite as we remembered her; she was this vaguely sour woman who may or may not have been dating the evil son of the evil Romanian dictator, and who was hanging around with a "manager" who was actually a Hallandale roofer who abandoned his wife and four small children. We were disillusioned; it was as if the vice squad had picked up Tinkerbelle on 79th Street for soliciting. But we should have expected it, here in the swirling vortex of the DeSillers Effect.

* The Tragic Tourist Murder Case *

Maybe you remember this one, from 1987. It's nighttime in downtown Miami. Police find a rental car containing a West German tourist named Dieter Reichmann, appearing dazed and distraught, next to the body of his girlfriend, 31-year-old Kerstin Kischniok, who has a bullet in her brain.

The story in the next day's *Herald* is a gut-grabber and a half. Riechmann has told police that he and Kischniok had left Bayside, then got lost. He said he saw a pedestrian and drove over to ask for directions; the man said something Riechmann didn't understand, then shot Kischniok.

"He remembers his girlfriend wheezing as he sped through the dark streets in an alien city," the *Herald* story says. "He remembers feeling her blood on his hand."

Riechmann tells the *Herald* that Kischniok "loved Miami, you can see her smiling in the videotapes I made, so happy."

Here's how the story ends:

Riechmann and Kischniok were to return to Germany Wednesday.

Now Riechmann is going home alone, with a question:

"Why do I earn this, coming here?"

It tears your heart out, doesn't it? I mean, here you have these innocent, decent, fun-loving people from a place where nobody even litters, and they come here and ask somebody for directions and this poor woman gets murdered for God's sakes. WHAT THE HELL IS WRONG WITH THIS TOWN?? That's what people were screaming on the talk-radio shows. WHY CAN'T WE DO SOMETHING?? WHEN ARE WE GOING TO GO AFTER THESE

DAMNED CRIMINALS who ROAM THE STREETS and prey on LAW-ABIDING PEOPLE who . . .

ZAP! Turns out that poor old distraught Dieter Riechmann stood to make $1 million in insurance on the victim's life. Turns out, according to evidence presented in court, that the victim was a high-class call girl and poor old Dieter was her pimp.

Turns out that he got convicted for murder.

That's how things turn out down here.

* The Police Officer From Hell *

This would be Metro police officer Alex Marrero, who was the chief defendant in the 1979 beating death of black businessman Arthur McDuffie. Marrero and three other officers were acquitted in 1980 by an all-white Tampa jury; this verdict touched off the 1980 Miami riots that left 18 dead. Marrero was fired from the force, and in a normal place the story would end here. Instead, Marrero was arrested in 1989 by federal agents on charges of conspiring to protect a cocaine shipment.

But wait, there's more. Hours after his arrest, a major fire broke out in the Everglades; investigators later discovered that the fire was caused by somebody igniting gasoline-soaked files belonging to: Alex Marrero. The fire destroyed 12,000 acres, spread thick, choking smoke over much of South Florida, required the federal government to bring in firefighting crews from as far away as California, and forced the evacuation of 748 illegal immigrants from the Krome Avenue Detention Center to Bobby Maduro Miami Stadium (which a few months earlier had housed several hundred Nicaraguan refugees).

Other than that, it was a routine case.

* The Curse Of The Giant Christmas Trees *

This is one of my favorite examples of the DeSillers Effect. It's November 1989, and there is holiday excitement in the air, because the World's Largest Christmas Tree is being erected in Bayfront Park. The World's Largest Christmas Tree always used to be in Lantana, home of the *National Enquirer* (of course the *National Enquirer* is in South Florida), but the *Enquirer* stopped doing the tree last year, so a businessman is bringing it to Miami and everyone is very proud.

And now ZAP it's December, and guess what? The businessman can't pay the contractors and the World's Largest Christmas Tree has filed for bankruptcy. Yes! Bankruptcy! A Christmas tree! Is that wonderful, or what? Could that possibly have happened in Cedar Rapids, or Macon, or Butte, or any place else back on the planet Earth? Of course not! It had to happen in South Florida. I'm surprised the contractors didn't retaliate by breaking the tree's limbs.

Miami is also the home of the World's Largest Flocked Christmas Tree, which appears each year in Tropical Park at Santa's Enchanted Forest, which has to be the World's Least Subdued Christmas Display. And last year we had another memorable holiday event at the extremely tasteful Fort Lauderdale Thunderbird Swap Shop, where a crowd including Fort Lauderdale Mayor Bob ("Free, White and an IQ of 21") Cox had gathered for the official lighting of the World's Largest Inflatable Christmas Tree, which actually looked like a 14-story-tall green tent. But just as the big moment arrived, ZAP, along came a gust of wind, which ripped a seam in the tree, which collapsed and sank to the ground.

"Certainly it's embarrassing when you get it inflated and it goes back down," stated Thunderbird Swap Shop owner Preston Henn, speaking for many of us.

Anyway, the DeSillers Effect appears to have a negative impact on giant Christmas trees, which makes you wonder what could happen in the upcoming holiday season:

HUNDREDS INJURED
IN YULE TREE BLAST

Of course nobody knows where the DeSillers Effect will strike next. That's the fun of living here. But I do think the Manuel Noriega situation is already showing signs of being affected.

Theoretically this was a case about issues such as drug dealing, human-rights abuses, U.S. foreign policy, etc., but when it came to South Florida, it mutated, under the DeSillers Effect rays, into a case almost totally about how the lawyers would get paid. For months now this issue has obsessed the legal system. The reason for this is that the Noriega case involves a great deal of "legal complexity," by which I mean "$20 million in various foreign bank accounts." Because of this complexity, Mr. Noriega has required a great deal of "due process," meaning "five lawyers making about $300 per lawyer per hour." It looks as if we're going to have due process for as long as the complexity holds out, which could be many years. God alone knows how the case will come out. It wouldn't surprise me if the final deal involves formally changing the name of West 132 Avenue to "Manuelnor Parkway."

You laugh, but there is no predicting what the South Florida legal community will do in any given situation. Remember The Case Of Claude The Sheep Dog? Here's what happened: One day an attorney named Frank Furci was walking his Doberman pinscher, Ginger, through his affluent Broward County neighborhood when he encountered a sheep dog named Claude.

Guess what happened next.

If you guessed that the dogs got into a fight and were separated by their owners and that was the end of it, then you are clearly not familiar with South Florida.

What happened was that Furci pulled out a .45-caliber handgun (of course!) and shot Claude in a fatal manner. He was charged with cruelty to animals and aggravated assault. But it just so happens that Furci's law partner is (of course!) famed local defense attorney Roy Black, who mounted a defense effort comparable in scope to the Normandy Invasion but probably more expensive. As *Herald* columnist Carl Hiaasen described it:

(Black) hired a private investigator. He got aerial photos of the crime scene. In 43 separate pleadings and motions, and 17 depositions, he and lawyer Mark Seiden hammered at the character of Claude the sheep dog.

They demanded records of his breeding, birth and pedigree; of any dog shows he'd won; of any previous bites or attacks. Claude's background, they asserted, was "of critical importance in formulating the accused's defense."

At one point—I am not making this up—Claude was thawed out and autopsied by Broward County's chief medical examiner.

Finally they worked out a deal whereby Furci pleaded no contest to animal cruelty, and the assault charge was dropped. The *Herald* story stated that Furci had to do some community service, and "has already spent 35 hours visiting nursing homes with puppies and kittens for the Humane Society's 'pet therapy' program." The story didn't say whether Mr. Furci took his .45 along to the nursing homes, in case one of the puppies got out of hand.

But that is not the point. The point is that this is a wondrous, classic South Florida story. I contend that there are more stories like this per square inch in South Florida than anywhere else in the United States. The key to enjoying yourself here is to accept this, to stop wishing it would be more like where you came from and start enjoying the fact that the entire region is one vast entertainment medium. Every day you should wake up and say, with pride in your voice: "I am fortunate enough to live in the weirdest area of the United States."

You should stop complaining about, for example, the quality of government here. Yes, we seem to have more than our share of political leaders with the ethical standards of toenail dirt. But look at how entertaining they can be. Surely you enjoyed watching Miami Beach Mayor Alex Daoud attempting to explain that there was nothing suspicious about his appearing before the Metro Commission in support of David Paul's dock. David Paul, of course, was the chairman of The CenTrust Savings And Loan And Real Nice Art Collection, and naturally a man of that stature could not have an ordinary little weenie of a dock. No, a man who is screwing up a multibillion-dollar operation needs a really big dock, a major dock, and Mayor Daoud was there to help him, but NOT because Daoud got $35,000 from companies controlled by Paul. No, he did it because it's a mayor's JOB to help make sure that his constituents, no matter who they may be, obtain the dock size of their choice, and as taxpayers we should all be glad he did because I think Mr. Paul's dock belongs to us now.

Mayor Daoud recently made the news again by obtaining several semi-automatic weapons from firms competing for a city contract. Once again we need to stress that there was nothing unusual about this. A LOT of political figures down here are armed. In 1987 Miami Mayor Xavier Suarez had his personal handgun stolen from his car. Politicians down here need to be packing heat, because they never know when gunfire might erupt during a meeting with the Chamber of Commerce.

Yes, they must be vigilant, our political leaders. Remember when Commissioner Victor De Yurre alertly spotted the Penis Carrots? That was a close one! What happened was, the City Commission was looking at the Downtown Development Authority's latest promotional brochure, which featured, for some artistic reason, an arrangement of broccoli, peppers and carrots. When Victor saw this picture he got very upset because he thought the vegetables looked, as the *Herald* put it, "too much like lower male body parts."

"What the hell does this have to do with Miami?" De Yurre asked, showing a stunning lack of understanding of Miami.

"It's a marketing tool," stated Matthew Schwartz, executive director for the development authority, in a quote that I am not making up. I could go on and on, but you see my point, which is that we have, pound for pound, the most dependably comical politicians in the country down here. The trick is to stop viewing the government as a government, and start viewing it as an entertainment medium. Be thankful for the weirdness. Embrace the weirdness.

Even the nature here is weird. The other day I was reaching out my hand to open a door and YIKES there was a grasshopper sitting on the handle. Ordinarily I am not afraid of grasshoppers, but this was the biggest one I had ever seen, definitely large enough to prey on adult squirrels. I made scary noises at it, but it just sat there, totally unafraid of me, using contemptuous grasshopper body language to convey this message: "So, Mr. Suburban Homeowner, you THINK you live in a civilized metropolitan area, but as far as NATURE is concerned you live in a GIANT, EONS-OLD SUBTROPICAL SWAMP and you have NO IDEA what's living in here with you HAHAHAHAHAHA."

One time I was picking my son up from school, and suddenly the air was filled with dragonflies—thousands of them, everywhere you looked. It was as though the finals of the Insect World Cup had just been held, and the dragonflies had won, and they had all left their little dragonfly TVs to rush outside and celebrate. Next day they were gone.

Of course everybody knows about the Giant Death Toads we have here, the kind where if you lick them you could die. "Never lick the toads" is the first piece of advice we always give to house guests.

And as if the native South Florida nature weren't strange enough, we have people bringing in all kinds of bizarre nonlocal nature. Earlier this year, for example, the *Herald* reported that Pompano Beach commissioners were considering an ordinance that would require residents to leash their bobcats, ocelots, etc., because "a cougar escaped from a private home and briefly chased a small boy."

A local painting contractor told me that one of his men was once chased out of a yard by an emu, which is a very large ostrich like bird.

"He was on the radio, scared to death," the contractor said. "He was shouting, 'There's a GIANT CHICKEN in there!' "

Last year a man driving on the turnpike right around the Broward-Dade line had a head-on collision with a buffalo.

Really. There was a buffalo herd loose.

"Certainly Miami is not the place to have buffalo roaming up and down the highway," a state official said. But of course he was wrong. Miami is exactly the place for this.

It's also a magnet for giant snakes. It seems as though every two weeks you pick up the newspaper and read about some family whose children are just distraught because their 14-foot, 275-pound boa constrictor named Louise has escaped, and they're looking all over for her because they love her so much and she's so sweet and she hardly ever eats anybody. Sometimes you hear about these snakes being re-captured, but sometimes you don't, so I figure a lot of them are still out there.

You never know what's out there. We found this out at our house during the Falling Lizards Incident. I'm not talking about the cute friendly little lizards that you see constantly down here, sitting on your toothbrush, standing upside down on your ceiling, etc. I'm talk-ing about a completely new brand of lizard that we discovered on our property last Christmas. This was during the Major Cold Wave when the temperature got down to a life-threatening 30 degrees and we were introduced to the "rolling blackout" by the folks at Florida Pow-er & Light (Motto: "Our Motto Is Not In Service At This Time").

On Christmas morning we walked outside to find large, bright-green lizards falling out of our trees. I mean large lizards. I never even knew they were up there, and all of a sudden WHUMP WHUMP WHUMP they were raining all over the lawn, a lizard storm. They looked dead, but they weren't. I know this because my son and I picked some of them up and put them in a box and brought them inside, and after a while I reached in to touch one and YIKES he suddenly opened his mouth really wide and hissed at me and I set a new world's record in the Leaping-Backward-While-Wetting-Your-Pants event.

When the weather warmed up we took them back outside and they disappeared. I imagine they're back up there in the trees, possibly with an escaped snake the size of Rhode Island, but I don't really know. All I know is that they helped make it a memorable holiday for us—a time of gathering comatose lizards off the lawn; of waiting excitedly for the arrival of the "rolling blackout"; of listening for the festive discharge of firearms that accompanies all South Florida holidays including Arbor Day; and of imagining that, if we listened carefully, we could hear, faintly in the distance, the unmistakable holiday sound of a Christmas tree going bankrupt. In short, it was a classic South Florida experience, the kind you couldn't get anywhere else in the country.

So I say the hell with those official lists of the Ten Safest Places, or the Ten Quietest Places, or the Ten Places Where Strangers Are Least Likely To Flip You The Bird, whatever. If they had a list of the Ten Least Boring Places, Miami would have to be at the top. So don't be ashamed of living here. Don't apologize. The next time somebody from back on the planet Earth asks you how you like Miami, don't make excuses. Think about the good things, the weird things, and then look that person right in the eye, and answer, with pride in your voice: "Stick 'em up."

POSTSCRIPT: Right after I turned in this story, a Dade County grand jury indicted Leonel Martinez—you remember, the drug dealer and former leading citizen—in connection with the murders of two men. Martinez had been a suspect in two drug-related murders, but these were NOT the ones he was indicted for. He was indicted for the 1978 murders of two kitchen-appliance salesmen. Tell me how this case could get weirder.

Never mind, I'll just wait around and find out.

PERMISSIONS

Audubon, John James. "Death of a Pirate" from *Ornithological Biography*. Edinburgh: A. Black, 1834, Vol. 2.

Banks, Russell. "Primal Dreams" from *The Condé Nast Traveler Book of Unforgettable Journeys: Great Writers on Great Places*. Copyright © 1995 by Russell Banks. New York: Penguin Press, 1995. Reprinted by permission of Russell Banks.

Barry, Dave. "Run for Your Lives!" *The Miami Herald,* August 19, 1990. Reprinted by permission of Dave Barry.

Bishop, Elizabeth. "Florida" from *The Complete Poems, 1927–1979*. Copyright © 1979, 1983 by Alice Helen Methfessel. New York: Farrar, Straus and Giroux. Reprinted by permission of Farrar, Straus and Giroux, LLC.

Buntline, Ned. "The Fast Duel: A Sketch from Life" from *The Family Friend*. Monticello, FL: April 20, 1861.

Crane, Stephen. "The Open Boat: A Tale Intended To Be After the Fact. Being the Experience of Four Men from the Sunk Steamer Commodore." *Scribner's Magazine,* 21, no. 6 (June 1897): 728–40.

Dos Passos, John. "Under the Tropic" from *The Best Times: An Informal Memoir*. New York: New American Times, 1966. Reprinted by permission.

Hemingway, Ernest. "Who Killed the Vets?" *The Masses,* September 17, 1935: 9–10.

Hiaasen, Carl. "The Last Days of Florida Bay." *Sports Illustrated,* September 18, 1995. Copyright © 1995 Time, Inc. Reprinted by permission.

Hurston, Zora Neale. Box 2, Folder "Atrocities Perpetrated Upon June 1938" (WPA Papers), Florida Negro Papers.

Johnson, James Weldon. "Lift Every Voice and Sing" from *James Weldon Johnson: Complete Poems*. New York: The Viking Press, 1927.

Kennedy, John F. *Inaugural Address of John F. Kennedy*. Washington, DC: Government Printing Office, 1961.

Lardner, Ring. "Gullible's Travels" from *Gullible's Travels, Etc.* New York: Charles Scribner's Sons, 1917, 1925.

Muir, John. *A Thousand-Mile Walk to the Gulf.* Boston: Houghton Mifflin Company, 1916.

Remington, Frederick. "Cracker Cowboys of Florida." *Harper's Weekly,* XXXIX (August 1895): 339–44.

Runyon, Damon. "Palm Beach Santa Claus." *Collier's,* December 24, 1938: 9, 10, 27–29. Copyright © 1938 by Crowell Publishing Company. Renewed copyright © 1966 by Damon Runyon Jr. and Mary Runyon McCann. From *Guys and Dolls* by Damon Runyon. Used by permission of Viking Penguin, a division of Penguin Group (USA) LLC.

Singer, Isaac Bashevis. "Alone" from *The Collected Stories*. Copyright © 1982 by Isaac Bashevis Singer. New York: Farrar, Straus and Giroux. Reprinted by permission of Farrar, Straus and Giroux, LLC.

Smith, Patrick. "Fried Mullet and Grits" from *A White Deer and Other Stories*. Panorama Studios, 2007. Reprinted by permission.

Stevens, Wallace. "Cattle Kings of Florida." *Atlanta Journal,* 14, December 1930.

Stowe, Harriett Beecher. *Palmetto Leaves*. Boston: J.R. Osgood, 1873.

Thompson, Hunter. "The Gonzo Salvage Company" from *A Generation of Swine*. New York: Simon and Schuster, 1988. Reprinted by permission.

Verne, Jules. "Florida and Texas" from *From the Earth to the Moon*. New York: A.L. Burt, 1867.

Whittier, John Greenleaf. "The Branded Hand." Salem, OH: The Anti-Slavery Bugle. 1845.

Williams, Tennessee. "The Diving Bell" from *The Collected Poems of Tennessee Williams*. Copyright © 1977 by the University of the South. Reprinted by permission of New Directions Publishing Corporation.

BIBLIOGRAPHY

Audubon, John James. *Writings and Drawings*. New York: Library of America, 1999.

Banks, Russell. *Lost Memory of Skin*. New York: HarperCollins, 2011.

Breslin, Jimmie. *Damon Runyon*. New York: Ticknor & Fields, 1991.

Carr, Virginia Spencer, and Donald Pizer. *Dos Passos: A Life*. Evanston, IL: Northwestern University Press, 2004.

Davis, Linda. *Badge of Courage: The Life of Stephen Crane*. New York: Houghton Mifflin, 1998.

Hadda, Janet. *Isaac Bashevis Singer: A Life*. Madison: University of Wisconsin Press, 2003.

Hendrick, Joan D. *Harriet Beecher Stowe: A Life*. New York: Oxford University Press, 1994.

Hurston, Zora Neale. "The Eatonville Anthology." *Messenger 8* (September, October, November 1926): 261–262, 297, 319, 332.

Kaufelt, Lynn Mitsuko. *Key West Writers and Their Houses*. Sarasota, FL: Pineapple Press, 1986.

Kennedy, John F. *Profiles in Courage*. New York: Harper & Row, 1964.

Kerstein, Robert J. *Key West on the Edge: Inventing the Conch Republic*. Gainesville: University Press of Florida, 2012.

Lane, Jack, and Maurice J. O'Sullivan. *The Florida Reader: Visions of Paradise.* Sarasota, FL: Pineapple Press, 1994.

Levy, Eugene D. *James Weldon Johnson: Black Leader, Black Voice.* Chicago: University of Chicago Press, 1977.

Ludington, Townsend. *John Dos Passos: A Twentieth-Century Odyssey.* New York: E.P. Dutton, 1980.

McCarthy, Kevin. *The Book Lover's Guide to Florida.* Sarasota, FL: Pineapple Press, 1992.

McCarthy, Kevin, ed. *Florida Stories.* Gainesville: University of Florida Press, 1989.

McIver, Stuart B. *Florida Chronicles: Touched by the Sun.* Sarasota, FL: Pineapple Press, 2001.

McIver, Stuart B. *Hemingway's Key West,* Second Edition. Sarasota, FL: Pineapple Press, 2002.

McKeen, William. *Mile Marker Zero: A Moveable Feast of Key West.* New York: Crown, 2011.

Moylan, Virginia Lynn. *Zora Neale Hurston's Final Decade.* Gainesville: University Press of Florida, 2011.

Murphy, George, ed. *The Key West Reader: The Best of Key West Writers, 1830–1990.* Marathon, FL: Tortugas Limited Publishing, 1990.

Parmet, Herman. *The Struggles of John F. Kennedy.* New York: Dial Press, 1980.

Proby, Kathryn Hall. *Audubon in Florida.* Coral Gables, FL: University of Miami Press, 1974.

Samuels, Peggy, and Harold Samuels. *Frederick Remington: A Biography.* Garden City, NY: Doubleday, 1982.

Sorensen, Ted. *Counselor: A Life at the Edge of History.* New York: Harper, 2008.

Stallman, R.W. *Stephen Crane: An Omnibus.* New York: Knopf, 1958.

Stevens, Wallace. *The Collected Poems of Wallace Stevens.* New York: Alfred A. Knopf, 1936.

Tebeau, Charlton W. *A History of Florida.* Coral Gables, FL: University of Miami Press, 1971.

Tofel, Richard J. *Sounding the Trumpet: The Making of John F. Kennedy's Inaugural Address.* Chicago: Ivan R. Dee, 2005.

Wagenknecht, Edward. *John Greenleaf Whittier: A Portrait in Paradox.* New York: Oxford University Press, 1967.

Walker, Jonathan. *The Branded Hand: Trial and Imprisonment of Jonathan Walker.* New York: Arno Press, 1969.

Yardley, Jonathan. *A Biography of Ring Lardner.* New York: Random House, 1977.

PHOTO CREDITS

INDEX

Here are some other books from Pineapple Press on related topics. For a complete catalog, write to Pineapple Press, P.O. Box 3889, Sarasota, Florida 34230-3889, or call (800) 746-3275. Or visit our website at www.pineapplepress.com.

The Florida Reader, edited by Maurice O'Sullivan and Jack C. Lane. Historical and literary introduction to our state's rich and diverse culture—from early Spanish myths and Seminole and African-American folktales to the latest descriptions of modern Miami. Features John James Audubon, Zora Neale Hurston, Zane Grey, Wallace Stevens, and Marjorie Kinnan Rawlings.

Florida in Poetry, edited by Jane Anderson Jones and Maurice O'Sullivan. A collection of poems from some of the earliest Europeans to encounter *La Florida* to contemporary poets who write of the beauty and degradation of the state. Includes Elizabeth Bishop, Walt Whitman, Langston Hughes, Donald Justice, and Marjory Stoneman Douglas.

Shakespeare Plays the Classroom, edited by Stuart Omans and Maurice O'Sullivan. This guide for teachers and lovers of literature and theater is an original collection of essays exploring the idea that Shakespeare's plays are best approached playfully through performance.

Dog Island and Other Florida Poems by Laurence Donovan. Miami poet-artist Donovan contemplates sea, sand, and sky in his words and etchings. In his foreword, Donald Justice calls Donovan "doubly gifted."

Presidents in Florida by James C. Clark. Presidents have played a major role in shaping Florida. Andrew Jackson came to fight Indians when Florida was still a Spanish colony and then became the first territorial governor. Abraham Lincoln came up with the plan to get Florida back into the Union in 1864 to help his reelection chances. Regular visitors have included Calvin Coolidge, Herbert Hoover, Harry Truman, FDR, Richard Nixon, and JFK.

200 Quick Looks at Florida History by James C. Clark. Packed with unusual and little-known facts and stories about the Sunshine State. For example, the inventor of air conditioning died broke and forgotten; Florida printed $3 bills in the 1830s; and Florida's first tourist attraction featured ostrich racing. A crash course in Florida history!

The Florida Chronicles by Stuart B. McIver. A series offering true-life sagas of the notable and notorious characters throughout history who have given Florida its distinctive flavor. **Volume 1**: *Dreamers, Schemers and Scalawags*; **Volume 2**: *Murder in the Tropics*; **Volume 3**: *Touched by the Sun*

Florida's Past Volumes 1, 2, and 3 by Gene Burnett. Collected essays from Burnett's "Florida's Past" columns in *Florida Trend* magazine, plus some original writings not found elsewhere. Burnett's easygoing style and his sometimes surprising choice of topics make history good reading.

The Edisons of Fort Myers by Tom Smoot. Discover the fascinating story of Thomas and Mina Edison during the forty-six years they wintered in Fort Myers. Visit the extensive botanical gardens Thomas created and tended, as well as his famous laboratory. Learn about his friendship with carmaker Henry Ford and tire magnate Harvey Firestone.

CPSIA information can be obtained at www.ICGtesting.com
Printed in the USA
BVOW03s2237081013

333253BV00005B/11/P